Born in 1930 in a Manchester slum, the youngest of seven children, Joe Brown left school at fourteen to be apprenticed to a plumber. However, his exceptional climbing abilities soon became apparent as he discovered the gritstone outcrops of the High Peak. After doing his National Service, successful expeditions in the Alps and the Himalayas in the mid-1950s established him as the top British climber. He was employed by archaeological expeditions to open up seemingly inaccessible caves in Persia and at Petra. He worked as an instructor at an outdoor adventure school, before setting up his own climbing equipment shop at Llanberis, where he still lives, combining the business with guiding and with climbing for film and television. His website can be visited at joebrownonline.co.uk.

The Hard Years

JOE BROWN

PHOENIX

A PHOENIX PAPERBACK

First published in Great Britain in 1967
by Victor Gollancz Ltd
This paperback edition published in 2001
by Phoenix,
an imprint of Orion Books Ltd,
Orion House, 5 Upper St Martin's Lane,
London WC2H 9EA

Reissued in 2007

3 5 7 9 10 8 6 4

A CIP catalogue record for this book
is available from the British Library.

ISBN-13 978-0-7538-0279-9

Printed and bound in Great Britain by
Clays Ltd, St Ives plc

www.orionbooks.co.uk

CONTENTS

ILLUSTRATIONS

Following page 160

Following page 208

ACKNOWLEDGEMENTS

I must thank various sources for permission to use copyright photographs, as follows: I. G. McNaught Davis for the colour picture on the jacket and No. 21; the BBC for the frontispiece and No. 38; J. R. Edwards for No. 12; Ken Wilson for Nos 15, 40 and 42; *Manchester Guardian* and *Evening News* for No. 27; Kangchenjunga Expedition for Nos. 28, 29, 30 and 31; *Daily Herald* for No. 32; Tom Stobart for No. 33; *Manchester Daily Mail* for No. 34; Edgar Siddall for No. 41. No. 14 was a photograph taken by the late Rosemary Soper.

My thanks are also due to Secker & Warburg Ltd for permission to reproduce a passage from *High Peak*, by Eric Byne and Geoff Sutton.

PROLOGUE

MOST CLIMBERS TRY to spend as much time in the mountains as possible. Particularly when young, merely getting to the hills absorbs a great deal of effort. Planning trips, thinking and talking about them, occupy a lot of time. The whole business is a vicious circle and eventually one comes to the conclusion that the only satisfactory solution is to go and live in the mountains. The problems are obvious, unless one has a lot of money. Living involves working, and there is usually very little work in mountain areas. However, over the past decade a number of climbing centres have been opened, providing many jobs, both temporary and permanent, for those who are keen enough to forgo the "pleasures" of living in a city or a non-mountainous area.

My first opportunity to work and live in the hills came with a job as an instructor at the White Hall Centre for Outdoor Pursuits. At first the life was terrific, with plenty of interesting things to do spread over most of the British Isles. But the disadvantages soon appeared: there is little compensation for being in the hills if you still have to work and cannot make the best of the position. Of course it is pleasant just to be there, but in some respects one tends not to appreciate the surroundings so much as during a normal weekend when one has spent the previous week working at a desk in a city, or, as in my case, doing property repairs in Manchester.

The idea of opening a shop to sell climbing equipment had been at the back of my mind for some time. Then one weekend a chat with Frank Davies, who had a shop in Ambleside and was just expanding to Birmingham, galvanised me into activity. Val, my wife, hadn't really been keen on moving to White Hall, but she immediately became excited at the prospect of a shop. There were few places left in the country which were not already comprehensively covered by other shops. A letter next day, to a friend in the estate business on the North Wales coast, brought a speedy reply saying that there were two properties available —one in Bettws-y-Coed and one in Llanberis. We took a day off the same week, and two days later we had decided to buy the property in Llanberis. I think both Val and I were rather surprised by the rapid turn of events, but at the time we were too busy to think much about it, and we were soon lost in a multitude of plans and ideas.

Llanberis would not entice many people as a place to live in and to work. To the tourist and casual observer it must seem a particularly drab and uninteresting town. The giant terraces of the slate quarries scar the hillside and the tips dominate the town. Most of the buildings are old, with walls several feet thick and their austere appearance reflects both a native taste for simplicity and the hardship of former times.

But for me Llanberis was an ideal choice. It is the focal point for climbing in Snowdonia and surprisingly there were no other shops there to supply climbers with equipment. Like most climbing centres, the town bursts into a hive of weekend activity for the greater part of the year, bringing business to the shops, pubs, hotels and of course Joe Brown's climbing shop! Having done a lot of my earlier climbing and exploration in the Llanberis district, I was particularly pleased at the prospect of going to live there. Feelings about the mountains and climbing are always more intense when one is young, and Snowdonia, and particularly Clogwyn du'r Arddu, will always have a special meaning for me.

The door from the hallway opened and Peter Crew came into the room. He settled down in an easy chair, pulled out a crumpled cigarette carton and threw a Gauloise to me.

Outside it was getting dark. Across the back garden a neighbour's light came on. A woman standing at the window drew the curtains. I had been living in Llanberis for nearly a month, getting the shop ready to open for Easter.

"Thought we might have a chat about the book," said Crew deliberately. "You'll soon have some time to work on it."

"Well, I need time to get used to the idea," I told him "—why I'm doing it at all. I have never written anything before."

"Why exactly are you doing it?"

"Not really for any specific reason—I need the money and it is good publicity for the shop."

My visitor laughed. "You had better not say that. I expect you've realised that some of the lads might not want you to write about them. After all, you are in rather a special position."

"Yes. I can't help that—I don't like writing about myself either, but so many other people have written pieces about me and made a mess of them, that I am sure I could do better myself."

Crew looked thoughtful and blew out a jet of smoke. "Moving to Llanberis is really the end of the story. You need a starting point—something besides 'I was born in' or 'Once upon a time'."

"No, I see it as a beginning. Llanberis is where I came in. I first started climbing here and I have started again with this shop. Nothing has ended, in fact I am going to carry on just as I did before."

"Well in that case, how about ending on the same idea— you could say that you have always wanted to live here and now here you are at last."

"But it wouldn't be completely true," I replied, "because it has not been possible till now. It has more or less just happened; I didn't plan it this way. Anyway, it doesn't matter very much where I start or finish, it won't alter what I have to say and that is presumably what people will want to hear."

"All the same the story will need a shape to make it clear that you have reached an important phase in your life, even if the next phase looks just as good."

"I agree, it adds up to that. The main point is that I shan't be able to give the reader the sort of stuff he imagines is the real me. I am not at all like my popular image—I hope. Everything I have done in life has been for my own satisfaction and not to inspire or impress others. The reader will have to take what he gets."

"Fair enough," declared Crew enthusiastically. "So you kick off with a description of Llanberis, a typical Welsh slate-quarrying village between Snowdon and the sea."

"Won't everyone know that?"

"Depends on what you tell them. You have seen all the changes since the end of the war and you've helped to cause them in fact. The older folk in the district don't really understand what has happened. The whole economy of this area has changed because of the increasing interest in climbing and because of the large numbers of people who come here regularly. You can make something out of that."

"Well, it wasn't done deliberately. I can't write about it in those terms. It's the sort of idea that will have to come out between the lines. Of course it's absolutely true that when I first started to come here there was hardly a soul to be seen. Climbers in those days went to Bethesda and the Ogwen valley —in fact I did myself for a couple of years. Llanberis was a very dead place then, much quieter than it is now. I think the only visitors must have been the people wanting to go up Snowdon on the railway."

"To me this would be one of the most revealing statements in the book—the fact that your background is entirely traditional in so far as you came to Wales at weekends and stayed in Ogwen—because that was *the* place to go—like everyone else."

"Yes. At that time, just after the war, all the people I knew went to Ogwen. We had no transport of our own to explore other places, so we just had to go wherever it was easiest to get to, and stay there."

"Exactly, so the shift from the Ogwen valley to the Llanberis one will be shown by your explorations that encouraged others to follow. The opportunities for exploration happened to be here and Llanberis was the nearest place of any size."

Crew interested me because he was more concerned with the consequences of what I had done than trying to put me on a pedestal like an idol. My trouble was that I felt no responsibility for the consequences. Besides, many others had been involved. The Beatles didn't set out to dominate the pop world. They made a sound that everyone liked. If the reception had been otherwise the sound would have been just the same. That was how it was with me.

"The real trouble," I began, "is that writing a book exposes you to comment. It is safer not having a book for people to quote from. As far as I am concerned the less people know about me the better. I just like being what I am and doing what I can, and think nothing more of it."

"Have you always felt like that?"

"Not really. When I was younger I had a desperate inferiority complex. As I became well known, if anyone congratulated me I was really embarrassed. Anyone who can just stand there and be told that they are marvellous, without feeling a little awkward, would be a very cold and strange person. After a while I became used to all the praise and quite enjoyed the sensation that other people thought I was somebody different. Then I began to wonder about it. I thought, it can't be that I am so good, it must be that other people are easily impressed because they aren't too good themselves. I suppose you'd say my reasoning was pretty confused but I was getting tired of all the publicity. Finally I came to the conclusion that I was the only person who could really judge my ability. Now I take little notice of what other people say about me."

"When you are actually climbing, do you always feel on top form?"

"Well, you've got to bear in mind that no two days are alike either for beginner or expert. One day you might be feeling a bit off colour and everything seems to be more difficult than it should be, while the next day you are feeling really great and the hardest routes are just no problem at all."

Val came in and said that tea was ready.

"Would you like to stay for tea, Pete?" Val asked.

"No thanks," said Crew, "I'm going over to the Padarn for a game of darts. Coming over, Joe?"

"I'll join you when I've had my tea," I grinned at him.

"Great, we'll find Robin Collomb and get his tape recorder. It will help you remember the introductory themes and should make the writing much easier."

"Fine, let's do that."

Crew stood up to leave. "We mustn't forget that this book is about mountaineering. In a way it's the story of developments in British climbing in the past twenty years."

"If you say so," I added. Pete darted into the hallway and skipped down the backstairs into the garden. I went into the kitchen for my tea.

The Padarn Lake Hotel is a few minutes' walk up the main street. As I approached it I became aware of a dull droning noise. The forecourt of the pub was jammed solid with vehicles —mostly old vans and station wagons full of climbing equipment. Shuffling through the car park the sound increased, and opening the inner door a shattering roar hit me like an explosion. A smoke-filled room, milling with casually dressed climbers, tables piled high with empty glasses, beer slopping everywhere: Saturday night at the Padarn!

Until recently winter weekends in Llanberis had been quiet, but with the mounting interest in Welsh rock climbing over the past seven years or so, all that had changed. Now a fairly representative cross-section of the British climbing community seems to gather in the Padarn Lake on a Saturday night all the year round.

It was too crowded for anyone to play darts, and I found Crew and Collomb huddled in a corner. A small conference was held, in which half a dozen of us were pinned against a wall with handfuls of beer, shouting to make ourselves heard above the racket.

Suddenly Robin Collomb bawled out: "I can't stand this any more." We all looked at him as if he had said a dirty word. but the point was taken. "It's chucking out time anyway, come to my place," I said. "We can carry on talking and drinking there."

A couple of minutes later we had parked ourselves in the sitting-room and Collomb spilled a glass of whisky on the carpet. It rather confirmed the view that everyone was in high spirits. There was no point trying to put over, at this hour, what I had in mind for an autobiography.

When the party broke up I was left with a tape recorder, a pile of debris and a lot of empty bottles.

"Why do we climb?" Mallory's classic answer to this question, "Because it is there", explains nothing of the complex reasons for climbing. Most men if not all have a spirit of adventure which needs an outlet. Many of the better-known sports, such as motor racing, sailing, etcetera, require a lot of money; but climbing needs nothing more than a pair of gym shoes and some old clothes, to start with at least. One of the good things about climbing is that it is possible to enjoy it in any form, from messing about on small practice cliffs, to struggling up a huge Himalayan peak.

Climbing is probably one of the greatest of all emotional stimulants; and without emotions man may as well be a vegetable. To a non-climber, the obvious emotion triggered off by climbing is fear! If this was true, climbing would never have become the popular pastime that it is today. Fear is something that all climbers feel at some time. Without it there would be no caution. But I certainly don't enjoy climbing when I am frightened, although I tend to remember the frightening climbs more clearly than ones which had no tension of any sort.

For me, the most enjoyable part of climbing lies in the adventure. Difficulty, as a thing in itself, is merely a by-product of any climbing that I have done. I have rarely gone out of my way to look for difficulty—if it does occur then fair enough, but the enjoyment of a climb is not spoiled for me if it turns out to be easy.

A popular misconception of climbing is that it requires great strength and nerve. If that were true then the strongest men would be the best climbers, which is not so. Strength is obviously an asset to a climber, but the most important thing is a combination of the mental ability to work out technical problems, physical suppleness and agility and the right amount of confidence. The first two of these qualities are quite common, and are demonstrated on the small boulder problems which are found below most crags, but a combination of all three is quite rare.

To the people who are bitten by the climbing bug, it becomes more than a pastime. It is a way of life. One tends to become discontented at work and to live only for the weekend's climbing. Many climbers have given up good jobs which interfered with climbing. For quite a large number of my friends it has become the custom to finish work in the spring and tour Europe climbing until September, then to get a job until the following spring.

It is very difficult to analyse the reasons for climbing. Each person feels differently about it, and feelings change from day to day. Perhaps it isn't necessary to have a reason. Many times I have heard climbers say, "What would life have been like if we hadn't started climbing".

The next best thing actually to climbing is to talk about it, and consequently the social side of climbing tends to produce many wits and line-shooters. Line-shooting can take many forms. The most common form is to exaggerate the difficulties and dangers of a climb; but this is usually when the listeners have not done the climb in question. The other way round is to make a climb sound easy; and this is usually when the listeners have done the climb and found it hard. I was climbing with Nat Allen once, and two other members of the Rock and Ice joined us. Nat asked what they had done and they replied, "Vember, Red Slab, Octo and White Slab" (all extremely difficult routes), and Nat said, "Well, we didn't have a very good day either". It is difficult to be a line-shooter in such company. Perhaps the worst line-shooter of all is the second man who falls off nearly every move on a climb, and when he gets to the top says, "That was nice, I wish I had led it".

Most people, especially climbers, tend to exaggerate slightly when telling stories. Consequently when a tale has been passed on several times it only bears the slightest resemblance to the original. Recently on Anglesey, my second couldn't follow a particularly overhanging pitch, so he shouted to someone else on the cliff to come and take his place. Yet, a few weeks later, we heard the "London version", which was that I had lowered my second off the cliff, and it was so overhanging that he landed in the sea. He then had to walk two miles back to the car park and drive to Llanberis to find someone who was daring enough to come and follow me. Meanwhile, I was supposed to be sitting on a minute ledge, waiting for the tide to come in and cut me off!

One weekend Nat arrived at the camp-site in Langdale. He had just been to the Old Dungeon Ghyll, and whilst in the pub he had overheard a whispered conversation between two climbers who thought that he was me. The conversation went as follows:

"That's Joe Brown over there!"

"No it's not, it can't be. Brown has bandy legs, teeth like tombstones and hands like bunches of bananas."

This amused us so much that we faked a photograph to fit in with the description!

The worst offenders at distorting the truth are journalists, and after returning from a big expedition it is not unusual to be met by a dozen or more reporters all eager to get the "human touch" into their articles. Number One human touch is the love story. As this is such an everyday occurrence it seems pointless that they should want to write the same old drivel. When I got married I think we had more reporters than guests at the reception. Like most newly weds, when we arrived at the hotel we thought that no one could tell we were just married. But we soon found out how untrue this was; when next morning the papers arrived, in almost every one there were photos of Val and myself draped with coils of rope. So much for the old married couple.

Number Two human touch is the local boy makes good. This is considered really good news value if you have a Coronation

Street background, which I had. I was frequently billed as the
Manchester Climbing Plumber.

Collomb and Crew sat solemnly in the sitting-room for two
hours, listening to the first of the tapes on which I had recorded.
I had spent most of the previous week talking to myself into a
microphone, so I left them alone to hear the result.

I brought some tea in. It was mid-afternoon and a moderately
good day—we should have been out climbing.

"Great stuff, Joe," exclaimed Crew. "Now you can start on
the story."

Then Collomb said: "I think it could do with a little more
about yourself apart from these controversial matters that you
might weave into the narrative."

I thought to myself, I shall never understand the language of
these publishing types, nor will they understand me.

"What do you suggest?"

"The social significance is missing. You know, that mountaineering isn't an exclusive upper crust recreation any more.
You must have some views on that. Also more about what you
think the motives are for taking up climbing."

"That's very difficult actually to analyse," observed Crew.
"It's the kind of idea which will come out much better in the
course of the book."

"Agreed, but so will lots of other things that Joe has touched
on already."

I butted in: "Well, I feel as if I have already gone beyond
the point of no return. I don't really mind. The die is cast
and all that."

We wasted the rest of the day in idle chatter.

THE HARD YEARS

CHAPTER ONE

CHILDHOOD AND EARLY SCRAMBLES

I was born in September, 1930, the seventh and last child to arrive in a family living near the railway viaduct in the Manchester suburb of Ardwick. We occupied a very small terrace house in the middle of a large slum area, and the hooting and roaring of passing trains was part of our industrial environment.

Even at that time Manchester and Sheffield were the two great centres in Britain for climbing activities. The outskirts of both cities encroached on the moorland perimeter of the Peak district, which was studded with gritstone outcrops and limestone tors. These rocks had already been coveted by two generations of climbers.

We were poor but respectable. My mother took pride in keeping the house clean and tidy. This was essential because we had only four rooms in which to squeeze a large and growing family.

The accommodation consisted of two rooms upstairs and two down. In this confined space my brothers and sisters were drilled in simple routines for keeping the house in functional order throughout the day. The kitchen was cell-like and contained one of those shallow slop-stones resting on a pile of bricks in place of a sink; the lavatory was situated in a small yard at the back.

My father died when I was eight months old. He had been in the building trade throughout his life, and for many years between times had been a sailor. An accident aboard ship had resulted in gangrene of the foot, which caused his death.

My two brothers' and four sisters' ages were spaced fairly evenly at intervals of about two years. Only my eldest brother Jim was working when my father died. During the seventeen years or so that my mother had been having her family she had never had the opportunity to look for work. So with six of us to feed she had to take in washing to make ends meet. When I was old enough to be left in the care of brothers and sisters she went out to work regularly, charing in local business premises.

In those days our adversity was a common condition in the north of England. We were no worse off than many of our neighbours. Mother was very proud of the fact that she always managed without the dole or national assistance of any kind.

Building was the family trade. There was no shortage of hands but work was discontinuous and it was a struggle to provide a steady income. In the absence of better prospects both my brothers became builders and in due course I showed an aptitude for woodwork at school which propelled me in the same direction.

My impressions of our struggle in the 1930s are few and hazy. My feet remind me of the doorstep and the flag-stones that covered the floor downstairs. The ritual of scrubbing and sanding them with a sandstone was one of the many knee-cracking chores that I escaped as a boy. When the housework was in progress we were warned in no uncertain terms to keep out and to return with clean feet when we dared re-enter.

Then I hardly ever had shoes. I always wore plimsolls, for they were much cheaper. My trousers were second-hand or cast-offs from an older brother. In fact all my clothes were very raggy. Even if we had been able to afford new ones it would have been a waste because I was always fighting and playing roughly, and tore my clothes. The Bisto advertisement displayed on billboards all over the country before the war personified my appearance.

Luxuries like birthday presents never seemed to go beyond a "dinky" toy. Jim married and left home while I was still very young but I was eleven before my eldest sister married. So in the beginning we all lived at home. Anyone who was earning had to give mother all their wages and they would be given something back for spends.

A fatherless upbringing and a hard but happy home life

encouraged me to fend for myself. As a passive and unreligious person my mother had a profound influence on my character over the years. A strong tradition of Catholicism rooted in my father's side of the family was instrumental, through well-meaning relatives, in having me sent to a Catholic school. The first was St Aloysius. I am unlikely to forget it because I was smacked for some reason on the first day and came home tearful. This experience probably had the effect of putting me against school for the rest of my childhood. Later we moved from Ardwick to Chorlton-on-Medlock, where we occupied a larger house at the back of the post office. I attended the Holy Name school about a mile up the road; I used to run this distance every day.

Catholic schools questioned children about church attendance. Right away I took a great dislike to this part of school life. Church had never appealed to me and there was no power at home to induce me to behave according to the faith. When I eventually thought seriously about religion I decided that if God was as good as people made him out to be, he could never be as paltry as to send you to hell for not saying prayers or attending church on Sunday. In school we were taught that God was everywhere. As a boy it always puzzled me that if this was the case, why was it that we were constantly pressed, even threatened, to attend church to talk to him.

So I stopped going to church.

The narrowness of interests in and experience of the world beyond our neighbourhood was widespread and unshakeable. The great hiking movement, which had mushroomed across the north in the 1920s, was flourishing. To many people the moorland heights often framed at the end of dreary streets were merely a boundary marking the limits of a place on earth. We had no contact with informed circles in the community that were making excursions into the countryside a short distance away. If the notion had been laid before us we would have been too poor to afford the thought.

It was probably not very remarkable that I discovered the

pleasures of the countryside all on my own. My equipment was a growing sense of independence and a yen for leadership. As the youngest of a large family I was pampered to some extent in the house, but more often humoured as a plucky little lad. A desire to explore the outside world was already planted in my soul. Play friends were easily led to the claypits where shoes were lost in the mud and clothes were torn. The upshot was that parents forbade their children to play with me. Not to be discouraged, there were plenty of adventurous lads who could be recruited at school or in the street.

The zoo at Belle Vue lured us on many occasions. At one time it had been a prison and there was a high wall round it. We found a way over the wall where part of it had crumbled away. It led on to a roof then into a passageway. The first time we entered in this unorthodox manner we went through a door at the end of the passage and found ourselves in the bison's den. But for the dozy state of the animal the fate of Albert stared us in the face.

The main object of making an unauthorised entry was to play on the fireworks island in the middle of the lake. Firework displays, like "The Storming of Quebec", had been held there. The undergrowth was littered with scenery framework and spent fireworks. To reach it we had to cross a rickety, unsafe bridge, but once this had been negotiated we were quite isolated and unlikely to be detected. Rummaging through a small hut on the island we found some costumes from "The Storming of Quebec". One day all the gang dressed up in these costumes, with tall hats, swords and lances, and spent the afternoon wandering round the zoo dressed as Wolfe's soldiers. Nobody passed any comment and we eventually walked through the turnstiles and went home in the costumes.

One night during the big Manchester blitz of 1940 we were bombed out. When the air raids were in progress we used to cower under the dining table, listening to the sirens, the bangs and crashes. On this night, the last I was to spend in the house at Chorlton-on-Medlock, there was a rattle in the chimney and we heard a scream next door. An incendiary bomb had fallen down their chimney. Moments later all the windows flew out of the house. There was no noise of an explosion, just a terrific crash of glass flying everywhere. Not lacking in imagination I thought it must be a time bomb. I panicked and dashed out of the house into the yard. My mother and sisters chased after me and we closeted ourselves in the lavatory for five minutes while mother pondered on the next move. We could not stay in the lavatory and there was no point returning to the house; the building was visibly sagging. So we went into the street and hurried down a nearby shelter.

What had happened was that we had been surrounded by a triangle of three landmines. One had blown down my school, which was an agreeable piece of news. Another had landed near a row of houses where my best friend lived; I don't think he was killed but I never saw him again. Our house was not completely destroyed but the floors had fallen down and the windows had gone. I remember vividly walking through the streets next morning on our way to stay with relatives at Longsight, treading through glass and piles of rubble that lined scenes of ruin and destruction.

After this I was sent to another school that soon met the fate of the last one. There were so few schools and so few teachers that it was all done on a part-time basis. Sometimes we were going only for one day a week and at busy periods we attended for half-days all week. None of us took any examinations.

The war certainly made a mess of my education. I was not exactly lazy at school—disinterested would be more accurate. Occasionally I played truant; after being caught and punished a few times I chose the less painful course of resigning to authority. My position in class usually came somewhere in the first eight. My best attainment was third and I never sank below tenth place.

Organised games bored me more than anything else during school life; football and cricket failed to arouse any enthusiasm in me. Out of doors my release was to be found in the countryside—doing anything—walking, fishing, messing about in general. This was how my friends and I occupied ourselves whenever the chance arose.

Within a few months of arriving to stay with relatives in Longsight we managed to get a house with ten rooms. By our standards this was a mansion. A widening pool of incomes improved our circumstances sufficiently for us to make it reasonably comfortable. This house has been my mother's home ever since.

By my twelfth birthday I knew that going into the country was far more satisfying to me than anything else. A constant problem was getting approval from my mother to go camping and, indeed, persuading friends to accompany me.

One could go to the city limits for a fourpenny tram ride. We asked for a halfpenny ticket but stayed on the tram until it reached the terminus. Sometimes we were caught and the conductor threw us off, so that we had to walk the rest of the way.

The collection of rough and ready gear carried on these trips was incredibly antiquated; an old patched up tent and a thick felt cover for a groundsheet. The cover (taken from a table) soaked up water in wet fields like blotting paper. Discomfort of this kind both contradicted and complemented the lure of open-air life. Four of us used to lie in the tent, shivering and our teeth chattering, on sleepless weekend nights. The party cooked on a big oil-stove with a cast iron base; the cooking pans were also enormous and very heavy. Our kitbags bulged with all this useless gear which we carried round like some comedy act wherever we went.

In the daytime we enjoyed ourselves immensely. At Middlewood near Stockport we discovered a stream that flowed in a deep channel. A rope was fixed to some trees beside the stream and we used to swing, Tarzan-like, for 50 or 60 feet and about 20 feet above the water. This was quite exciting and kept us entertained till dusk. We also tried our hand at fishing—the usual bent-pin variety—and digging out wasps' nests; in fact we were game for anything with an element of danger in it. Needless to say our condition on arriving home was invariably filthy—from sitting over open fires and mishaps with the oil stove.

Then I heard about the mines at Alderley Edge from some of the lads at school. They were fifteen miles away and there were shafts about 50 feet deep with a sandy floor at the bottom. We cycled there and used our cycle lamps to go down the mines. The police had rather misguidedly thrown all sorts of rubbish into the shafts to discourage children from entering them. Despite this the mines were popular with schoolboys and there were quite a few accidents.

On one occasion we had just reached the main shaft at the cross-roads of two tunnels. In our direction you could walk over the shaft on a plank—it was called the Plank Shaft. Another party was coming down the other tunnel. To gain the far side entailed a jump about ten feet across and three feet up; I doubt whether anyone had cleared the gap. A girl in the other party attempted the leap but she didn't even touch the far side. Before our eyes she fell to the bottom. Luckily she missed all the planks, railway lines, sleepers and other deterrents and landed on a small patch of sand. Unhurt and shouting to be rescued, all we had to do was pull her out with a rope.

We now carried a rope everywhere. At first we merely walked round the passages, for the prospect of getting lost appealed to us. Then one of the lads found a better rope beside a hole in the road, so he coiled it up and brought it along. We began to lower ourselves down the shafts with this rope, with the object of trying to get out at a different level. But I found it much more satisfying to climb up the vertical sides of the shafts without using the rope.

One of the most impressive caving exploits tried in my younger days took place at Eldon Hole on the edge of the Peak district close to Manchester. This was a few years later, after I had begun climbing with Slim Sorrell. Eldon Hole was a vertical shaft about 180 feet deep. Six of us went there, tied all our ropes together and slithered down them. On the way down there were two or three resting places, but after the half-way point one could not touch the sides and dangled freely. The bottom was still full of winter snow, blocking the entrance to the main chamber, so we climbed out hand over hand. This was probably the most dangerous escapade I have ever undertaken. I shudder to think what would have happened if one of us had lost grip on the rope. When I was working at White Hall many years later we took a party of students down the hole with elaborate caving equipment. The ladders reached the bottom of the 180 ft pitch. I was astounded at the trouble they had, just climbing down and back up the ladders with safety ropes attached. It was hard to visualise that six of us had made the descent with nothing more than a crude fixed rope consisting of pieces tied together like knotted blankets.

The rough and tumble of my boyhood was not completely lacking in the facets of a normal childhood. I spent several happy months in the Scouts, but even here I came adrift. Fencing and boxing were encouraged and both activities suited my temperament. The swords had rubber bungs on the end and these were always coming off: somebody went home after every meeting with a bloody face. In one of the boxing matches I was fighting the biggest lad in the troop; quite by chance he walked straight on to the end of my arm which was extended rigidly. He went down flat on the canvas like a log. When he got up, some time later, he had the biggest black eye I have ever seen; I think he was even prouder of it than I. I had nursed a secret longing to be responsible for giving someone a really good "shiner" and I achieved it by accident. After this incident the Scoutmaster displayed his annoyance by putting on the gloves and knocking the stuffing out of me. In the end I was expelled from the Scouts for refusing to go on church parade.

When I left school I was four feet eleven high, and even when I came out of the Army after National Service I was still only five feet four.

The war was in its final stages when I took my first job as an apprentice with a plumber called Archie. He was a Jack-of-all-trades and consequently so am I. I started with him as soon as I left school at the age of fourteen and the association continued, off and on, for ten years. My interest in woodwork and the family background of the building trade satisfied my mother that it was a fitting occupation.

The pay I received was ten shillings a week at first, and my mother gave me half-a-crown back for spends. Over a period I saved enough to buy the equipment I needed. At one stage I had put aside thirty shillings towards a pair of boots that would cost five pounds. Archie heard about this, presented me with the rest of the money and sent me out to buy them. As an employer Archie was angelic and generous in many ways. He recognised that climbing consumed lots of time and gave me time off to pursue my growing passion. Unintentionally I was thoughtless enough to reward him with one calamity after another. The damage I caused during the first month must have cost him six months' wages for me.

While reslating a roof some planks had been put across the ceiling joists, on which the old slates could be placed. Instead of walking along the joists I chose to tread about on the ceiling and went through it in several places. This meant that we had to replaster the ceiling when the slating was finished. On the same job one of the men working on the roof dropped a slate pick which slid behind a chimney stack. I volunteered to recover it. I slid down and retrieved the hammer but the pitch of the roof was so steep that I could neither walk nor crawl back up. So I placed my feet in climbing fashion against the chimney to gain some leverage; the whole lot heeled over and fell through a lavatory roof below, which we had just reslated. Another time I was playing see-saw on the job with one of my mates, using Archie's 45 ft ladder; we ended up with two 22 ft sections.

Looking back on those days I cannot understand why Archie tolerated my behaviour. When we first began working together there were two men and two lads besides Archie himself. Before long the responsibilities of running a business overwhelmed him. He worried more and more; less and less work was done until the business ran right down and he had to sack all of us. Five days later he came round to my house to ask if I would consider coming back to work for him. Of course, I agreed. But Archie continued to fret and worry and did even less work. By the time I was sixteen I was working almost entirely on my own; this had its compensations because I enjoyed the independence and responsibility. My opinion of Archie was as high as ever. I was in the habit of telling everyone that he was a "terrific bloke" because I was quite attached to him. Eventually the balance sheet of our little operation tipped the wrong way. The jobs we tackled were far fewer; Archie complained that he could not support his family and pay my wages at the same time. Fortunately I was fairly thrifty and had saved some money; when Archie couldn't pay the wages my mother and I made do with what I had saved.

At the end of ten years Archie owed me about £70. He had just had a nervous breakdown and was in a terrible state. I had started doing odd jobs on my own initiative and felt that I could not press him for the money. Finally I forgot about it. The loss meant much less than the three pounds ten he had given me years before to buy a pair of boots.

The mines at Alderley Edge brought us into contact with youngsters who had explored more distant corners of the moors beyond Manchester. Four of us—the remnants of earlier parties —teamed up together for weekend jaunts; these grew in scope and ambition. The period between my fifteenth and seventeenth birthdays was a voyage of discovery.

When the great freeze of 1946–47 gripped the country with an icy hand we endured the hardships of coal queues and cold breakfasts and suppers by candle-light, and awaited weekends with an impatience akin to children yearning for Christmas Day. We trekked into the hills above Hayfield where there were houses completely buried in snow. The amount of snow was astounding and the moors could pass for the most desolate Antarctic landscape. We tried our skill at sledging and once went to the summit of Kinder Low.

Our first climbs were made in gritstone quarries. The loose rock and an inclination to wander over the faces independently, making our own way to the top, was disagreeable and curiously unsatisfying. Then we noticed something that intrigued us; it was the waterfall on Kinder Downfall, which blew upwards in a strong wind. No time was lost in making an investigation. The waterfall was at the back of a long ravine enclosed by steep cliffs. In hobnailed boots and with cumbersome rucksacks on our backs the ascent was distinctly awkward. I climbed the rocks beside the waterfall with a heavy brewer's rope coiled round my shoulders. On reaching the top I threw it down for my companions to follow with its protection.

This deep fold in the mountain, lined by the steep Kinder cliffs, impressed us so much that we were eager to return. I happened to read Colin Kirkus's book *Let's Go Climbing* before our next visit. Proper management of the rope was evidently necessary if it was not to prove a menace in the hands of clumsy and ignorant novices like ourselves. I now had a sash cord as well, discarded as a washing line by my mother, who considered that it had outworn its usefulness. It was very thin, bleached white and strong enough to give the second man a tug; it seemed quite adequate to us at the time.

I was on a ledge about ten feet from the top of the cliff when a climber strolled across to watch us.

Looking down at me he inquired: "Is that one of those new nylon ropes?" Nylon was just appearing as a vastly superior material for making climbing ropes. Of course I didn't know it at the time. He thought he was addressing a well-informed party because our rope was white and much thinner than hemp, which was used by the majority of climbers.

"I really don't know. It's just a rope," I replied, trying to appear matter-of-fact and not foolish. I was hoping he would go away.

"There's a good belay behind you," he called out. In other words a rock spike on which I could secure myself with the rope. I shrugged my shoulders, tried to puzzle out what he was

driving at and prayed that one of the lads below would not
hurl some rude comment at him.

"It's all right," I said, "I can hold the others if they fall off."

I had failed to grasp the instructions given in Kirkus's book.

The climber went away. After I had brought up the others I
noticed him again, sitting beside the Shelter Stone near the
"gates" at the top of the Downfall. Being anxious to unravel the
secrets of this belaying technique I plucked up courage to ask
the stranger to explain them. This he did and I have used the
same belaying methods ever since.

A few weeks later we ventured to the Lake District. Albert,
Derek, "Ludder" (Keith Ludbrook) and myself set off on ten
days' holiday with enormous loads on our backs. The party
carried thirty tins of food each—three for each day in the
mountains; sleeping-bags of old tarpaulins sewn up with cord;
a large canteen, cooking stove, tent and accessories, besides
mountaineering equipment and personal effects. Each pack
must have weighed close on one cwt. The rucksacks could
hardly be seen for extra packages strapped on the outside.

Coming up Eskdale on the little train from Ravenglass to
Boot, Ludder started to get himself fit by opening the carriage
door, jumping out and running alongside the moving train.
By the time he had finished he might have saved himself the
fare. We took three days to cross from Eskdale over Scafell into
Wasdale, then over Black Sail pass to Pillar Rock, our main
objective. The terrible weight of our packs caused the delay
and we ate far too much food too soon. Before we reached
Pillar we were feeling a bit like wolves.

"You can't eat those pilchards," I told Derek who was
savouring the sight inside a can that he had just opened. He
hadn't many left.

"Why not?" he said.

"Well, look at them. They are bad. Aren't they, lads?"
The others crowded round and agreed. Shaking my head, I
said: "Throw them away, Derek, you'll just have to go without."

Derek, who was rather gullible, tossed the tin away. We immediately recovered the pilchards and with big grins shared them out evenly amongst us.

The guidebook to climbing on Pillar Rock was the only one available to Lakeland crags. Pillar was 400 feet high but our training on gritstone diverted us from the long climbs and we chose shorter routes on the low side of the rock. On the last day we ascended the New West Climb, some 300 feet of exposed walls, slabs and chimneys, and then realised how much the holiday had been wasted. All the same we managed to get up a Very Severe route on the shorter side of the rock; at the time this was the highest grading of difficulty applied to rock climbs in Britain.

At sixteen years of age I was completely ignorant of the traditions, conventions and, more importantly, standards in rock climbing and mountaineering in general. None of my acquaintances were mountaineers and for a while I relied on instinct. If a climb was not scraped by boot nails we thought it must be new. Having just started climbing we assumed that everyone else must be better than ourselves, instead of merely regarding them as more experienced.

One day we were on Kinder Downfall when a large party swarmed along the base of the crag. In the course of an exchange between the two groups it was plain to see that a tall dark-haired lad, with a knowledgeable air and commanding tone in his voice, was the leader. In a few minutes he had told us all about Kinder Scout. There were extensive climbing grounds on the other slopes, which were like a foreign country to us. He was Thomas Merrick Sorrell, a nineteen-year-old pipe fitter from Stockport. We got to know him as "Slim" and we all decided to go out together the following weekend.

Although Slim had probably started climbing only a few months before we had, his knowledge of the High Peak was far superior. He had visited distant outcrops and had made friends with other groups of climbers. He was very much someone to look up to, especially because he had three years over me in age—a big difference when you are in your teens. He was friendly and chatty with everyone. He had a flair with people that earned him a position of respect. My attachment to my own group soon frayed; for Slim's part, he too made an effort to ensure that we combined as a team that planned a weekend's climbing beforehand, instead of going somewhere and pottering about aimlessly.

In the first few weeks a party composed of all sorts of hill-goers clambered round Kinder Scout. We visited Edale and fell in with a band of youths known as the Edale "Yips". Slim knew them well but did not appear to be one of their regular members. These boys and girls gathered in Edale at weekends, slept in the open air or in barns and played with shotguns, knives and axes. I was never clear about their intentions; I suppose they fitted the description of layabouts. Sometimes they went walking or made half-hearted attempts at climbing or caving; but the main purpose of gathering was the "social life" they made for themselves in the evening.

"It's bad for the serious climber," observed Slim.

Another of Slim's revelations was reducing gear to a minimum. I had developed the habit of carrying everything except the proverbial kitchen sink.

"Chuck that tent away," he announced one day. After that I found myself sleeping under boulders or in one of the disused shooting cabins perched along the Edges. Slim was thoroughly practical and resourceful.

An argument with him won me my first down-filled sleeping-bag. Slim had two sleeping-bags, one down, the other kapok. I slept in the latter, which was barely half as cosy and warm as the other. One day we disagreed about the price of a tent I fancied buying. Slim was adamant that it cost about half as much as the price I claimed for it. I knew I was right because I had been browsing recently through a catalogue listing the tent in question.

"Bet you what, Slim," I challenged him, "your down bag for the kapok one that my price is correct."

"You're on!" he exclaimed confidently.

When we returned home I produced the catalogue and he

conceded defeat. After that I slept in the down-filled bag while Slim regaled his friends with a story concerning "Big Head Brown" and how he, Slim, was once the proud owner of two sleeping-bags, but now he slept in the poorer of them.

Slim also preferred to stay in Youth Hostels if they were strategically placed for climbing operations. However, the restrictions did not agree with me, especially the work duties handed out by the warden before one could leave. During our first trips to Ogwen in Wales, in deference to my wishes, Slim had to be content with bedding down on the flagstones in the porch of the old chapel next door to the Youth Hostel. The porch was cold and draughty and this forced us to go climbing in all weathers. In mid-winter we occasionally crept into the hostel for a bit of comfort. Slim tried all ways to get our parties off the chapel porch and into the hostel. His favourite ploy was an authoritative statement to the effect that dead climbers were brought to the chapel and laid inside until the hearse came to fetch them.

My first sight of Wales came at Christmas, 1947. The train arrived in Bangor at 2 a.m. Normally one slept on a waiting-room bench until the first buses were running, but after an hour I became impatient and set off on foot. A post office van gave me a lift to Bethesda where I curled up in a shop doorway to await the others. My companions appeared much later, having walked the five miles from Bangor. It was then learnt that there were no buses going higher up the valley; so we all walked the four miles to Ogwen through a steady drizzle and in a thoroughly disgruntled mood.

Four days of sleet and snow chilled us to the marrow. Camping in such weather, clothes could never be dried and no one got a proper wash until he returned home. All the routes on the Idwal Slabs were climbed before the party was stopped by the Holly Tree Wall. This piece of rock was much steeper. It was snowing and we were wearing gym shoes. Nearby a party of Oxford types stretched out in Javelin Gully was having a difference of opinion about the merits of climbing in gym shoes in

the prevailing conditions. In a high voice the leader was order-
ing one of his companions to get off the rope because he was
wearing gym shoes. The conversation between them was most
unfriendly. We wondered if this sort of conduct was normal in
climbing relationships because it was the opposite to our
behaviour with each other.

In the following spring Slim and I went absent from work for
a few days and returned to Wales. The weather was perfect and
the mountains looked most inviting. We polished off all the
routes on the Holly Tree Wall and the Gribin Facet, which left
us feeling elated and full of confidence. While climbing on
Glyder Fach our imagination was fired by Lot's Groove;
this climb was alleged to be one of the most difficult in the
district. We merely goggled at the sheer corner and turned
away.

On the next visit we met John Disley and John Lawton
outside the Ogwen hostel. As two of the best climbers in the
country, their presence in the neighbourhood had been
mentioned to us. We inquired about the real difficulty of Lot's
Groove and Disley advised us to try it on a top-rope. This
meant that one of us should work round to the top and lower a
rope for the other. If we managed comfortably, he said, we
were then to eat a bar of chocolate (to give us energy, I suppose)
and climb the route again without the moral comfort of a rope
hanging from above. Having no bar of chocolate we dispensed
with a top-rope inspection and climbed the route on sight. We
couldn't understand what all the fuss was about.

Fresh from this success we turned our attentions to Tryfan,
where the Munich Climb presented a similar challenge: a
number of people had been killed attempting the ascent. The
difficulties were short and hardly more serious than the stiff
gritstone problems we wrestled with in the Peak.

On both these climbs I probably made greater use of cracks
in which the hands could be jammed to raise myself; as a
technique hand-jamming had not been fully exploited by
cragsmen. Used properly one could hang on for quite a long
time without a conventional hold. I employed hand-jamming

at every opportunity and it was to prove a cornerstone in my future climbing.

Glorious mountaineering was to be found in Scotland during the winter, when conditions similar to the Alps were reproduced. The clue that sent my pulse racing was shown in several photographs of snow-covered Scottish peaks that illustrated the Pelican book, *Climbing in Britain*. These photographs inspired me to make the long journey to Ben Nevis at Easter, 1948. Ludder was my companion. As one of the foursome who had suffered badly from the crippling loads carried on the Lake District trip, he was relieved to learn that I was planning a light-weight expedition. We bought ex-army ice axes for 2s 6d, borrowed the smallest tent we could find and agreed to share one sleeping-bag between two. The general idea was to hitch-hike to Fort William and set up a camp high on the slopes of the mighty Ben.

On the first night we failed to get a lift and eased ourselves into the sleeping-bag a few miles outside Manchester. In the morning we were awakened by a group of workmen standing over us, wondering what kind of creature might be sealed inside the cocoon-shaped object lying on the ground. Our luck changed and we reached Glasgow and then Fort William on the same day.

We camped on the plateau half-way up the mountain. From this base we could walk each day to the towering north face, a cliff some 2,000 feet high: the sheer size and complexity of its buttresses, ribs and gullies, now encrusted with snow and ice, took our breath away.

Our first climb was the gully known as Number Three. The snow was in excellent condition, hard and crisp, and a set of steps cut by a previous party made the climbing effortless. We practised cutting steps for ourselves until we noticed another party descending unroped. Suddenly one of the figures, about 1,000 feet above us, fell and spun all the way down. We rushed towards his line of descent, not knowing how we might assist. The helpless figure went straight past and became a small dot at the bottom. Happily he stood up and waved to indicate that he was unhurt. Not a good omen, I thought.

We pressed on to the top and after an interlude for exploring the summit observatory commenced the descent to our tent. The shortest way followed a snow-filled gully called the Red Burn. Some way down this we were sliding for speed on the steep snow bed when a gap blocked with jagged rocks loomed up. I succeeded in stopping myself but Ludder was not so fortunate. He careered into the rocks and fell over. He looked little worse for the experience and said that he had injured an ankle. The verdict was a bad sprain.

I helped him down to the tent where we remained for five days, hoping for an improvement in the condition. Ludder's discomfort grew worse. The fifth day dawned with a green sunrise, which cast an eerie light across the mountains. In half an hour a terrible blizzard sprang up. A wind of hurricane force lashed the tent and it started to disintegrate. My hands froze in a desperate bid to avert disaster by tying up the flapping ends; I had to abandon repairs while the tent was torn to shreds.

Two fleeing climbers came across to us. With their assistance we evacuated the spot, retreated in disorder towards the valley and headed straight for the Youth Hostel. In the bottom of the valley the bridge across the River Nevis had been washed away. The river was in spate and at this point was some 80 feet wide.

By now Ludder was virtually an invalid and the party was generally exhausted. I made three attempts to carry a line across the stream. Three times I was swept off my feet. Chest high and bitterly cold in the water, I was played back to the bank, more below the surface than above it, by the other two holding the rope.

Our plight was noticed by a climber walking along the road on the opposite side. I waded into the water again, caught a rope thrown from the far bank and returned with it to my companions. The rope was strung well above the water between two trees. For safety a second rope was arranged as a pulley beside the fixed one. Came Ludder's turn to cross, he began by pulling himself hand over hand along the fixed rope. He could not stand upright on the river bed because his leg was so painful. About three-quarters of the way across he slipped below the roaring waters. Both ropes sagged and we could not see where he had submerged. A hand came to the surface; I rushed into the water and started to haul with all my strength on the pulley rope. His head popped up; by pulling myself farther into the water against his weight on the rope I reached out and grabbed him and we were hauled to safety by the others.

Meanwhile the proceedings of this drama had been reported to the hostel, and the warden had telephoned for an ambulance. When we lifted Ludder on to the roadside it was waiting: without further ceremony he was put inside and taken away.

The following day I went to see him in hospital. Ludder's sprained ankle had been diagnosed as a *broken leg* and he greeted me with a somewhat forlorn grin across a huge plaster cast.

But there was worse to come. The nurses had brought him a pile of morning newspapers, recounting the events of the previous day. The main headline read of an heroic deed of bravery by one Joseph Brown, who had "dived 4,406 feet into the River Nevis" to rescue his companion. According to the newspaper reports Ludder had fallen a distance that any schoolboy could determine as several thousand feet underground. Other details of the story were also exaggerated beyond recognition.

How had the news leaked out? The two climbers who had assisted us down from the camp-site were journalists by profession!

The Peak District is a huge tract of moorland, high at its northern end where our early visits had been concentrated and falling away to the south in a maze of dales, either fortified by limestone cliffs or scarped along the upper edges by elongated tiers of millstone grit. It was on the gritstone edges that I learned to climb. Our rough and ready approach to climbing also prepared us for most of the hardships one might face elsewhere in Britain. Our favourite edges were Windgather,

Laddow, Yellowslacks, Stanage, Froggatt, but there are a host of others. Every weekend was spent exploring these crags and slowly we built up an impressive list of new routes.

At Windgather we had to keep a sharp lookout for the farmer who owned the grazing rights to the land surrounding the rocks. He had gone to extraordinary lengths to rid himself of "climbing pests". He had poured tar over sections of the crag that he regarded as popular. He had chipped off holds, not realising that there were probably more holds on this crag than any other in Britain. A few less was no bad thing! If he caught you on the rock face it was quite normal for him to stand at the bottom, throw stones with a notable lack of accuracy and deliver a torrent of abuse, until you fell off or scrambled to the top and ran away.

A climb at Windgather called Portfolio was the scene of my first fall. I had done the climb before, making the first ascent in nailed boots when it had been quoted as impossible in anything but gym shoes. Demonstrating the ascent for a second time, I fell off backwards from the overhanging top. With no conscious effort I managed to land on my feet in a standing position on the ground 30 feet below.

Peering nervously over the top Slim shouted, "You must go straight back on to the climb." Slim looked slightly amazed at my rapid recovery. He had invoked an old adage in mountaineering that after a fall one should attack the problem without delay (injuries permitting!) to avoid losing confidence. There was a grain of truth in it. By paying attention to detail I romped up on the second try. Curiously enough Slim's brother fell off at exactly the same point a week later. He landed on his side and only dented his cigarette tin.

Most of our gritstone climbing was done in nailed boots. The awe in which some of these gritstone climbs were held—so far as climbing them in traditional footwear was concerned— was still a little baffling to me. At Laddow I led Easter Ridge and Tower Face in boots. I had an audience composed of members of the Manchester Karabiner Club, who plied us with advice. An occupational hazard of climbing on outcrops is having to perform before a gallery of critical watchers, themselves resting between climbs. Warning shouts that this or that piece of rock was "hard" or "V.S." confused me because I did not find them difficult. In any case I was uncertain what the terms meant. People had a mental blockage about "hard" climbs.

At the bottom of Laddow Rocks someone nudged me and said: "See those three coming along the path over there, they are Cloggy climbers." An impressive hush descended over the gathering. Approaching us were three climbers who had made ascents on the most feared cliff in Britain. Even I could not help feeling some admiration and envy for them. In those days such men were regarded with reverence as great as if they had climbed on Everest.

As our horizons broadened in the Peak district so did our contact with other climbers. Towards mid-summer in 1948 we met a group of Derby climbers and spent the holidays with them. Wilf White and Nat Allen were the prominent members, and with Slim, myself and two or three others from Manchester it was not long before we joined the Valkyrie Club, the forerunner of the Rock and Ice. Wilf was already at home with a broad section of the mountaineering community and he was on friendly terms with Peter Harding, who was then acknowledged as the leading rock climber in the country. Information about modern climbing trends reached us for the first time and we were able to relate the difficulty and quality of the routes we had been doing with established standards. We also had a yardstick to measure our own performances.

It was Wilf White who introduced us to Froggatt Edge near Sheffield. He went into raptures about fantastic walls and slabs of rough gritstone. "All blank, they are, and nobody has touched them." We were disinclined to believe him but it was true. There were only a few routes on the crag; we worked along the edge making dozens of new routes. Some of them were extremely hard, such as Brown's Eliminate. The rock was friable and I top-roped the face three times before leading it. The holds were microscopic and the climb was only possible in nails, which could be hooked perfectly on to tapering flakes that were uniformly about one-eighth of an inch wide. These flakes broke off in time, leaving a larger gripping edge and the route has gradually become easier.

At Stanage, also near Sheffield and probably the most frequented of all gritstone outcrops, we climbed the famous pair of Unconquerable cracks on the same day. Byne and Sutton have reported accurately in their classic history, *High Peak*: "The twin cracks . . . gradually became known as the Unconquerables. Although the left-hand crack is in fact the harder of the two it looks less bleakly formidable, and at last a determined effort by Albert Shutt and Tom Probert was successful. The problem is to pass a sort of blunt beak of rock perhaps 30 feet up which overhangs in two planes, and the holds are so exiguous that, though decisive climbing is essential, there is relatively little time available in which to arrive at decisions. The right-hand crack still proved impregnable. At length came the inevitable visit of the Valkyrie. Extreme severity on a rock climb usually implies technical severity coupled with exposure, sometimes strenuosity, and frequently an embarrassing lack of protection for the leader, all of the characteristics the Unconquerables certainly possessed, together with a reputation. Knowing nothing of Probert's earlier lead of the left-hand crack, Brown, seconded by Sorrell, proceeded to climb both of them with ease."

The story of these two climbs circulated only several years later. A yarn was transformed into a controversy that sought to discredit the validity of our "first ascents". That we made no claims ourselves did not alter the situation; other people had done it for us. The argument centred around our admirers and their opponents and it was up to both sides to extricate themselves.

The adventure of these gritstone climbs was an unforgettable experience. I was impressed by Wilf White from the start. He had been born with a double club-foot and had not walked until he was eight. Now ten years later there was no sign of the handicap; he climbed superbly. He was the ideal companion for me because he acted with exceptional drive and determination when a route looked like defeating him. Wilf was slightly taller than the rest of us. He was endowed with brawny arms which may have owed their development to childhood exertions.

As climbing partners Slim and Wilf were poles apart. In a critical situation Slim would say: "Oh well, that's it, let's pack up and go back." With Wilf an impasse had the opposite effect. He would talk and talk and drive himself to greater heights of effort. On the other hand Wilf hated defeat. If Wilf failed on a climb he made life unbearable for everyone. When he was glum his mood infected the party for several days and no one could speak to him. If the leader coped and his followers failed, then Wilf remained fairly cheerful. Unfortunately there were times when Wilf fell off while the rest of the party struggled up.

The most fanatical climber to join us was also the youngest. He was Fred Ashton, who had started climbing with Ron Moseley at the age of eleven or twelve. He invariably rose from a ditch on the moor *before* dawn, breakfasted and threw himself at the crag before anyone was awake. The success of Fred's day depended on how many routes he could tick off before nightfall; he went up and down them all day without stopping.

Not the least of Fred's faults was the language he used. As a matter of course he swore incessantly, totally unaware of what he was saying.

One day Slim brought his young lady to Froggatt. As they approached Slim called out: "Watch your language, young Fred."

Fred jumped up. "You've got a bloody nerve," he snorted loudly, "I haven't said a f. . . . . thing yet!"

On Dovestone Quarry Fred reached the end of his tether and capacity for uttering purple language. Slim and I were taking him up the route called Brown Corner. Dusk was falling when we reached the top; water was streaming down the rock, the cracks were filled with mud and the climb finished on a band of extremely loose shale. Fred was terrified and spluttered that he would never climb with me again.

But Fred broke his pledge when he joined me for a day on Wimberry. I proposed that he should do all the leading; that way we should avoid any dispute. "All right," he said, "follow me, Brown!"

Walking along the crag Fred stopped at a crack and confidently announced: "We'll do that. Piece of bloody duff!"

Fred must have had a brain storm because there was a fierce-looking overhang in the crack some 25 feet up. All the same, for a twelve-year-old he had plenty of nerve. I said nothing.

After an unmentionable tirade of expletives Fred dropped to the ground.

"You have a go at the bugger!" he spat out.

The overhang was a tough problem. I jammed a fist in the crack and leaned right out on it, raising my feet high enough to explore over the top and find a fist jam for the other hand. The position was extremely precarious and the climbing painful. On this type of movement one could easily injure the hands. My hands were numbed by the cold day and all sensation had gone when I pulled up at the top. I examined my hands but could see nothing wrong with them.

Fred followed on the rope and had a desperate struggle on the overhang, tearing his hands to pieces. As I cranked him over the top I felt a sharp sting on the back of one hand. A circle of blood about the diameter of a penny was oozing out on the first knuckle. On touching it a skin-flap fell back, revealing a deep wound, from which the flesh had been gouged.

Fred vowed again that he would never climb with me— another promise he broke. A piece of Elastoplast was stuck across the hole in my hand, and for the next three months it reminded me to avoid all climbing propositions put by young Fred.

Fred Ashton's enthusiasm for climbing was quite unique and he could lead Very Severe climbs at the age of twelve. As a youth of fourteen he followed me on harder climbs in Wales, which must be something of a record.

Of all the people with whom I had a long climbing association, J. R. "Nat" Allen was the most memorable for steadiness and lack of temperament. Nat was "with it" from the beginning: thoroughly reliable, a perfectionist without being fussy or annoying to companions, eternally cheerful and a soothing influence in the midst of disputes. Safeguards and modern rope techniques were second nature to him. A plumber by trade, his short stocky figure worked day and night like a perpetual machine, always ungrumbling, shoving aside enormous problems with alacrity. He enthused everyone with witty remarks and his mettle improved in proportion to the inches of rain and feet of snow.

In the New Year I received my call-up papers. The date named was 20th January. The thought of joining the Army left a hollow feeling in my stomach. The recruitment office wanted conscripts to volunteer for the undermanned Catering Corps. I was only too glad to listen to alternative suggestions. Having learnt that there was no mountaineering regiment and that I would have to sign-on to become a Marine, I chose the Ordnance Corps.

The weekend before I was due to report to barracks a farewell party was held on my behalf at the Church Hotel in Edale. Slim, who was a talented song writer, had composed a sad little melody for the occasion. I felt more homesick at this gathering than at any other time in my life. It seemed like the end of the world. I was floating in a vacuum and the singing and merriment around me were beyond reach. My mother packed a case, knowing that I would forget half the essential articles that I would need to look after myself in the Army. This was not the same as preparing for a bivouac on a mountainside.

At Aldershot there really was a big Sergeant in glistening boots and razor-sharp uniform to welcome me at the gate with a broad friendly smile. Inside the barracks he assumed, as I had been warned in jest, the proportions of a monster who barked at "little men" and addressed the platoon as "you horrible lot". True it also was that a thunder clap shook the billet every morning at 5.30 a.m.; that within five minutes the voice of terror boomed, "outside in two minutes". Rushing round the camp in vests and shorts at this hour in mid-winter was absolute torture.

After basic training I was posted to Portsmouth. All the trains from Portsmouth headed north, filling me with an urge to desert and run away to the hills and hide. I finished up at Leamington Spa as Private Brown, Storeman in charge of receiving and issuing ammunition.

All my leaves were spent rejoining friends in the mountains. In the Peak we camped in caves or slept on the moor in the open. Just before one weekend when I was due to go to Froggatt there was a rush for tea in the canteen at Leamington as the urn was wheeled in. In the ensuing scramble I was knocked over and broke a leg in three places, which put me out of action for three months. While convalescing Wilf wrote me a letter, mentioning a particularly stubborn climb at Froggatt which had beaten everyone. He thought that he could now do it.

Wilf was not there when I arrived at the crag, still limping and on tenterhooks as to whether my ability to climb was impaired. Mercifully the leg gave me no trouble on the rock-face. I was just easing myself over the crux of the route when Wilf appeared hurriedly below.

"Ahrrr . . . You treacherous swine, Brown. What happened to your crutches!"

The Army posted me to Singapore. Even privates were important people there. The time was passed in sunbathing and swimming. The men were ordered not to work because there were coolies for that sort of thing. We were also ordered not to disturb old planks and tarpaulins, under which snakes and scorpions nested. So turning over planks and tarpaulins was a pastime for this bored Army. Apart from nearly being sacrificed to a swarm of blood-sucking flies and having a running encounter with a shoal of Portuguese men-of-war, I saw no excitement in the Far East. A troopship steamed into Southampton in the spring of 1950; a month later I was demobbed.

1. "has bandy legs, teeth like tombstones and hands like bunches of
bananas"

2. Valkyrie Club meet on Kinder Scout in 1947 *L. to R.*: A.N.O., Brown, Wilf White, Nat Allen

3. Climbing *The Dangler* on Stanage Edge

4. Fixing a runner on *Treewall*, Curbar Edge

5. Climbing *The Great Crack* at Curbar Edge

6. Don Whillans on *Esso Extra* at Stanage Edge

7. *Sloth*, a roof climb on the Roaches

8. *Green Gully* in winter conditions on Ben Nevis

9. *left*
Don
Roscoe

10. *right*
Joe
(Morti-
more)
Smith

CHAPTER TWO

THE VALKYRIE

THE VALKYRIE CLUB had only recently been formed when I joined it in 1948. The nucleus was composed of a splinter group from a cycling club, the Derby Mercurys. I joined because it was the logical outcome of friendships I had struck up with people like Nat Allen and Wilf White. By other club standards the Valkyrie hung together loosely; we were more concerned with getting things done in the mountains than looking for recognition as yet another post-war climbing club. The real difference could be spotted in the level of activity shown at meets. In climbing circles organised meets were notorious for the leisurely attitude adopted by those attending. Socialising often took precedence over climbing. The Valkyrie climbed in all weathers because the effort to get out to the hills was so great. We felt it was always worth doing something even in the worst conditions.

The techniques acquired from our gritstone exploration were easily applied in the mountains of Snowdonia. The Welsh cliffs had size and scope for rock climbing on a grand scale while the roughness and soundness of the volcanic rock added materially to the attraction of finding new routes.

At Ogwen during Christmas, 1948, the Devil's Kitchen cliffs were fluted with an organ-pipe formation of icicles. This was the first time that we had seen these cliffs in such wintry conditions. The thing that attracted our attention was the area of cliff to the left of Hanging Garden Gully. The lower 100 feet of this section was scooped into a great overhanging wall, with another 100 feet of vertical wall above. Draped down this was a cascade of ice—the top part attached to the rock, but the lower part hanging in space like a chandelier. We tried to traverse on to the ice but it was very brittle and our nerve failed at the prospect of climbing the ice stalactites. So we climbed Hanging Garden Gully instead.

Whilst descending from the Idwal Slabs, Slim pointed out Suicide Wall which was then the hardest route in Wales and certainly one of the most impressive. Although we were well aware of our inexperience, having only previously done two or three V.S. climbs in Wales, we decided that there was nothing to be lost by trying it on a top rope. We all found the Wall too close to our limit to entertain any thoughts of leading it, but it made us realise what the upper limits of climbing were like at the time.

Some years later we went to the Carnedds to climb on Llech Ddu and turned back because the weather was so bad. While we were recovering with a cup of tea in the chapel porch, we decided to have another look at Suicide Wall. Remembering all the tiny spikes on the wall, we cut up a thin nylon rope into several lengths for running belays. After the first easy 20 feet I overcame the hardest moves of the climb by using one of these rope loops as a handhold. Higher up the climbing was easier, but every loop I put on was blown off by the strong gusts of wind. When I reached the stance in the middle of the wall I put in two pegs for belays. Then I decided that these were too unsafe, so I continued to the top. When my second started to follow me he fell off on the first hard moves and both pegs fell out! When we returned to the road mender's hut where some of the lads were sleeping a friend called Ginger Cain was there and he asked us what we had done. "Suicide Wall," I said, trying my hardest not to grin; but of course he didn't believe me and thought I was shooting a line.

The Pelican book *Climbing in Britain* contained photographs of all these Ogwen cliffs and of some others in the Llanberis Pass, in the next valley. One was of Dinas Cromlech which was cleaved by a huge corner. Wilf White and I rode pillion round the Glyders on the motor cycles of two acquaintances who dropped us at the Cromlech Bridge in the wildest stretch of the pass. This valley was narrower and much darker than the Ogwen one and it was very desolate. The imposing columnar cliff of Dinas Cromlech frowned above us, its striking central corner—Cenotaph Corner—acting like a magnet on our impulses.

We scrambled up the rough scree slopes to the foot of the cliff —there was no path to speak of in those days. Where the two vertical rock walls met at right-angles, a long thin crack ran up in the back of the corner. It looked about 100 feet high but this was an underestimate. Having calculated that I would need every piece of equipment we had brought with us I took stock of the gear: five assorted pegs, a variety of snap-links and numerous slings. With any luck the pegs could be driven into the crack at average intervals of 20 feet. The snap-links could be used either attached to the eyelets of the pegs or to slings that might be hooked over rock spikes. Alternatively a sling could be passed round a stone jammed inside the crack, using a snap-link to join its loop-ends together. The purpose of these devices was to clip the climbing rope into the snap-links, threading it to fixed points on the cliff. The rope always ran freely through the snap-links so that the leader could protect himself as he climbed farther away from the second man paying out the rope. In one form or another this device is called a running belay (runner, for short).

Bit by bit I jammed and bridged my way up the corner. The climbing was quite hard to within some 30 feet of the top. Here there was a shallow scoop in the rock, and the exit from it, leading into the final part of the crack, was overhanging.

I had just banged in a peg with my mason's hammer, which I put between my teeth to leave my hands free to fiddle with the rope. It was no easy matter to hang on while clipping the rope into a snap-link. Having successfully arranged the runner I twisted my head round to shout to Wilf at the bottom that he should hold me up against the runner by pulling on the rope. I forgot about the hammer. It slipped from my mouth and hurtled below. Proof that the corner was vertical from top to bottom, the hammer did not touch rock and gave Wilf a glancing blow on the forehead. He let out a scream and collapsed on the ground. Using the runner as a pulley I climbed down as fast as I could.

When I reached the bottom Wilf had recovered from the initial shock. I merely had to mop up the blood trickling down his face. After we had reassured ourselves that he was not going to die Wilf's true concern became evident when he snarled: "Get back up and do this bloody thing!"

I bridged up the scoop into a niche below the overhanging exit. I was now only 20 feet from the top and could see that the first 10 feet were formidable. At least one more peg would be needed and I had none left. So with considerable reluctance and a heavy heart I retreated, removing the pegs as I went down.

News of our attempt on Cenotaph Corner spread rapidly. Peter Harding, who knew the cliff well, had dismissed the Corner as "for another generation with fewer scruples". He believed it could be climbed but not without some degree of artificial assistance. Encouraged by my comparative success a number of experts mounted attacks on the great corner; all failed to get higher than 20 feet above the bottom. I had been prepared to use pegs to protect myself whereas the previous contenders had not. Having come quite close to reaching the top, at least I knew that the five pegs I had used would not all be necessary. Fewer should suffice. It was subsequently shown that only two were actually needed.

The Valkyrie Club held an Easter meet at Llyn Llydaw. I was in the army and managed to get leave to join them. I thumbed a lift from Caernarvon to the top of the Llanberis Pass and asked a Welshman for directions. This side of Snowdonia (the peak of Snowdon itself) was new ground to me. There were about a dozen in the party, camping beside the lake. On the first day we rambled up to Lliwedd. This satellite of Snowdon has a cliff nearly 1,000 feet high. The hardest route on Lliwedd is Central Gully Direct, grooving the centre of the face. It had been climbed once, before the war, by the pioneer explorer of the Llanberis Pass, J. Menlove Edwards.

We had a perfect day for our attempt although the fine weather had brought out swarms of other climbers. As we neared the start of the main difficulties excited chattering and blows from a peg hammer drifted to our ears. Then we heard a chilling "twang" and "ping". A peg had shot out and buzzed through the air, landing in the anorak hood of a member of our party. As one voice we raised a hearty cheer; this stimulated a host of watchers to applaud with loud clapping and for the next minute the revelry echoed round the cliffs.

The main pitch of Central Gully was a steep slanting crack, overhanging at one point and furnished with poor inverted holds. Wilf yo-yoed below the overhang for an hour before coming down to rest. We changed places. I raised myself above the overhang and discovered a rusted peg; it was Edwards'. The climbing was now extraordinarily delicate. I edged up gingerly on suspect rock. Every movement was a concentrated mental effort and I began to worry about the absence of a ledge for resting and belaying. I came to an uncomfortable sloping place where it was possible to wedge myself in the crack. I had to chip the edge of the crack with my hammer to make a notch on which to secure the rope.

Ernie Phillips tied on as second man and in due course reached my stance. Thirty feet of this crucial pitch remained. Ten feet higher I was stopped by a huge loose rock lying in the crack. I could not see how to circumvent it; if I continued the rock would be dislodged and crush Ernie. Realising the situation Ernie turned very pale.

By now Wilf and one other had climbed around the Direct pitch and were gazing over the top, making improper suggestions. They lowered a rope and Ernie went up, skirting the obstacle, on the tight rope held from above. As I went past I gave the rock a kick and sent it to the bottom: the danger had been removed permanently.

That night at camp it rained. The morning was cold with a thin drizzle. The lop-sided pyramid of Snowdon was veiled in mist. Llyn Llydaw, locked in a deep cwm below the pyramid, and the long serrated arms of Lliwedd on one side and Crib

Goch and Crib y Ddysgll on the other (forming the Snowdon Horseshoe), enclosed us.

With no clear intentions we decided to pay a visit to Clogwyn du'r Arddu. An aura of mystery surrounded this cliff. While we had information about a dozen climbs, it was spoken of with bated breath and one seldom met anyone who had climbed there. Those who had were looked upon as gods. There was no question that "Cloggy"—as it is affectionately known—was the most continuously steep and near-impregnable rock-face in Snowdonia, perhaps in the country.

We traversed the airy crests of Crib Goch and Crib y Ddysgll and crossed the depression contoured by the mountain railway between Snowdon and the Clogwyn dome. As we approached the spur where the cliff lay hidden, slowly, one by one, a concertina of blank vertical walls loomed through the mist. It was the most dramatic sight that I had ever seen. We hared along the bottom, rising from one grass terrace to another, eagerly trying to pick out natural faults between the immense walls that might be climbed.

The party congregated at the foot of Curving Crack. I had just embarked on the first pitch when another party arrived. It was led by none other than Peter Harding; his partner and equally fine climber, Tony Moulam, together with several other Derbyshire-based climbers and a South African, were in the group. A tremendous feeling of excitement surged through me as I jammed up the famous first pitch, a thin vertical corner crack. The rock was greasy but this did not upset me unduly; its roughness compensated for the conditions. Again I found the climbing no more difficult than other hard routes we had done in Wales. On the other hand the position of Curving Crack was infinitely more impressive and nerve-racking. It steepened and became more exposed as it rose, and the final pitch was the most sensational piece of climbing we had encountered. On the climb we tended to talk a lot, unable to control ourselves. I have since noticed that many people are affected in the same way on their first visit to Cloggy.

Collecting our rucksacks at the bottom we noticed two deep

holes in the turf. The South African in Harding's party had fallen from the top of the first pitch, spraining both ankles and leaving two holes a foot deep (this turf has long since disappeared with the passage of trampling feet).

That summer (1949) I spent three days climbing on Cloggy in glorious weather with Slim and a girl called Edna. We camped on the old moraines in the hollow below the 500 ft cliff. A vivid reflection could be seen on the sombre lake of the Black Hollow which gave its name to the cliff. Since 1927 some thirteen routes had been made on the main East and West Buttresses. Nearly all of them had been graded Very Severe—still the ultimate in difficulty at that time. There was tremendous variety in the character of the routes: walls, slabs, chimneys, cracks and, occasionally, ridges. Slim and I climbed all thirteen routes while Edna made a third person on the rope for three of them.

The interesting feature of this short and successful holiday was that I led all the climbs until the last day. The last route was Bow-Shaped Slab. I had led the introductory pitches and was at the end of the traverse section below Narrow Slab. Here I paused beside an enormous rock-flake leaning against the face; it was an ideal place to belay. To drop the rope behind the flake and secure myself I had to climb up it. Slim joined me and I suggested that he might care to lead through to avoid changing places. He continued along the traverse and climbed to the next resting place.

Following him, I had to layback up the edge of the flake to remove the belayed rope. No sooner had I done this when the entire flake heeled over. The rock and I went flying through the air. I somersaulted. I sensed the rope drawing tight to jerk the life out of me; my puny body would be smashed against the cliff. I landed face down against a patch of grass clinging to the face. Making a frantic effort to grab the grass I slowed down just as my weight came on the rope. Slim felt only a slight tug; he was well belayed and could not be pulled off. All the same, having seen the rock and me depart from the cliff, accompanied by an explosion reminiscent of a cannon discharge, he was a little upset. We composed ourselves and pushed on without further incident to the top.

One of the first breaches we detected in the defences of Cloggy, that might reveal a new route, was the climb now known as Vember. I had first noticed it when climbing Curving Crack. Vember was the name of Mrs Williams' daughter and the family looked after the Half-Way House on the Snowdon Mountain Railway. During the period of strict rationing after the war they helped us with items of food and an occasional bucket of coal to keep the fire burning in a derelict house that the Valkyrie sometimes used near the railway. We were also given addresses where bacon and other scarce foodstuffs could be bought without producing a ration card. The reception extended to our parties earned the Williams family our undying gratitude. Mrs Williams and Vember had remarkable eyesight. They would keep a watch for us coming up the track. Long before another human being might spy us we had been identified and tea or a light snack, according to the time of day, would be ready when we tramped into the café. Mrs Williams addressed Slim as "The Climber"; his voice could always be heard above the rest of us.

The line of Vember is close to Curving Crack. It is a crack-line with smooth blank walls on either side, and in bad weather the first pitch becomes a waterspout. The weather was foul on our first attempt which dragged on for several days. We struggled in the vertical and sometimes overhanging crack with water pouring into our sleeves and shooting out of trouser legs. The shock of cold water running across my chest made me wince. The first 20 feet of the crack is smooth and holdless and the filthy mess of dirt inside it felt as if I were climbing on soft soap.

On the second pitch the deluge was more like a waterfall. It looked even worse than the first although there is only about 30 feet of climbing to the next ledge. Again the crack is about two inches wide and slightly overhanging all the way. I started up it trying to jam my hands but progress was very slow and I felt far from safe. Even the texture of the rock was smooth and my stockinged feet were not gripping very well. After several attempts I managed to fix a runner at fifteen feet. Although I was now much safer the crack above was too greasy to get any sort of hold. Before giving up I decided to have a look round the corner to my left. By leaning against the pull of the rope held by the party below, I stepped on to the face. Slowly, on very small holds, I gained a few inches. I ended up in a position where my arms and stiffened fingertips were at full stretch on the edge of a small ledge. My saturated feet, on mere ripples in the rock, were slowly slipping out of the stockings. I could see what my hands were gripping but I couldn't feel them. They had gone quite numb. In the next instant I became airborne.

No one was surprised when I fell off. The rope, a new hemp line, was sawn along a sharp vertical edge. Examined afterwards it looked as if it had been chewed up in a piece of machinery. I plunged into a knot of figures on the stance below; like a ball thrown into a scrum my supporters collapsed on me and we all helped one another. Licking our wounds and commiserating, it was, as Slim put it, "a narrow squeak".

It rained all week without stopping. Some of the party retired behind the walls of an old mine building. Stone shelters were erected round the inhabitable tents, to the level of their ridges, and other tents were stretched across them for additional protection. But the tents were so poor—in fact none of them was waterproof—that rivulets snaking over the ground entered everywhere. Once the bottom end of your sleeping-bag had become soggy the damp crept higher, until you had to curl up in a ball at the top end.

Life in these conditions was squalid and miserable but no one complained. Such was the passion for climbing in the Valkyrie. Nat Allen had a wonderful knack of taking round tea just when morale was sinking. Wilf White amused the company with a nasty habit he had acquired of taking wet clothes into his sleeping-bag at night. He had practised this trick for some time and the discouraging smelly results provoked much laughter.

My first new climb in Wales was made not on Cloggy but in the Llanberis Pass. It was more by chance than design. So much depended on being in the right place at the right time: a place where a new route could be made, and finding oneself there in the right frame of mind when the weather and conditions on the rock-face were acceptable.

The Pass bristled with cliffs. Those on the north side, like Dinas Cromlech, could be reached in anything between five and twenty minutes from the road. The Grochan face was among the best of these. Its main features were smooth walls and boiler-plate slabs rising in an unbroken sweep of 300 feet. We had spotted a particularly fine and intimidating groove in one part of the face where the rock was gently overhanging for 150 feet. It would make a magnificent climb. On an early attempt I went at it in nailed boots. Some distance up the rope caught on a holly bush which sprang back and spiked me in the eye. I tried to push ahead with the eye shut; after nearly falling off I excused myself and retreated on a doubled rope.

In May, 1951, Slim Sorrell, Ray Greenall, Fred Ashton and myself climbed the groove in excellent conditions and almost in the atmosphere of an anticlimax. Fred Ashton was only fourteen years old. The rest of the party was severely pressed to stay in contact with the rock; the difficulties were unusually sustained and everyone resorted to a certain amount of brute force. The ascent surprised me by the small demand it made on my margins of reserve.

It was John Lawton, an acquaintance I met from time to time in Wales, who suggested the name of Hangover for the route. A route of that name had been made in the Lake District, he said so why not even up the score.

Conversations with the Greenall brothers and John Lawton provided me with a rudimentary education in the traditions of British mountaineering. They also acted as couriers, bringing information abaut the activities of other climbers, especially in the Lake District. The curious perennial topic of the "Welsh School" versus the "Lakes School" was thus brought to my attention. When it was first mentioned, in connection with the naming of Hangover, I thought it might be a leg-pull. This long-standing controversy had been handed down from generation to generation and accounted for the specialisation of some climbers in one region or the other. The "schools" (of opinion) took sides on questions of whether the climbing was better in Snowdonia or the Lake District, and whether the leading Welsh climbers of the day, and their finest achievements, were more outstanding than those of the Lakes. The whole idea struck me as being spurious and silly.

At this time no one doubted the supremacy of Arthur Dolphin, a Yorkshireman, as the climber who was making the most notable ascents in the Lake District. He hardly ever appeared on the Welsh scene and one concluded that the label, "Lakes School", was firmly attached to him. The reason was, of course, that he lived much closer to the Lake District, and it was natural to concentrate his efforts there. Like ourselves he was trained on gritstone; he favoured the outcrops farther north, such as Almscliffe near Harrogate.

Our Welsh explorations were varied not infrequently by short trips to the Lake District. We wanted to sample the routes that Dolphin was making. At least three of these became great classics: Hell's Groove on Scafell, Kipling Groove on Gimmer Crag—so named by Arthur because it was "ruddy 'ard", and Deer Bield Buttress. I did not meet Dolphin until shortly before his tragic death in the Alps in 1953.

Dolphin based himself in the Langdale area. Langdale was also the most convenient centre in the Lake District for Manchester-based climbers—there was a bus journey of fifteen miles from the railhead at Windermere. Between 1948 and 1951 we repeated most of Dolphin's routes; the small, steep and compact crag of Deer Bield charmed us most of all.

We first went to Deer Bield because its Crack was reputed to be one of the hardest climbs in the Lake District. The crag was also noted for drying off quickly after prolonged bad weather. The party was Slim, Wilf, Nat and Don Cowan. As we approached the crag, which could be seen a long way off, a mystery developed. The crag was shining green, like an old

Norman tower pitted with lichen. The rocks were coated with green slime. No one liked the look of it at all.

We had intended to climb in boots for we had nothing else with us. In these conditions no other footwear would afford a purchase. I had lost the nails from the inside edge of one boot, having ripped them out when I stumbled running down from the top of Cloggy. The boots I wore would nowadays be laughed at, as were Chaplin's; there was more paper and board in them than leather and they oozed like a sponge.

The crux of Deer Bield Crack was a smooth, narrow chimney. Being short and agile I brought my knees up into the chest and wriggled up in a wedged position, moving a few inches at a time. When the others arrived at the most difficult place in the chimney a tinkle of nails dropping out of their boots joined the sound of their grunts and groans. Wilf came first, fell off fifteen feet below me and elected to haul himself up on the rope. He sprawled on the stance in a black mood. I wasn't going to say a word to him. Don Cowan made a furious scraping noise; his nails clattered down the chimney in a small shower. As soon as Don skidded off, the rope went tight and Wilf brightened up.

"Didn't I tell you, Don," he yelled, "the only way to get up this lot is to pull on the rope!"

Nat Allen put up a tremendous struggle; the sounds of a fierce battle drifted up.

"Who are you fighting with down there," called Wilf.

Then Don chipped in: "It's dead easy if you hold the rope and swarm up it!"

Now everybody was shouting instructions to the weary warrior. If this was calculated to make Nat fall, it succeeded. In a spirit of frivolity the entire party came up like sacks of potatoes. We were a dreadful sight, covered with grease from the crag.

Slim and I went to Deer Bield to climb the Buttress. This was the third ascent and it was probably the hardest route that I had done. Peter Greenwood, who made the second ascent, put us up to it. In telling his tale he confessed that he had fallen off the last pitch and had unrolled the green caterpillar of grass that grew in the upper groove. I was not overawed by the difficulty of Deer Bield Buttress; the climbing was serious enough but the pitches were short and there was an adequate number of running belays.

Crossing into Eskdale we took in a couple of routes on Esk Buttress and set up camp below Mickledore in readiness for climbing on Scafell. Previously Slim and I had been rained off Scafell and we thought that our chance had come at last. It was not to be. Black cloud swirled into Eskdale and blotted out the landmarks. Pouring rain imprisoned us in the tent for two days. On the third day we were so fed up that a walk across Mickledore to Wasdale for afternoon tea was proposed to cheer us up.

We set off in thick mist, crossed the pass we believed to be Mickledore and trotted down the other side towards Wasdale. Emerging from the mist an unfamiliar and desolate valley was spread out below. In the bottom we saw a tiny tent and wondered who would be mad enough to camp in such a lonely place, because there was nothing of interest to be seen in any direction. It never occurred to me that a valley such as this could not exist in the Wasdale direction if we were on the right course. Moments later Slim realised what had happened. He sat down absurdly, like a dummy, and burst out laughing. He laughed hysterically for a long time. I had to shake him to bring him to his senses.

"What's the joke," I demanded.

"That's our tent," he said, choking on the words, and relapsed into another fit.

CHAPTER THREE

THE ROCK AND ICE

THE VALKYRIE CLUB was disbanded three years after its formation. The membership was scattered over a wide area and began to drift in separate directions. Our activities had already attracted some attention and when other climbers recognised us we began to respond to their interest. Those of us living in the Manchester area met climbers who were not attached to any particular group or club—the astonishing thing was that several of them lived within a radius of five miles of my own home.

The fusion of these individuals did not happen overnight. I met Ron Moseley through the Greenall brothers whom I saw from time to time in Wales. Moseley's prowess had been described to us by Fred Ashton. Setting off from his house for a weekend in the hills Moseley took a short-cut across a large croft to reach the bus stop. The tracks made in the earthy path by the hobnails in his boots had been seen by a pair of climbers who used the same short-cut. Moseley's tracks remained a mystery for a long time. The other pair walked across the croft nearly every weekend but the person who had gone ahead of them was never seen. They bumped into each other after many months and Moseley introduced himself to Eric Price and Don Roscoe. In conversation it was revealed that Price and Roscoe lived round the corner and 50 yards away from Ron at the bottom of the next street!

The disintegration of the Valkyrie was final when Don Whillans joined the Manchester group. We had heard of Whillans long before anyone had met him; even in 1951 the reputation of one of Britain's greatest mountaineers in the making had something of a mythical quality about it. A story was told that this exceptionally powerful lad had fallen from the top of Twin Eliminate at Laddow Rocks. He had jumped from wall to wall in springboard style, landing at the bottom, 50 feet below, in an upright position and without a mark on him. Other stories of miraculous escapes and a charmed life aroused our curiosity. Nat Allen saw him climbing at Froggatt; he wrote to me, saying what a brilliant climber Whillans had shown himself to be. Whillans eventually started to come out with us, accompanied by Leslie Wright, Dick White and a couple of other lads.

The size of the Manchester group grew to fourteen in number. All of them were capable of leading Very Severe climbs. Only Nat Allen survived from the original Derby group; he took a job at the Orthopaedic Hospital in Oswestry and usually attended our Welsh gatherings.

Living close to one another about eight of us became inseparable. Every Wednesday evening we went to the Y.M.C.A. in Manchester to play billiards or table tennis and plan the weekend's climbing. Around midnight we trailed off to Moseley's house and drank tea into the small hours. None of us drank beer and in those days not many of us smoked. (I had started smoking as a youth but contrary to the popular image of a cigarette dangling perpetually from his lips Don Whillans did not start smoking until many years later.) If we went to a pub the group ordered a jug of orange and sipped it from small tumblers, making it last all evening. Rum and orange was indulged in at Christmas to comply with the superstition that one should be merry and gay.

Planning weekend trips in Moseley's front room began with an examination of funds. The average wage of the group was about £7 a week. I had about £4 a week to spend. The biggest expense was travelling to the mountains. We had to budget carefully and keep a reserve for replacing costly equipment. A weekend in Wales was a special occasion, and most of the time we could only afford to go out into Derbyshire. Preoccupied with this business the meetings frequently broke up at four o'clock in the morning. I lived about 400 yards away but the Greenall brothers and Doug Belshaw had to walk two or three miles home.

I cannot remember who mooted the idea of forming a club. I clearly remember being against the idea from the start. One evening the group went to the cinema and sat through the show discussing the subject. We came out into the street and the "Rock and Ice" had been born.

My objections hinged on the belief that a club formation was unnecessary to keep the group intact. I pointed out that we would spend half our time tied up in red tape and rules: a club committee tends to busy itself with fund-raising schemes to purchase a hut or other permanent trappings, whereas I wanted the group to continue the self-initiated policy of sleeping where we found ourselves at nightfall and not become tied down with responsibilities. Deliberations on a meets programme and indoor functions at home, such as an annual dinner, promote stuffiness and argument. The reasons for wanting to start a club struck me as being futile because we were already pursuing all the functions successfully without an official committee telling us what we should do.

A committee was formed and I was elected to it. Then as now I never did a stroke of work while in office. After I was struck off the Rock and Ice committee it was easier to take an active part in club affairs by voicing complaints as an ordinary member.

All my prophesies came true. The meets programme was disrupted by the stronger influence of personalities who diverted enthusiasm for attending an official location in the mountains to another of their own choosing. Club dinners were disastrous. An after-dinner speaker delivered his speech to a handful of people (the club membership never exceeded thirty at any time) in the self-conscious atmosphere that torments an entertainer standing in a near-empty auditorium. These events were an acute embarrassment to all concerned. Not even one guest speaker's talk on sex being the downfall of all-male climbing clubs saved the occasion.

All the same the Rock and Ice was a close-knit body, intensely active in the mountains and avoiding the usual relationships with other clubs. We were not represented in any national mountaineering issues or debates and it was not surprising that other climbers viewed us as a secret society. The solitary purpose of the Rock and Ice lasted six years before chinks appeared in the armour of its single-minded members.

The rules we obeyed were those invented extempore in the open air. If someone misbehaved in camp he was fined "brews" —that is to say ordered to make the next billy-can of tea. A fine in brews might be several in number, extending over a period of days, according to the seriousness of the offence. Clumsiness was a common reason for imposing fines. If someone kicked dirt over supper he was liable to be fined.

We were once staying in crowded conditions in a barn. Moseley was cooking a piece of steak. It fell off the stove into the hay, so he took it outside, washed it in a stream and put it back on the stove. Later someone stepped over the place where he was cooking and some clotted hay fell off the culprit's boots into the frying pan. Moseley washed his steak again and put it back in the pan. Just as it was ready for eating someone else stood up and brushed off the hay clinging to his trousers, sprinkling the stuff over the steak. He washed it in the stream for the third time and finally ate it!

The most incorrigible offender during the early years of the Rock and Ice was Joe Smith. He joined the group almost in the capacity of an apprentice. Don Roscoe's mother had met a woman who mentioned that her fifteen-year-old son wanted to go climbing. When Don was told to take the youngster out on trial we cringed at the thought of acting as nursemaid to one so junior to ourselves. But Joe Smith endeared himself to the whole group. He had a gravel-like voice, reminiscent of Louis Armstrong, and he shambled about like a little bear and was characteristically playful and good natured.

If anything went wrong Joe Smith was usually to blame. He was fined brews all the time. The problem was that he could not be trusted to make tea without knocking over the billy-can! In camp we took the precaution of pushing him to the back of the tent on the assumption that he could do no harm there. He would sit in the back with a dreamy, far-away look on his

c

face and unconsciously tug at the groundsheet, pulling the stove over.

When he came to Ben Nevis with Nat Allen, Nip Underwood and myself, we were battered by blizzards which confined us to a hut for long periods. A place for everything and everything in its place was the order of the day. Joe had committed all sorts of unpardonable acts, effectively reducing him to our dogsbody. I felt terribly guilty sending him out into the howling storm to fetch water from a stream that ran between the walls of a deep rock crevice. If he spent a long time away on these chores we had to go out and look for him in the darkness. Reappearing clad in a ghost-like shroud of snow we had to brush him down before he could be allowed inside. Altogether Joe fetched fifty buckets of water.

This was the holiday when I had fallen in Point Five Gully. Nat had injured a knee during the accident. To ensure that Nat would not have to go outside we found a tin in which he could urinate. Joe knocked it over when it was rather full. Having been told to mop up the mess no one noticed until it was too late that he had surreptitiously borrowed Nip Underwood's scarf to do the job. On the same day Joe was emptying the teapot and cast round for somewhere to throw the tea leaves. For our main meal we had started a continuous stew into which something new and different was added every day. Joe absent-mindedly tipped the tea leaves into the stewpot. On the last day of the holiday we had enough tea and cocoa left for two cups each. Joe brewed the tea and put cocoa into two of the cups and then poured tea on top of the cocoa.

Joe Smith became an expert rock climber and one of the most popular members of the group. He was noted for his endurance and resourcefulness. Before he joined the Rock and Ice at the age of fifteen he hitch-hiked alone to Chamonix and back with £12 in his pocket. Out of this he managed to pay his fare across the Channel, which was £2, buy a pair of French boots costing £9, and live for two weeks in the Mont Blanc range on a theoretical balance of £1. He climbed Mont Blanc and other peaks. He would have undoubtedly become one of the leading climbers in Britain, if he had not had a serious motor cycle accident. He had great natural ability and the strength to match.

Soon after Joe Smith came to the Rock and Ice it was patently obvious that two Joes on the rockface would lead to confusion in the general run of shouting this and that to one another. The group had always been amused by the accents of Oxbridge types one saw on the crags; we called them "light-coloured voices". The lads impersonated them; on the cliff they called to each other with phrases such as: "Raighto, I've got a bloody belay now, Cecil. Doo come hup." In the course of amusing ourselves with these funny accents Joe Smith was labelled "Mortimore", or Morty for short. This suited everyone and after this he was addressed by his nickname. Several members of the Rock and Ice were given nicknames, such as The Villain (Whillans) and The Count (Neddy Goff)—because he sounded like a Russian count.

The competitive spirit of the Rock and Ice among its own members was cultivated in the surroundings of the camp-site, the barn or the boulders under which shelter was taken. There were no idle or dull moments. Someone would pick up a heavy stone, lift it above his head or toss it a few yards. A challenge had been thrown out to the rest of the company.

Continuous press-ups, and pull-ups on snap-links, were among the more exacting tests. Ron Moseley pushed a pen all day in an office yet held the record of twenty-six pull-ups. Don Whillans, who was generally acknowledged to be the strongest, achieved sixteen. The best I could ever manage was thirteen.

If a handicap system could have been devised Morty would have taken first prize for press-ups. His strength-weight ratio surpassed everybody. His party-piece was press-ups; I once saw him make nine with someone of his own weight of nine and a half stones sitting on his shoulders. When I tried to repeat the feat, handicapped with someone of my own weight on my shoulders, I couldn't even raise myself. It was as if I had been screwed to the ground. Once, out of interest, we decided to size up Morty with a tape measure, to compare his vital statistics with my own. Morty was three inches less round the chest and seven inches more around the shoulders. The aggregate gain of ten inches in the shoulders explained the advantage.

As a rock climber of unusual ability Ron Moseley suffered from extremes of form. One weekend he could lead the hardest routes imaginable, the next he might be reduced to ordinary routes on a tight rope. His standard fluctuated wildly for no apparent reason.

Moseley's inconsistent climbing was probably due to his ups and downs in enthusiasm. As with Don Whillans and myself Ron's standing in the Rock and Ice was founded on his persistence for attempting new routes. He excelled at this. Like ourselves he disliked acting as a second and therefore regarded our company as a waste of time. He wanted to identify himself as an independent leader, planning his own campaigns. My best climbs with Moseley were winter ascents of Welsh gullies: Black Ladders Western, Schoolmasters', and Kitchen South. The latter contained the finest ice pitch I have ever done in Wales.

In reality there was hardly any friction between members of the Rock and Ice. The episode of who was entitled to make the first ascent of White Slab on Cloggy was the only instance when tempers frayed. Here again outside observers have made much more of the incident than the facts warranted.

As an all-rounder Don Whillans was more than just a brilliant climber. He was, and still is, a genius. Of sallow complexion, with hair brushed straight back over a large forehead, Whillans stood five feet four in his stockinged feet, broad in the shoulders and chest and exceptionally lively on his feet, like a middle-weight wrestler in miniature. He lived in the Salford part of Manchester and his family background and occupation were almost identical to my own; he was a plumber and general handyman in the building trade. He began studying at night school for examinations but gave up attending the course. His employer was not as generous as Archie in giving time off and

Don couldn't leave for the mountains until mid-day on Saturday. On the other hand he owned a motor bike and soon caught us up.

The stories circulating about Don Whillans over the past fifteen years have undergone so many colourful twists that no one can say where fact ends and fiction begins. Don always gave the wrong impression of himself. He was lackadaisical yet dynamic, contented yet cunning. He was not exactly two persons; there were two sides to his nature and most of the time one overlapped the other, producing a mixture of he-man and saint. He had a deep-seated love of animals and pets and couldn't bear to see them ill-treated.

The tough-guy stories attributed to this remarkable figure were and still are without parallel in British mountaineering. The "dobbing" of the bus conductor probably started it all. At the age of fifteen Whillans was taken before the magistrate to account for punching a bus conductor who had been laid out cold. The court was informed that Whillans had not hit the man with anything except his fist; on that point the magistrate doubted the evidence. Don had been getting off the bus; the conductor had demanded another halfpenny fare; Don had refused, stating that he made the journey every day to work and had paid the correct fare. The conductor got hold of him and tried to prevent him leaving the bus; whereupon the mighty fist of the tiny Whillans shot up from the ground and felled the man.

On another occasion Whillans had a slight altercation with a 6 ft guardsman. He leapt at the soldier with a flying tackle, wrapped his legs round the guardsman's arms, pinning them to his sides, and proceeded to "knock hell out of him".

This tough reputation spread like wildfire in climbing circles. True or false it had a salutary effect on other people. During the early fifties, for instance, when hordes of climbers slept rough in the Wall End barn in Langdale, Whillans quelled a riot of noise late at night by shouting, "Pipe down and go to sleep". This order was greeted by indignant comments, such as, "Who the bloody hell do you think you are!" Whillans replied

in a whip-cracking voice, "Whillans", and silence fell instantly
upon the rowdy company.

Don was four years younger than I: he was seventeen when
he joined the Rock and Ice in 1951. He was a born rock climber.
The ascent of rock-faces of every description was completely
natural to him; he did not have to learn the craft, he had
simply to familiarise himself with it. He could lead Very Severe
routes, or harder, virtually as soon as he started climbing.

The spiky side of Don's nature was dormant on the mountain.
He was easy-going and took my advice as readily as I took his
on matters of route finding. Dissension in a party on questions of
route finding had led to many broken friendships. But Don
always listened to reason; he was content to accept an opinion
that was probably not entirely consistent with his own and I
believe the same was true of me.

Don's climbing style was similar to my own. If anything, his
prowess was built on an ability to "float up" overhangs; yet
many of his masterpieces were triumphs in delicate slab
climbing (for instance, Slanting Slab on Cloggy). Don made
fewer first ascents than I but all his routes were nothing short of
magnificent; they were virtually devoid of protection in the
form of good running belays, and a unique boldness and their
improbable outcome placed them immediately among the most
serious undertakings in Britain. He exemplified more than
anyone in British mountaineering the image of a "hard man".

The plain fact about climbing with Don Whillans was that if
you got into difficulties, or couldn't manage to get up at a
particular point on a climb, the chances were that he could pull
something out of the bag. It followed that mountaineering with
Don was much safer than with anyone else. He is the best rock
climber that I have ever known and he is equally strong on
snow and ice on mountain ranges abroad.

My career was shaped with the Rock and Ice, and the Rock
and Ice in those days was synonymous with Cloggy. The
verticality of the great dark cliffs on the north side of Snowdon,
with their ferocious unclimbed cracks and slabs, presented a

marvellous challenge. Cloggy had a special place in my aspirations; just being there made me feel excited.

In 1951, apart from the climb called The Sheaf, there had been no new routes discovered on either of the two main buttresses for ten years. It was significant that after J. Menlove Edwards had made his Bow-Shaped Slab on the West in 1941, The Sheaf (1945) was regarded as something of an eliminate, both as an ultimate in difficulty and in route finding. Then Peter Harding girdled the West Buttress and that seemed to clinch the matter. These climbs, and earlier ones, were concentrated at the left side of the buttress where the cliff is 600 feet high. Farther right the face was still inviolate, protected along its slanting base by a huge fault in the rocks—an overhang several hundred feet in length.

As for the East Buttress it is even steeper than the West, being often vertical or overhanging. The face is split by cracks or narrow chimneys, and the obvious ones, like the Chimney and Curving Crack, had been climbed. The face rises 350 feet to a grassy gallery below a triangular wedge of rock called the Pinnacle, also vertical and a further 200 feet high. The last climb made on the East had been Sunset Crack in 1937.

In 1951 I made two new routes on the East and one on the West. All three were appreciably harder than anything else put up on the cliff to date. My predecessors had certainly done their job well, for one always hoped to uncover a good climb of reasonable standard that might have been overlooked.

In June I went up to Cloggy to try the line of grooves in the face to the right of Chimney Route, which eventually became known as Diglyph. I did not get very far up before returning towards the Chimney. There I noticed a crack splitting the right wall. Having climbed some way up it I got myself into an awful mess and could neither advance nor retreat. In the jargon I was "committed". The crack was filled with grass and dirt. This had to be removed to make room to jam both fists inside to hold on. Nothing as good as a handhold was in sight. I was carrying my peg hammer on a wrist loop and it became wedged between my knee and the crack and I couldn't get it out. My position was perilous; I was sweating profusely and my throat was bone dry. It was a miracle that I didn't fall off. In the ensuing struggle I wrenched the hammer free, moved up a foot or two to a good ledge, but I was so tensed and gripped up that I banged in a peg almost without thinking. I had been doing everything at a furious pace and my only thought was to rest—the peg relieved my aching arms and restored confidence. The next few feet were equally vicious but I was now in control of the situation and thinking clearly. The fight to gain height above the peg was only a matter of careful planning; some little spikes of rock came within reach and put an end to the desperate part of the climb. Above the spikes the crack ran up in a marvellously exposed position on the face to a good ledge.

Eric Price, my second, having watched my antics with mounting trepidation, refused to follow. "I'm not going to try that," he yelled up. Slim Sorrel had gone to climb Bow-Shaped Slab, and I decided to wait on the ledge until he returned. In due course Slim tied on to one end of the double rope while the other piece was fixed so that he could use it for a pull. I think Eric may have warned him about the difficulty of the crack, and the fixed rope gave him confidence to start up the climb. Slim arrived on the ledge in the middle of the cliff, feeling more out of this world than in it. Above, the groove steepened and looked very unpleasant, but a series of big holds led out to the edge of the groove, overlooking the huge central wall of the East Buttress. The finish was really exhilarating and we reached the top feeling very pleased with ourselves, the struggles of the lower section soon forgotten.

By the autumn I had teamed up with Don Whillans. The pair of us were determined to launch an all-out attack on my old rival, Vember. Conditions for the ascent were ideal. The lower part of the climb was so familiar that, without a gushing water-spout, it seemed much easier than before. At the place where I had fallen in 1949 a sling that I had jammed in a crack was still in place and came in very useful. The chimney above was unknown ground; a narrow slot just wide enough to insert a shoulder. Squirming up it was a maddening fight in trying to raise my hands above shoulder level; the chimney pinned the arms to my sides. After a desperate struggle I pulled out on top and lay panting on a ledge. From there the next section looked worse. I was so shattered that I could not imagine it possible to climb anything harder. Don secured himself with great thoroughness while I waited until my heart stopped pounding. How much easier all climbing became when one was composed and rested. The final chimney-crack was difficult but quite straightforward. Now we were really excited for there were no more serious pitches above. Vember was a route at last.

A fortnight later I was back at Cloggy with Ron Moseley and a friend of his. The previous weekend Ron had climbed Kaisergebirge Wall in the Llanberis Pass without using pegs. The route had previously been done with several pegs—eight being used on the first ascent. So he was feeling very pleased at having made the first "clean" ascent.

I wanted specially to look at the Boulder. This piece of rock, about 350 feet high, forms a cornerstone at the left edge of the West Buttress. The name is something of an understatement. My curiosity had been aroused by the rumour that Chris Preston, a wartime explorer of Snowdonia, had tried to climb it. He had come away declaring, it was said, that fifty pegs would be needed to force the ascent.

I climbed up the left edge of the Boulder for 40 feet and saw a traversing line of holds rising across the sheer face of the cliff. The traverse was awkward to start with, but difficulties eased after 30 feet and I eventually came to a stance beside the Black Cleft. This was the dank vegetated gutter separating the Boulder from the main mass of the West Buttress.

I secured myself, then Ron and his friend tried to climb across the initial hard moves on the traverse. Neither of them could get across and they went back, shouting that if they fell off they would pendulum well over 100 feet and be smashed against the lower part of the Black Cleft. They had a point because I had not been able to fix any runners along the traverse.

I was now in a bit of a predicament. I wanted to continue. I had overcome a lot of the uphill part of the climb and the rumour about fifty pegs was preposterous. I hadn't enough rope to lower myself to the bottom of the Black Cleft. The thought of reversing the traverse was so repulsive that descent was out of the question.

There was no option but to ask Moseley to tie on another rope. The friction and drag from the combined length and weight of two ropes were unnerving. As I proceeded up the Black Cleft I arranged the unwieldy rope in running belays by tying knots in it. At each runner the knot took the weight of the rest of the climbing rope below it. The problem with this system was calculating the distance between each running belay before reaching it, and knotting the climbing rope accordingly.

In this fashion I worked up the Black Cleft to its prominent overhang. I had run out close on 200 feet of rope. The overhang was split by a crack. I jammed my right fist into it and heaved. Feet braced against a holdless slab, I swung up into a horizontal position. Then my anorak hood caught on a downward spike and no amount of wriggling would free it. Meanwhile I had a clear unobstructed view to the screes 400 feet below, with the rope hanging in loops down the big slab of the Boulder. There was not a soul in sight at the bottom and I felt very lonely.

There was nothing to do but swing down and unhitch the hood; this manœuvre cost me a great deal of energy. The infuriating thing about the overhang was that if I had been facing the other way, as I discovered on a later visit, it would have been considerably easier. Sometimes it was impossible to sum up all the possibilities and hit on the right one. If I had had a second man below me I would probably have found the correct solution straightaway. But I went back to it in the same position as before and after a short fight I got over the bulge. I was greatly relieved to see in front of me an easy slab, then a scrambling slope leading to the top. I had run out 270 feet of rope. Ron appeared at the top and helped to pull up the rope and runners, which could now be lifted off by remote control, thanks to the knots.

Throughout the year Rock and Ice parties had been busy in the Llanberis Pass. The right wall of Cenotaph Corner seemed to offer a possible route near its right edge. This edge was gently overhanging for 200 feet. I was not quite ready to try the Corner again but Don Whillans was game to inspect the line of cracks that split the edge of its right wall.

I led the first pitch and took a stance just above a holly tree. I say "took" because there was no ledge, only a couple of footholds scarcely large enough to accommodate half a boot. I hung on to slings attached to poor spikes sticking out of the rock a few feet higher. This was the first stance in slings, as it is called, that we had taken. The position on the face was very sensational and frightening. I brought up Don and he was flabbergasted. "Christ, this is a gripping place," he muttered hoarsely. Neither of us seemed able to move. Then it started to rain and we both breathed a sigh of relief. To get down we had to descend on a doubled rope with our hearts pumping. Running down the screes to shelter from the rain we decided that we must return as soon as possible to strike while the iron was hot. We were now mentally prepared to accept this fly on the wall situation.

A week later we took a stance in slings again. We couldn't change places so Don led the second pitch which was truly hair-raising. All the way up it little flakes of rock broke off when we pulled or stood on them. The redeeming feature of the climb was an abundance of running belays; if one of us fell his flight through space would be short, or so we told ourselves. I led through and climbed the third pitch, losing a pair of socks from a pocket. The socks floated straight down without touching rock and I thought, My God, what a hell of a place! The third pitch vanished up and round the corner of the edge on the right. Don had to wait, without news, on his uncomfortable stance, for the outcome. After 30 feet of continuously amazing climbing I yelled, "It's in the bag!" A line of big holds led up the last stretch of rock that was merely vertical. There was no mistaking that we had cracked it. Don let out a shriek of triumph. Never before or since have I known him to show emotion in this way. He was normally taciturn after making a new route. Now he was bubbling over with pleasure.

Going home that night on the motor bike we saw a bus in Chester with Cemetery Gates on its indicator. This seemed to fit in with Cenotaph Corner and Ivy Sepulchre (the routes on either side), so we decided to call the climb Cemetery Gates.

While climbing in the Llanberis Pass the Rock and Ice bivouacked under boulders or slept in a road-mender's hut. In August, 1952, Doug Belshaw and I left the hut and went to Cenotaph Corner for another attempt.

Compared with the first attempt I now had superlative equipment and a keener eye for running belays on which to protect myself. I avoided using pegs up to the point I had reached before, but pulled on a sling to overcome the first hard move at 20 feet. I found the climbing just as difficult as ever and tore my trousers from knee to ankle in the crack at 70 feet. Getting into the niche at 100 feet was absolutely gripping— very much harder than I remembered it from the previous occasion. The exit crack jutted out above. I tried an assortment of pegs; none seemed to be the right size for the crack. I buckled half of them and thought, Oh, damn it, you'll have to bridge up across the bulge to gain a little height and bang one in higher up, where the crack appeared to be more regular. To make this move I stuck a peg loosely into the crack and pulled side-ways on it. This movement was as hard as any I had done in my life. The last thing I expected was to be able to stay suspended in so fantastic a position and hammer in a big wrought-iron peg above the impending rock. This was what I had to do and it was done. The peg remained there for eight years. However, the strain of planting the peg must have dulled my senses. I leaned away on the crack and pressed my feet against the left wall to raise myself. I pivoted up almost horizontally. In this shattering position I knew that I would be down in seconds. I was climbing in socks and vainly tried to hook my feet on to rugosities below a large patch of moss, oozing with water. Until then I had forgotten that conditions on the cliff were bad and the corner was very damp.

There was a large jug-handle hold above. If I used it, releasing a hand from the crack would swing me off. But I had to use it or fall off in any event. Grabbing the jug-handle I swung back into a vertical position. The wrench drained the strength from my overworked arm. I got my other hand on the jug and pulled with all the strength I could muster. I shot up like a missile from a catapult and thrust a foot firmly on the big hold. The exclamation "Phew" was never more appropriate than at that moment.

My bag of routes on Cloggy during 1952 was six. Three of these were on the Pinnacle above the East Buttress. The Pinnacle Face was noted for its great flake; Harding was alleged to have climbed to the top of the Flake and dismissed the final wall as impossible. The Pinnacle Flake had exceptional exposure and very little protection. Both Don and I were rather pressed on the mantelshelf movement at the top of the first pitch, owing to our short reach. From the top of the Flake, where Harding had turned back, a short traverse left led to easy ground, though Don returned some time later and climbed the final wall.

The Black Cleft was in another class. Don and I had made a reconnaissance in deep snow at Christmas. We had taken off our boots and pranced up the first pitch in stockinged feet. A gardening trowel found at the top of the introductory pillar was a mystery unsolved to this day. In those conditions further progress was impossible.

On the day we pressed home the attack, a torrent was flushing the gutter. The Cleft was full of luxuriant vegetation and turfs loaded with water. Don excavated the first pitch slowly and tortuously, water running out of his trouser bottoms. When I reached him he was chattering with cold, wet through and shrivelled up. On the next pitch the vegetation was really fantastic. I stripped if off in huge lumps, as heavy as lead rolls. Earth and debris rained on Don, spraying him with dirt from head to foot. He was in a sorry state on joining me at the Boulder stance. He stood there deliberating whether to continue. The last pitch was his. "Oh, to hell with it," he growled. As soon as Don started moving he was back in top gear. There was no stopping him now and in this sort of mood he rarely if ever made a mistake. He sailed over the overhang facing right, demonstrating what a mess I had made of the pitch when I had climbed the Boulder.

A week of rain preceded the ascent of Llithrig with Nat Allen. We were climbing Sunset Crack and I decided quite casually to break out on to the right wall. An overhang and a crack took me out of sight, so that Nat had no idea what lay in store for him. Confronted by a blank wall I saw the possibility of continuing the route ten feet horizontally to the right. I fixed the rope on a runner, swung across with feet skidding wildly on the rock and grabbed the edge of the continuation crack. This led easily up to a good stance but the belay pegs only went in for about a quarter of an inch. (These pegs are still used today and I am sure that most climbers doing the route would be very alarmed if they knew how poor the pegs were.) Nat came up the pitch cheerfully enough until he saw where I was lodged and then where the rope was fixed. His eyes almost popped out of his head. This kind of manœuvre, called a tension traverse, always looked impossible at first sight. Nat was very pleased when he got across. The rest of the climb was a series of interesting cracks, dripping with water. We plodded up them steadily, little knowing that this route was to become one of the most popular on the cliff.

The last big climb was Cloggy Corner. This corner was not unlike Cenotaph in height and position and it stood at the right-hand side of the East Buttress. Some of us had already roped down the corner and opinion was favourable. The week of rain had damped our spirits so much that lethargy had taken possession of the party. On the morning in question we were roused to action by Ron Moseley, who had been off-form all week and had done precisely nothing. It was pouring down and he drove us up to Cloggy. We sheltered in the old mine buildings and looked up at the crag through driving mist and rain, thinking that Moseley must be crazy. "Come along lads," he nagged, "shan't get anything done by standing about here." We obeyed him and were shepherded to the crag, soaked to the skin.

Four of us plucked up courage to make the slippery scramble to the foot of the corner. We took our boots off and prepared to climb in socks. Even while I was grappling with the slimy corner a few feet up the first pitch Moseley had had second thoughts and was quietly roping down to the bottom!

I dug out yards of earth from the crack in the back of the corner. Patiently I forged ahead; it was not possible to be wetter, so that did not matter. I sprawled over the top, feeling as if I had waded through a mud bath.

Nat Allen and Doug Belshaw followed, and both arrived at the top soaked through and covered with mud. But despite the terrible condition of the climb we had all really enjoyed it. The socks we had climbed in were worn through, so we left them in a pile at the top of the Corner. The cairn of socks remained there for six years.

Routes multiplied thick and fast in 1953: another five on Cloggy, including a girdle of the East Buttress, and the Carpet Slab on the West, treading new ground at the right-hand side of the buttress. In the Llanberis Pass Whillans and I completed Surplomb, widely misreported as "a fierce ascent accomplished in nailed boots in a snow storm". These conditions applied to an earlier attempt. We had bright sunshine and wore rubber shoes for the ascent. Some unorthox tactics for moving while standing in slings were employed on the first pitch which was a very blank wall with tiny spikes.

Don Cowan and Eric Price accompanied me to the Grooves of Cyrn Las where the rock was decorated with rosettes of a thick, brown, blubbery fungus growth that one imagined only flourished in a primaeval jungle. Both Don and Eric fell off the second pitch and neither of them wanted to continue. Although we were on a comfortable grass ledge, the final 100 feet was just a great overhanging mass of rock with no obvious line. I was determined to finish the route. "Just hang on a minute," I said, "I'll traverse round the corner and have a look. If it's going to be hard I'll come back and we'll go down."

Confident that any exit from this place would be really hard the other two agreed, so I traversed off round the corner. The shallow groove above was very steep but it had good flake holds and I decided to continue. I don't know what my companions reactions were, but I can well imagine, because as I went up the pitch the rope hung farther and farther away into space.

Hemp ropes had gone out and nylon was in. Nylon cost three times as much. An advertisement pointed out that nylon rope buried in a dung heap for six months could be recovered intact and as good as new; hemp rope rotted and fell to pieces after two months. The most important consideration was the elasticity of nylon, up to 40 per cent of any given length under certain conditions of loading. This quality enabled the rope to absorb great shocks without breaking.

Pegs were either scarce or expensive to buy. They were made abroad and only a few types were imported because the demand from British climbers was small; their use was esoteric and misunderstood. Until the climate of opinion changed, a few years later, several people made their own from wrought iron and mild steels on the factory work bench. Snap-links were universally adopted for a host of techniques and ex-W.D. ones were available in Britain.

Pegs opened up new vistas in British rock climbing. By planting them with various attachments in "unclimbable" rock an artificial route could be made. Contrary to the impression of cheating, artificial climbing involved complex and precise techniques and was invariably strenuous. The climbing was also very sensational but usually quite safe because the climber was attached to the rock every few feet by the rope running through snap-links on pegs. The limestone cliffs in the lower Derbyshire dales were ideal for practice. Unlike the coarse gritstone, limestone cliffs were vertical, the rock hard and smooth and often loose. Free climbs could be made but many prominent faces and buttresses could only be tackled with the peg hammer and artificial techniques. The horizontally jutting overhang, called a roof, could be scaled by these methods.

Our first attempt at artificial climbing was made on the short side of the Ilam Rock in the famous beauty spot of Dovedale. Like most newcomers we banged in pegs at intervals of 18 inches and soon ran out of equipment. It was no good doing this because the rope could not be moved against the friction caused by so many snap-links. Proficiency was gained with patience and a lot of faith. We favoured High Tor at Matlock and Stoney Middleton near Grindelford. By 1952 we had graduated to driving in a peg completely upside down and swinging into space on it. Swinging about under a roof was very exhilarating; sometimes a peg popped out and one was left hanging from another with shattered nerves.

One such climb was the Kink at Stoney Middleton. Ron Moseley wanted to repeat my ascent and Ray Greenall and I offered to hold the ropes for him. Sitting at the bottom with nothing to do but hold up Ron in the runners and pulleys that he was attaching to the roof, we were carried away by the crescendo of a pop-song which we were singing at the top of our voices and forgot our duties. The next thing we knew was the trussed up body of Moseley dangling just above our heads. "What the bloody hell do you think you are doing?" he said furiously. He went back up, got over the roof now that we were paying attention to the ropes, and brought up Ray. As last man I removed the gear. Near the top I asked Moseley to lower me down, to avoid a long walk round the cliff-side. He started paying out the rope steadily, so I jumped off. I found myself falling unchecked through the air until I was five feet off the ground, when the rope was braked. A group of boys nearby goggled at this performance. Before they could comment I stood up and took off the rope as calmly as my nerves would allow, trying to give the impression that my dead-weight descent was normal procedure.

Burning round the ears I caught up with Moseley and echoed his vexation: "What the bloody hell do you think you are doing!"

"Let that be a lesson to you," he said with a smug grin.

On the limestone battlements of High Tor, Joe Smith and I had a spot of trouble with the law. A special constable was patrolling the pleasure gardens at the top when we arrived in this guarded domain by way of the cliff face below it. The constable saw us emerge from the depths and must have got the idea that we were trying to gain free access to the flowers and lawns.

"What are you names," he demanded.

I replied: "Joe Brown."

Morty answered: "Joe Smith."

Whereupon he gave us an enraged look and retorted: "You needn't think I care if you tell the truth or not."

The constable was only satisfied after an independent witness came up to vouch for us that our names were as we had stated.

CHAPTER FOUR

HARD DAYS IN THE ALPS

W E D R O V E I N T O the Chamonix valley at nine o'clock. It was dark and the shadows played tricks with the rain dancing on the ebony road. After a gruelling journey across France we were groggy and wanted to sleep. I had already bashed my ankle on a roadside bollard and had nearly fainted and fallen off the pillion seat.

A car edged out of a side-turning straight in front of us. The bike was travelling at fifty to sixty miles per hour. Jamming his brakes on, the car driver locked the wheels and failed to stop. We went into a long skid, were ejected from our seats as the bike toppled over, and shot along the slippery road in a sitting posture. In the helter-skelter situation I could see Don Cowan quite clearly. The bike spun round and he was silhouetted in the blazing headlight. He drifted into the bank at the side of the road at a terrific speed and vaulted over the top.

Picking myself up I made out the vague shape of Cowan splashing about in water. He had landed in the River Arve. Although he was quite close to the bank he was wobbling in a daze, knee-deep in water, and uncertain which direction to take. Don had been sitting in a cramped driving position for eight hours and had been lulled to stupefaction by the motion of the bike. No bones were broken and the machine was undamaged. Bulging packages of equipment and belongings strapped to the bike had cushioned it.

We remounted the motor cycle and drove on to the Biolay sleeping quarters in Chamonix. The pair of us staggered across the threshold like two prisoners who had just escaped from Devil's Island and had swam to freedom. A member of a party of Cambridge students looked up from his supper and eyed us reproachfully.

"I say, old man," he drawled, "you look as if you have been in the river."

I had saved £20 to go to the Alps. I would have liked to have gone earlier but could not afford a visit before 1953 as I had spent most of my earnings on buying equipment and on climbing at home. Several members of the Rock and Ice had already been to the Alps. Don Cowan, whose motor cycle got us there (just), was the most experienced alpinist in the club and he had a number of excellent climbs to his credit.

Chamonix was much as I had pictured it—large, unlovely and swarming with tourists. In those days the Biolay was little more than a doss-house suitable for climbers accustomed to rough quarters and not afraid of the occasional flea. The charge for staying in this converted barn was 2s a night. An assortment of mattresses and bunk beds lay around in a loft and meals could be prepared on your own stoves. There was a yard outside the back door where trestle tables and benches could be set up on a fine day for meals al fresco. Unfortunately the pleasure of eating outside was spoiled by the unpleasant smell from the lavatory, which was simply a hole in the ground. We soon learned not to carry wallets in our back pockets when using this toilet. The barn was situated adjacent to a large camp-site and all sorts of unwelcome folk (or so climbers thought) crept in when the weather was inclement. No one was sure of the ownership; the French Alpine Club was said to have a stake in it but their name was not conspicuous. Various bodies—but usually an old lady—called once a day to collect money. An inmate got the feeling that he was contributing to some charity. Needless to say *les anglais* made the Biolay their second home. I think it must have reminded them of living in roadmenders' huts and barns in the British mountains.

My first reaction to the mountains, foreshortened from the town, was that they were not particularly impressive. Of course in the bottom of many Alpine valleys all one can see is a deep forested corridor and the peaks are often screened behind it. Possibly I was unaware that Mont Blanc stands over 12,000 feet above the Chamonix valley, a height four times greater than any comparable situation in Snowdonia. Having read that the gigantic scale of Alpine peaks called for retraining in values of planning, method, and both physical and mental effort, I looked forward to judging these matters for myself.

Don Whillans arrived on his motor cycle looking suitably fit and confident. Our first climb was just about the smallest and most accessible peak in the neighbourhood, Pointe Albert. Short as the climb was it had the highest technical grading given in the Alps. The West Face is a sheer wall of granite, not a lot higher than Cloggy; the difference is that the bottom of the wall is 5,000 feet above the Biolay, through pine forest and over grass, scree and moraine. This was our first taste of the famous Chamonix granite, which is a hard red rock with plenty of cracks suitable for jamming techniques. We also resorted to some artificial climbing, using pegs and slings for standing in and pulling on to make progress. On the other hand there was nothing on Pointe Albert to match the technical standards on the artificial routes that we had been doing on the Derbyshire limestone.

For advice and guidance in choosing climbs we relied on Don Cowan. He suggested trying the East Ridge of the Crocodile. This was a longer and more serious route on a rock tower nearly 12,000 feet above sea level. It would give us a good introduction to the difficulties of a long glacier approach.

With my first taste of aching shoulders we tramped along the Mer de Glace to the Envers hut. On a hot day walking up these huge glaciers with a large rucksack on your back is really uncomfortable, and when you are unfit your entire body aches. The only compensation is the magnificent scenery. We found the Envers hut still in course of construction, and in the rather bare and unfinished building we had to fend for ourselves. The hut is perched on a rocky spine projecting from the base of the Aiguilles and commands a wonderful view across the glacier basin of the Mer de Glace. We gazed at some of the finest scenery in the Alps, a ragged tapestry of rock and ice, and retired to our bunks buoyant with anticipation.

Getting out of bed at 2 a.m. is one of the most unpleasant aspects of Alpine climbing. Rising early is necessary to cross the approach glaciers before sunrise and to ensure full use of all the daylight available to avoid a bivouac. One reads about other people feeling exhilarated by getting up at this unearthly hour and being excited with the day's prospects. I tend to feel the opposite way, and hope that the weather is doubtful enough for us to go back to bed, for a few more hours' sleep. In fact I found early starts so repulsive that it eventually became my practice to wander up to the foot of a climb on the previous day, make a comfortable bivouac and start climbing at first light next morning.

Our approach to the foot of the Crocodile was made easier by the steps of a previous party leading most of the way up the steep icy glacier. By daybreak we were standing below the ice gully that marks the start of the difficult climbing. I was leading and drove my axe into the upper lip of the big crevasse defending the entrance to the gully. As I pulled on it the shaft broke (ex. W.D. equipment of course!) and I fell back among my companions.

"That's a very good start, I must say," remarked Whillans dryly. The other Don said that the embedded piece of axe should be good enough for hauling ourselves across the gap; it was. Chopping steps in the gully ice, Cowan began a recitation hardly calculated to steady our nerves. He had been in the gully the year before when he was going up to do the Ryan-Lochmatter route on the Aiguille du Plan. On that occasion a block estimated as weighing half-a-ton had bounded down the gully and grazed his head.

"You make me sick," said Whillans, looking round apprehensively and expecting to run for his life at any moment. Anyhow, this cautionary tale spurred us to scurry up some rocks and traverse out of the danger area to the foot of the East Ridge.

All went well until we arrived at the hardest section of the climb. This involved climbing on pegs driven upside down into the rock.

The two Dons were standing on a huge flat-topped rock flake about 50 feet high. A deep subterranean crevice went behind it while the top supplied a first-class stance. I led across the artificial pitch above the flake, finding little difficulty, and entered a groove. Then the rope stopped coming. "Hang on, the rope's jammed," shouted Cowan. Ten minutes later they still hadn't freed it so I climbed down to lend a hand.

The rope had slipped down the crevice behind the flake. We could see it hanging down inside but could not get it out. No amount of tugging and shaking would free it. Nearly three hours were lost climbing up and down the cracks on both sides of the flake, poking the rope with axes and trying to undo the tangle. Eventually we managed to pull out to one side most of the rope and we chopped it off into several long pieces. I could have cried; our beautiful 250 feet rope had been reduced to four 60-ft-long pieces. Tying them together the knots caught on bits of rock all over the ridge and made it impossible to use running belays. It was very late when we reached the summit. We left almost immediately, descending on the doubled rope. The knots interfered with the descent quite seriously, slowing us down and wearing us out. Rummaging for food in a rucksack, a torch was dropped, reducing us to two axes and one torch between three.

After an eternity we got down on to the glacier. It was dark and the slopes now seemed twice as steep. After twenty hours or so of continuous climbing fatigue must take its toll. We had attached crampons (steel spikes) to our boots for gripping the icy surface. Stumbling down the glacier Don Whillans caught the crampon spikes in his flapping trousers and fell over. Within seconds he had knocked me over and both of us went flying down the slope. I braked to a standstill, trying to gather in the rope between myself and Whillans, but when the shock load came on the rope I could not contain it. I was jerked off my feet again. Having slowed the slide to some extent Cowan checked us with his rope at the expense of ripping two fingernails. Unluckily I collided with Whillans and punctured him in the thigh with my crampons; his bruised leg looked like the nozzle of a watering can.

Reorganised, we proceeded at a slower pace and reached the hut at 3.30 a.m., some twenty-five hours after setting out. During the last fifteen minutes I sank into an hallucination. I was convinced that we were in Scotland; we were hemmed in by dark forests, and as we dragged our heavy feet up the last leg of the track to the hut I saw myself approaching a castle. I must have been asleep on my feet and dreaming—a condition that other mountaineers have suffered after a trying day.

There was no question that Cowan had been the strong man of the party. He had kept us going. Now he sat down and fell asleep in a chair. Whillans and I tottered about making a brew and soon followed his example. I awoke at three in the afternoon. Still drugged with fatigue we ambled back to Chamonix. I had accomplished my first major Alpine route and reflecting on it over a glass of red wine in the Café National the effort had been worth it.

Browsing through the guidebook to the Mont Blanc range, we noticed that a crack on the Allain-Fix route on the West Face of the Blaitière was graded VIb. This is the hardest grade given to any rock pitch in the range and was in fact the only pitch of this grade in the guidebook. Although we hadn't climbed a pitch even of Grade VI at this time we all agreed to go and have a look at it. At the Biolay we met Geoff Sutton, who spoke fluent French and who probably knew as much about the Chamonix area as any Englishman. He pointed out that there had been a huge rockfall on the face and that it was now doubtful if the route was possible.

"I wouldn't mind joining you," he said, "then you could climb more rapidly as two pairs." We readily agreed, for Sutton had convinced us that an inspection of the face was a worth-while proposition.

At the foot of the Blaitière it was obvious that something had radically changed. A great scar about 1,000 feet high discoloured the rocks, where a huge pillar had fallen down.

We scrambled up the easy lower part of the face to the foot of the scar. A crack reminiscent of Curving Crack on Cloggy led to a good ledge at the foot of a vertical wall. This was split by a huge bulging crack leaning to the left. The crack looked deceptively easy and I set off up it with my rucksack. It was not long before I realised that the pitch was liable to be as hard as some of the big cracks on gritstone. It was completely holdless and had to be climbed by wedging one arm and leg inside it. The climbing was strenuous but straightforward up to a bulge, where I managed to fix an upside down peg behind a poor flake. Overcoming the bulge was even more strenuous and all of us tore the skin off our knees.

Another long and difficult crack brought us to a terrace about one-third of the way up the face. Here we rested and had some food. Don Cowan and I prospected to the left for a line through the vertical walls above. This sortie side-tracked us on to the pale-coloured scar marking the scene of the rockfall. The rock was brittle and unpleasant to handle. As an underlying skin, freshly exposed to the elements, it was completely unweathered. Whillans and Sutton pushed directly upwards from the terrace. They returned to report that the rocks looked exceedingly difficult. It was now too late to find the solution. The retreat was sounded and we roped down the cracks to the lower terrace. Darkness trapped us and we had to bivouac on a ledge overlooking the carnival of lights in the valley 6,000 feet below.

Ten days in the Alps flashed by and bad weather brought the holiday to an abrupt close. The experience of Alpine climbing haunted me. Back in Manchester I told myself that I might as well go back the following year for the whole of the season; three months. One would then stand a really good chance of making a number of major climbs. I would have to resign my job and look for something else when it was all over. Whillans, Moseley, Ray Greenall and others supported the idea although not all of us would be in the Alps at the same time.

In preparation for the event Moseley and I made a resolution: our general expenses must not exceed one shilling a week until we had saved about £100 each to pay for a long holiday. We dedicated ourselves to the cause. I gave up smoking and we cycled everywhere on weekend trips in Derbyshire. The shilling was usually spent in a café. Our friends tucked into big meals with a loud smacking of lips while we watched in silence. We used to ride away in disgust or because we couldn't trust ourselves. I was saving about £5 a week and Ron, after deducting his fares to work, was putting by a similar amount. Week after week we persevered, denying ourselves the pleasures and most of the necessities of life. The target was reached, but not before we had transgressed a little!

After many months of scraping, saving and waiting the summer arrived. Ten of us rode or walked into Chamonix only to be tied to the town by atrocious weather for several weeks. We pottered about on the practice climbs of the Brévent and did one or two short routes on the Aiguilles.

Among other things, the East Face of the Grand Capucin loomed large in our ultimate plans. Girdled by overhangs and roofs this magnificent wall had been finally scaled by the brilliant Italian climber, Walter Bonatti, in 1951. Bonatti and a companion had toiled on the precipice for four days, finishing in a storm.

To reconnoitre the approach we had been up to the foot of the wall, quite a long way from Chamonix, on several occasions. Cautious with our hard-won savings we walked to the Montenvers hotel, where the glacier trudge began, rather than use the railway. Expenses were also cut by avoiding staying in huts. Huge loads and sleeping gear were carried up the long glacier into the Géant basin where an igloo was built below the mountain. We might sit inside for two days, melting snow and making endless brews of tea while the snow fell outside. During one attempt to find the climb the party was lost in a white-out. As far as we knew we had marched across the glacier in a straight line. When the cloud lifted for a moment we were high enough to see our tracks curving in an arc away from the Capucin. The only good thing to be said for the long siege was that it kept us fit. We used to race down to Chamonix for fresh supplies and in descent the Montenvers train was regularly beaten on foot.

I had commuted up the glacier three or four times before our luck changed. Whillans, Moseley and I were lying in the igloo when the roof collapsed. The top melted, leaving the walls with ominous cracks splitting them. In this condition we spent another night in the shelter but it couldn't last more than another day. Early next morning some voices woke us. It was still dark but the weather was fine. The voices receded, we got up, and thinking we had the Capucin to ourselves, prepared breakfast leisurely as dawn stole across the grey-white glacier.

When it became light enough to see the East Face clearly, we noticed two figures already on the traverse about 700 feet up the face. By the time we had sorted out our gear the leader was just starting on the third difficult pitch. As we climbed on to the face ourselves over an hour later we were very surprised to find the second man still in the same place. In this time the party which had got in front of us had hardly moved at all.

The sun was blazing and the rock was fit to fry an egg. With sacks weighing 50 lb our pace slowed. Don kept shouting to Moseley to climb faster because he was taking longer to climb each pitch with all the pegs in place than the time I spent putting them in and climbing, and the time Don spent climbing and removing the pegs. The East Face was mainly sensational artificial climbing through and over some of the most improbable overhangs I had ever seen and it was important to recover the pegs progressively for use higher up. For some unaccountable reason I was sack-hauling without assistance and getting browned off. I was leading and hauling three sacks.

When I reached the first decent ledge on the face I was already thinking that we would have to bivouac much sooner than we intended. The appeal of the Grand Capucin was beginning to wane, even after waiting so long to get on the climb. I learnt that enthusiasm was more likely to fade under the mental stresses of Alpine climbing than at home. Our progress might have been better if a party had not been climbing immediately above. By our standards the Frenchmen were slow; yet they were not the real cause of our delay. Our morale was drooping and we voted to go down. To descend, however, was easier said than done.

Owing to the fact that I had just made a long traverse through some overhangs, it was impossible to rope straight down the face from where I was standing. Moseley, who was half-way across the pitch between Don and me, decided it would make our manœuvre easier if he took a stance in slings at the other end of the traverse. I sent the three sacks across to Moseley and then reversed the traverse to join him. There I found that both of us and the three sacks were hanging on the same peg. We hurriedly sent the sacks down to Don and started roping down ourselves. Approaching the edge of the couloir near the bottom of the face we found a good ledge and decided to bivouac there. Ron had been practising bivouacking all winter in hard conditions, so no one raised any objections. While Ron was making soup Don and I fell asleep and he must have felt that we were not being co-operative. In spite of his intensive training Ron remained awake all night, thinking to himself what a rotten pair of companions we made.

Later in Chamonix I commented to some Parisians on the slowness of the two Frenchmen who had been climbing the Capucin ahead of us. They insisted that I must be mistaken. The pair in question, they said, were two of the fastest climbers in France. A week later their argument was reinforced when the same Frenchmen made the second ascent of the West Face of the Dru in three and a half days. This climb ranked as a milestone in modern climbing in the Western Alps. The first ascent had taken seven days and a book had been written about it. Still we told ourselves that if the speed of the Frenchmen on the Capucin was better than normal, then we ought to be fairly capable of reducing their time on the Dru by half.

"What about having a look at the Dru?" I suggested to Whillans. "Well, there doesn't seem anything better to do, so let's go." With a vague description of the climb in my pocket he and I set off at midday with packs that dwarfed our figures.

The granite thumb of the Dru presented its West Face in full view of the drinking terrace of the Montenvers hotel. Turning our backs on all that, we crossed the glacier and made our way to the gully that led to the bottom of the face. The gully contained several hundred feet of clean ice. Each axe blow broke off large jagged chunks of the brittle stuff.

"Hey, mate, watch it!" shouted Whillans, who was below and unable to dodge the cannonade. "Chop it into smaller pieces."

Perhaps he thought that one could be artistic in cutting, like the figures illustrating a textbook on climbing.

We bedded down for the night on the terraces at the bottom of the West Face. We were tremendously impressed by the wall of rock soaring above us. It was nearly 3,000 feet high. It rained off and on and neither of us slept much. Our bivouac equipment consisted of a *cagoule*—a sheath-like anorak— which I had borrowed from Geoff Sutton, and a pacamac that Don had borrowed from me. The pacamac was more waterproof than the *cagoule*, but not as windproof, so by morning we were both very cold and damp.

As soon as it was light we started moving. With just the right amount of exercise to loosen stiffened limbs we stepped from terrace to terrace with an odd Grade III wall between them. Before long the weight of the sacks became purgatory. The serious climbing was just starting.

"This is useless," I declared, throwing my pack down. "Yes," said Don, "let's wear ourselves out the other way." After that we hauled the packs up the face on ropes.

The first Grade VI pitch was the Vignes fissure. We had been warned about its difficulty. Bar-room gossip in Chamonix was tinged with bated breath when the famous crack was mentioned. Don went up in splendid style, giving a running commentary on its merits. Calling out scornfully, the general drift of his remarks noted "big holds here, large holds there, jug holds above, piece of cake," and so on. Why the pitch should daunt so many ace French climbers baffled us. We thought that if this was the crux, then we were in for an easy climb.

A new power flowed in our veins. We really bombed up the face, pitch after pitch, without faltering. Sharing the leads I got the 40-metre crack which splits an incredibly smooth and overhanging wall. The start of this pitch is a traverse, so that the exposure on the rest of the wall is as sensational as any wall in the Dolomites. The crack was clogged with broken wooden wedges that set my nerves on edge. The wedges had to be treated very carefully, but Don just laybacked straight up the crack, using them as footholds.

We had a snack at the foot of the remarkable 90-metre corner, the most conspicuous feature of the face, which opens below a barrier of triangular roofs outlined darkly against the sky. The sky too was darker now, the rock colder and a woolly cloud-cuff had begun to grip the peak. The artificial climbing in the corner took a long time and I was getting cold. I put on my duvet jacket half-way up one of the pitches. This was distinctly awkward, sitting in slings and with no room to manœuvre. We were told afterwards that telescope watchers at the Montenvers now lost sight of us for good as the peak was smothered in cloud. Shut off from the world and with vast blank walls on all sides, our loneliness was heightened by the snow falling and the uncanny presence of a rope hanging down the face a short distance above. It had been placed there by the first explorers as an escape route on to the easier North Face. We had to find another rope up to the right, which was used to make a pendulum descent to a ledge in the middle of the face.

"My turn, I think," said Don, who was full of beans. He went up a blind crack that—just as it became hopeless—revealed a rotten-looking fixed rope trailing down a rock curtain into the mist.

"Come up now," he called. The stance at the top of the fixed rope was very insecure. "I'll test it," he said, yanking fiercely on the rope. He pronounced it good. Relying on me to guard two unsatisfactory pegs holding the rope, he jumped into space. Don and the rope vanished from sight. I was left in a suspense of waiting. If it doesn't work out, I thought, he'll have a hell of a job getting back up.

Presently a cheery shout rent the stillness. I went down to a big flake crack that we soon climbed to a little nest of a ledge that no self-respecting eagle would call its own.

"This will have to do for the night," Don announced. "Which side would you like to sleep on?" As if it mattered!

Neither of us could relax or stretch out. The ledge permitted only crouching in a variety of restless positions. Snow fell all night. I kept looking at Don, hour after hour, praying for daybreak. Don slept soundly through it all—I know not how—a hooded bundle huddled against the precipice. We were soon covered with a thick layer of snow. In the morning ropes and sacks were buried under snow; snow was melting everywhere and running water showered the rocks. With the equipment stiffened and weighted with water we started up a series of chimneys and cracks; before long we made our first error in route finding.

The estimated length of pitches we had climbed so far corresponded with the poor translation of a description of the route that we had procured in Chamonix. On the upper part of the face we realised too late that the description applied to sections as short as ten or fifteen feet. We had climbed too far up several slabs and cracks and were caught in difficulties more serious than anything else on the climb. Having regained our bearings, we discovered a caving ladder hanging in space. In his usual daring manner Don coolly bounced up and down on the lower rung and declared it safe. We learnt later that this curious and helpful piece of equipment had been removed from the Vignes fissure by the previous party and carried up to the overhang which it now adorned.

The top section of the climb goes on to the North Face. When we looked down the face it was all ice. The prospect upwards was quite the reverse—good clean rock. An explanation for this illogical condition on the mountain came to hand at the top of the first section. From below the landing appeared to be a flat ledge; when I got there it was banked up at 45 degrees with ice. The downward view had shown us similar ledges optically linked to represent an icy face. The top of every pitch was the same. You had to chip hand and foot holds before a standing position could be attained. Even then each stance was delicate and uncomfortable to stand on and we found no relief from the climbing effort.

About 200 feet below the summit a chimney was blocked by icy overhangs which Don avoided by traversing to the right. This was not the correct route and the traverse was the hardest pitch that we did on the West Face. The chimney was the correct route—a traverse line, not at all evident from below, went off to the left below the overhangs. As it was we searched for an exit to the summit. Bit by bit we girdled the top of the mountain, about 300 degrees of a circle. No breach could be found. Several hours were wasted looking for an escape before we hauled ourselves, dog-tired, on to the summit.

This was the lower of the two summits of the Dru and we did not know the way down. The question of descending from this point was debated. Don was clearly in favour of pressing on to the higher summit, albeit farther away, from where we had a sketchy description of another way down. So we climbed the upper rock bastion, another short climb in itself on a very exposed wall.

At the top, an interminable series of walls and chimneys swept down to the Charpoua glacier. Dusk had fallen when we reached the last rocks beside the glacier. Don had just leapt into space across the crevasse between the rock wall and the glacier.

"Come on," he yelled up. "It's all right." Not until I was dropping stone-like through the air did I realise that the jump to the glacier was a good 30 feet. One would probably never pluck up courage to jump down a place like this if it could be examined first from below.

The Charpoua glacier was a jumble of crevasses and ice walls, and never less than 40 degrees steep. We had neither torch nor crampons and had to cope with one broken axe between us. Our descent might be described as a controlled fall of 1,000 feet, taken in stages of one yard at a time—slip and stop, slip and stop.

11. At the foot of Cloggy after the first ascent of *The Corner*.
L. to R.: Doug Belshaw, Nat Allen, Brown

12. An early attempt (1951) on the *White Slab* of Cloggy. *L. to R.:*
Nat Allen, Brown, Ron Moseley, indicated by circles

13. First ascent of *Woubits* on the Far East Buttress of Cloggy

14. Attempt on a new route on the Steep Band, Cloggy

15. CLOGWYN DU'R
ARDDU—EAST
BUTTRESS

Traditional Routes: -----

1 Sunset Crack
2 Pigott's Climb
3 Chimney Route
4 East Buttress Direct
  Finish
5 Curving Crack
6 Pedestal Crack
7 Terrace Crack

Author's Routes: ·······

L Llithrig
D Diglyph
V Vember
N November
C The Corner
S Spillikin
PF Pinnacle Flake
→ Girdle Traverse links

16. Rock and Ice group in Chamonix (1954): *L. to R, standing*: A.N.O., Ray Greenall, Don Whillans; *Sitting*: Brown, Fred Ashton, Nat Allen, Ron Moseley

17. Don Whillans at the bivouac place on the West Face of the Dru

18. On the North Face of the Grands Charmoz in bad weather

WEST FACE
OF THE
PETITES
JORASSES

19. Don
Whillans at the
foot of the
climb
20. Morty at
the bivouac site

We missed the hut on a rocky peninsula in the lower part of the glacier and spent our third night in the open. We wandered into a crevasse-maze and it was too dark to extricate ourselves. We cut a ledge in the ice, spread out the gear and sat down dejectedly. In saturated clothes, and with nothing to eat or drink, severe cramp in the back and legs tortured us all night. Sleeping was an invitation to succumb to the penetrating cold. We exercised our legs by stretching out and then drawing them up to our chins with arms wrapped tightly round the knees to keep our backs away from the ice. This rhythmic movement kept the blood circulating. Overhead the sky was filled with stars as cold and remote as wandering for ever in space.

A light came on in the Charpoua hut. Later a party crossed the glacier barely 200 yards below us. We couldn't move immediately; we had to thaw out and force ourselves to stand up. Two frost-white figures, we finally got moving and trundled to the hut in ten minutes. The building was empty. We ransacked the place for matches to make a brew; there were none. After 40 hours on the mountain, with not more than six hours sleep, I pointed to the valley that was still some hours away. "Let's go, Don." He nodded without speaking.

On the way down we met Hamish Nicol, who congratulated us on achieving something for the "old country". With Tom Bourdillon, he had made the first British ascent of the North Face of the Dru in 1950. His welcome might have forewarned us of the reception awaiting us in Chamonix, but it didn't. In the valley we were hailed as heroes. We had no inkling that our ascent of the West Face of the Dru would have this effect on people.

Back at the camp-site we went into our tents and passed out. A violent storm broke loose during the night. Don's tent was flooded. He was lying in water with his head just above the surface. Far from waking up, he didn't stir and the salvage workers left him in peace. In another tent I was in much the same condition. Water was trickling over my face but I refused to wake up. Two friends dragged me to higher ground, saying afterwards that I was whimpering, and went away to attend

D

to more urgent matters. In the morning Don and I felt deathly. The storm had wrought havoc in the camp-site. Potato peelings, tea leaves and other rubbish had been washed among belongings and the whole place looked like a disaster zone after a hurricane.

Louis Lachenal, one of France's foremost guides, came to pay his respects. He was dressed immaculately and was escorting a gorgeous girl. He found the party lounging on the ground in filth and squalor, like a band of brigands. Goodness knows what he thought of us. Homage from one so exalted in the mountaineering *élite* was indeed a surprise. After this the Chamonix guides came up to us in the street to shake our hands.

A fall I took while climbing the Ménégaux route on the Aiguille de l'M could be attributed to over-confidence. By now I was feeling superbly fit and had unwisely dispensed with the normal procedures for overcoming an artificial pitch on the route. In result a boot slipped off a peg that I was standing on. Falling free after 20 feet, I flashed past a runner that carried some slack rope leading down to the second man. That is my rope, I thought. I grabbed it together with the end tied to my waist and stopped myself. The second man was unaware that anything had happened. I broke the fall and saved myself by a fluke, otherwise it could have been very serious.

Bad weather prevented any further attempts to climb the Capucin. My thoughts turned to the Blaitière. The job was unfinished. Could it be finished? The only way to answer that question was to go back on the face.

One afternoon Don and I strolled up to the West Face and bivouacked on the luxurious platform at the bottom of the cracks that we had climbed the year before (now known as the Fissure Brown). We had a most comfortable night and next morning we romped up the cracks with hardly any effort to the ledges near the rock-fall scar. I traversed on to the rotten rock again and spied a delightful crack running up through much better rock to an overhang. Putting in a peg below the bulge, I swung out to one side and lodged myself in an even nicer groove that broke through the beetling rocks. The climbing was hard but unbelievably straightforward. Don came up remarking on the simplicity of the key that unlocked the door to the rest of the face. Instinctively I felt that nothing could stop us now. Cracks, walls and ledges guided me to the foot of a truly massive wall. It was split by the most gigantic crack that I had ever seen. The wall was either vertical or overhanging for some 400 feet and the crack zoomed up to the heavens.

Two pitches up I was stopped by an overhanging portion, the like of which I had not met before. Even brought to ground level in gritstone surroundings, I doubt whether I could have climbed it. It was dripping with black water, greasy, holdless and devoid of cracks for driving in pegs. After 20 feet of desperately insecure climbing I came down feeling rather shattered. Changing places, Don's attempt was repelled with the same result. We descended to the bottom of the wall to look for an alternative. Only a minute or two away we discovered a short wall leading to a thin unbroken crack that rose to a dizzy height. This was the noted Fissure Fix, climbed before the landslip by the first ascensionists. It is two inches wide and goes straight up—more or less vertically for 100 feet—to a ridge. Fingers and toes were pressed inside as jamming or pressure holds; every upward movement was identical and really enjoyable. I could not remember when a pitch had given me so much pleasure.

Beyond the top of the ridge I slipped in a corner where the landing was on a ledge covered with stones. I fell a few feet, managed to jam a hand into the corner-crack and stopped myself. Soon it was dark and we moved cautiously on the last part of the wall below the summit. The ground was broken by dozens of little ledges, yet none of them would allow us to sit comfortably. We played about under the summit pinnacle for a while, more bemused by the revelation of having made a new and major route than putting our heads together on a course of action. A fresh breeze was blowing, we chatted, the lights came on in Chamonix far below and we forgot the time. Very much later, or so it seemed, a pale light stole across the horizon.

"Stir yourself, Don," I said, "dawn is breaking—let's get down."

"Oh, all right," he grumbled, "I was just getting comfortable and ready for a bit of shut-eye."

We packed the rucksacks and uncoiled the rope, ready to move off when the light was stronger.

Suddenly Whillans growled: "What the hell's that?"

I looked up and saw the moon rising above a dark ridge. The time was only about 11 p.m.

This made both of us so fed up that we couldn't stop talking about it for hours. Came the real dawn, we crossed to the head of the Spencer Couloir, which was in very good condition, and went down by the normal route. We re-entered the camp-site at seven-thirty, before anyone was up.

One of the worst post-war seasons in the Alps was 1954, a year that was remembered long afterwards for continuously bad weather. We had been lucky to snatch the climbing that we did before the season went completely sour. Six weeks of cat-and-mouse games with storms and gales blunted my patience, and Don and I agreed to return home to spend the rest of the summer in Wales. As it happened when we got back we were rewarded with three fine days in six weeks.

With money to spare I bought a lot of superlative French equipment. I carted my purchases home in a colossal suitcase, which was also stuffed with piles of dirty washing belonging to other people. The case was so heavy that two of us had to carry it with an ice axe pushed through the handle. In the customs shed at Folkestone the examining officer frowned suspiciously.

"Open this case, please," he said. He deliberately ignored our grubby-looking rucksacks. The counter was sagging under the weight.

I flicked open the catches. He can lift the lid himself, I thought.

"What have we here," he said in a flat tone, prising up the

top. The lid sprang back and a mass of sticky rags that we called clothes billowed up.

The most distasteful smell imaginable rose from the case. The officer's face screwed up in horror and he stepped back a foot or two, poked a stick inside, lifted up a corner and let it drop. He chalked the case at arm's length, he said: "Yes, that will be all".

CHAPTER FIVE

KANGCHENJUNGA

A TELEGRAM WAS WAITING for me at home. It read: INVITED KANGCHENJUNGA EXPEDITION STOP LETTER FOLLOWING STOP CHARLES EVANS.

I was completely surprised and very pleased about the invitation. A thousand questions buzzed in my head. Only a short time before going to the Alps I had been talking to some of the 1953 Everest team, and they had given me the impression that the Kangchenjunga arrangements for 1955 were settled. In fact I thought that the team had been chosen.

The letter arrived and I went to see Charles Evans, the expedition leader, in Liverpool. He explained that the expedition was primarily a reconnaissance; he wanted the party to be strong enough to ensure that the mountain was climbable. I listened attentively, for he was talking about the third highest mountain in the world and the highest unclimbed mountain at that date.

I attended various briefings at the Royal Geographical Society in London. At the first of them I met Alf Bridge. He had been Secretary to the successful Everest expedition and was now to organise the Kangchenjunga one in his meticulous and masterly way. From the late 1920s Alf and a few close friends—among them Kirkus and Linnell—had pioneered climbing on Cloggy. His services to mountaineering over the years were enormous. He went out of his way to help me prepare myself for a national mountaineering expedition, even to the extent of subsidising me. No one could have wished for a better friend and mentor. Equipment outfitters measured us for special boots, gloves and high altitude clothing and the expedition members met in Wales for rehearsals with oxygen equipment.

At this time I was broke. On returning from the Alps, and

after the sequel in Wales, I had started up in business on my own, working from home. I tendered ridiculously low quotations for repairs on houses—a third or even a quarter of competitive bids—with the result that I had to work at hectic speed to make a profit. In February, shortly before the party was due to sail for India, I asked Charles Evans if he could tell me something about the financing of the expedition, as is applied to individual members. He said that all expenses would be paid and that £20 pocket money would be ample. I couldn't tell him that I hadn't got £20.

The weekend before the boat sailed the Rock and Ice held a meet at Stanage. I went there with all the equipment I had bought in Chamonix and auctioned it. Walking down from the rocks I tripped and badly wrenched an ankle. I was sure that I had snapped the Achilles tendon. In pain, and limping, I boarded the boat convinced that I would be a cripple on the expedition, but the injury cured itself on the sea voyage.

The voyage was the most bracing and carefree holiday of my life. Delicious food was served at frequent intervals and between times we amused ourselves with competitive deck-games that were a trifle rougher than those played by other passengers. Tony Streather, who had served in the Pakistan Army and Chitral Scouts, held classes for an hour each day to teach the party Urdú. He spoke the language fluently and I think that I must have been his worst pupil. The boat eventually arrived at Bombay and we disembarked. At ports of call and on the journey across the plains the expedition was given unsparing assistance by the Himalayan Club. Our destination was a big tea plantation at 6,000 feet above sea level, the Rungneet bungalow near Darjeeling, owned by Jack and Jill Henderson.

Conditions in the mountains were still wintry when we arrived. Cloud swamped the valleys and there were no distant views to be seen. On the second day a shout brought me running outside. The sky was steaming with vapours and I could just discern the outline of Kangchenjunga. The size of big mountains had not impressed me deeply in the Alps. Now, in the foothills of the Himalaya, I was looking at a gigantic unearthly shape, boiling inside a tissue-thin bank of cloud. This was truly an incredible sight. I seemed to be looking up at an angle of 45 degrees at the mountain, yet it was nearly 50 miles away. Slowly the vapours trailed away and the mountain stood out diamond-sharp. When my eyes were adjusted to the total panorama and when all the cloud had dispersed, the mountain blended proportionately with the rest of the Himalayan range. It was the first dramatic sight that aroused the imagination.

We stayed at Rungneet for a week. Six tons of gear had to be broken down into loads that porters could carry towards the mountain. Boxes galore were laid out on the bungalow lawn to await the arrival of our sherpas. They had a long trek to make from the Everest region, which is their home. Charles Evans greeted the troop like a long-lost family and he knew most of their names. Other members of the party who had climbed with some of them on previous expeditions gave the sherpas a tremendous welcome and everyone was soon falling over in high spirits. The sherpas were wonderful company.

Supplies and equipment were loaded on lorries and we drove to the farthest possible point beside the Singalila Ridge. This ridge came down from Kangchenjunga, step by step, for dozens of miles, falling 23,000 feet in the process. The lorries took us up to 8,000 feet; after that the caravan of 12 sahibs, 36 high-altitude porters and 300 coolies set off up the ridge towards the mountain.

Each member of the climbing party was allotted a sherpa for his personal convenience. Mine was Ang Temba, a tough wiry man of about my own age. His log-book showed that he had been six times over 24,000 feet. The sahib wrote in the log-book on matters of the sherpa's behaviour and efficiency, as a record and reference for his next expedition-employers. Ang Temba was a really bright lad and we got on famously together.

For the first few days we journeyed along the ridge in stages of about ten miles. The weather was bad and continued unsettled for the next month. The climatic pattern was identical each day; fine in the morning, snow in the afternoon and most of the evening. After two days walking on the ridge, up to 11,000 feet, I began to appreciate the boon of having a sherpa for a manservant. The climbing party tended to loiter on a day's walk, taking photographs or leaving the trail to look at something interesting. Turning up in camp, all the tents would be pitched and ready for the night; your sherpa had laid out personal effects in a tidy order and he had inflated the Lilo and unrolled your sleeping-bag. You sat down in the tent and the sherpa entered and pulled off your dirty boots and socks, replacing them with clean ones. He then served tea and biscuits and asked if there was anything to be done. I was supposed to be in charge of the radio. Erecting the aerials was a fiddling job; Ang Temba watched me doing it on the first day, and after that the mast was already up when I strolled into camp.

Waking time was 5 a.m. We rose, had a cup of tea and started walking. Breakfast was taken at a halt along the way. This system suited the porters, who preferred to cover as much distance as possible in the cool of the morning.

On the third day we left the ridge and went straight down the side to breakfast in the valley. This was like stepping from a winter scene into the tropics. We put on shorts and gym shoes and continued in this dress for several days through the valley. The caravan turned into the entrance of the Yalung valley and paid off most of the coolies at a ruined Buddhist temple near Tseram village. The expedition was now at 13,000 feet. An acclimatisation camp was set up, about five miles from the Yalung glacier and perhaps fifteen miles from the base of the mountain. Freezing mist and drizzle, interrupted by snow flurries, screened the mountains, and we saw nothing of the views expected.

The effects of altitude were now noticeable. Walking up a gentle slope for 20 yards between two tents made me puff and pant. When the party pushed higher up the valley towards the glacier it was reduced to five miles, then two, a day. Wet snow was falling every day and the murderous boulder ground was slush-covered to a depth of one to three feet. This ground was very tiresome to cross. A moraine slope of 300 feet led on to the glacier. This was so bad that fixed ropes were laid in position and steps were cut in the cement-like grit. The glacier was three miles wide; it took a full day to traverse it. The terrain was appalling underfoot; ferrying a load from one bank to the other, I fell asleep on the glacier from sheer exhaustion.

The approach to the mountain was dull and dispiriting work. Murky weather spoiled the surroundings and the temperature was minus 25. Our equipment was designed to withstand the cold, so that low temperatures were no great hardship. Tinned food was frozen solid. Potatoes resembled balls of coalite all the way through. We stopped peeling them; cut up in a stew they turned the contents to a blackish-grey concoction. The meal was unsavoury to look at but if you closed your eyes the food tasted like any other stew.

At one of the approach camps beside the glacier there was a boulder some 20 feet high. A smooth overhanging face with a narrow crack in it aroused my interest. Throwing caution to the wind I fought my way up the crack on hand-jams and with feet flailing in the air. My high altitude boots were about as well designed for this type of climbing as a pair of boxing gloves. The effort was so great that I thought I must have damaged my lungs in gulping for breath. My throat was raw and at 16,000 feet it seemed ages before I recovered. Ang Temba had watched me using hand-jamming techniques to climb the crack and his interest was aroused. After a couple of practice moves, to my amazement he could hang freely from a hand-jam.

In the final stages of the approach we split into groups of four. Two ferried loads over one section, two over another either ahead or behind. Charles Evans, Norman Hardie—a New Zealander and deputy leader of the expedition—and I reached a point that was reckoned as one ferry-stage distant from the place we hoped to make our Base Camp below the mountain. We camped at this point in gale-force winds. We tuned in on the radio to the BBC and Radio India for the weather forecast. The transmission came over loud and clear. The announcer said: "This is the BBC calling the British Kangchenjunga Expedition . . . winds up to Force 10 can be expected in the area . . ." He was a bit late with the news.

George Band, an Everest climber, joined Norman Hardie in the other tent. The porters were sleeping in a dome tent. We had grown accustomed to a loud cracking noise made by the wind. One morning we heard a particularly loud crack followed by a crash. Charles stuck his head outside and saw the porters lying on the ground; there was no sign of the tent. Slumbering in their sleeping bags, none of the porters blinked an eyelid. Charles got out and went round kicking them into life. The poor fellows rushed round looking for their gear and dashed up the glacier to recover the tent, which was found 300 yards away.

Towards mid-April the first Base Camp was established at 18,000 feet. The glacier surface was slashed by huge crevasses and the ferry road through them looked like the trail of a drunken man. Some of the detours round crevasses were half a mile. Intent on straightening the route I took a party of sherpas and we heaved boulders into the crevasses to bridge them or block them sufficiently for a caravan to descend inside and reascend the far side. My "road" gang turned the route into a fairly straight line.

George Band and Norman Hardie tried to complete the entry on to the West (Yalung) Face of the mountain by using Kempe's Buttress—so named after a previous explorer. This approach led into an icefall that resembled a series of giant chandeliers which were so unstable that it would have been suicide to pursue this route. So a second Base Camp was installed on a pleasant craggy island more to the north. It was thickly snow covered at first, but a month later, after the snow had gone, mosses appeared and there were lots of little flowers.

To circumvent the icefall a somewhat less dangerous route was found in a steep corridor between ice cliffs about 800 feet high. At one point the route passed very close to the cliffs. A camp was made in the corridor and everyone was warned to keep away from the cliffs. Climbing to the camp in mist so dense that you could walk into a snow hump without seeing it, I was surprised to look back after the mist had cleared and see our tracks go within 50 feet of the cliffs. Crevasses notched the top of this ice precipice and at the end of the expedition the rim was collapsing and tossing lumps of ice as big as houses on to the corridor slopes.

The camp near these cliffs was sited in the closed end of a crevasse. We decided that this would be a good place to dig ice caves and thus save the tents for higher camps. After cutting through the ice walls we always broke through into other crevasses. I then decided to explore the main crevasse on my own. It was about 20 feet wide and 30 feet deep with several bends in it. After walking only a few feet the noise from camp could not be heard and I felt as if I was alone on the mountain. Continuing along the crevasse, which was getting steadily deeper and wider, I noticed a black hole ahead. Caution warned me to retrace my steps, but curiosity edged me forward. I crept along until I could see into the hole. On the opposite side the snow formed a thin fragile bridge and I knew then that I must be standing on a similar one. For the last few yards I had not been walking along the bottom of the crevasse, as I had thought; instead, I was standing on a board of snow bridging the crevasse. Through the hole I could see that the crevasse plunged into blue-green depths. I estimated that I could see about 200 feet down and there was no sign of the bottom. I was very frightened and had a great urge to run, which could have been disastrous. Rational thinking made me walk very carefully in the tracks I had made. It was nice to be back at camp.

Above the camp we had to cross an ice cliff; a ledge was hewn out and protected by a fixed rope. Above this, easy angled slopes led up to a ridge. On the opposite side a snow gully ran down into the head of the lower icefall on the Yalung Face. This gully was a marvellous piece of luck for it was the key to all our hopes for reaching the upper slopes of the mountain. A crevasse at the bottom of the gully was about three feet wide when we first

crossed it. A month later four ladders bolted together were
placed across it, 24 feet in all.

The next camp was positioned 300 yards from the bottom of
the gully. The first half of this distance involved intricate route
finding round massive ice blocks, over crevasses, and climbing
up ice walls 50 feet high. Ladders and ropes were fixed on the
vertical sections. Forcing a route through terrain of this nature
might take a whole day, but after the artificial equipment had
been positioned a man could negotiate it in two hours. Camp
II was raised on a level plateau at the top of the icefall and half
a mile away from the next icefall. The latter was a vast area of
rumpled glacier and there was no way round it.

Now at 20,500 feet the altitude slowed down our movements
seriously. The exertion of getting out of a sleeping-bag winded
me. I had to rest and breathe quietly. Sitting up and pulling on
boots was also sufficiently tiring to force a rest. I wondered if I
would ever get another 100 feet higher. It was some consolation
that even Charles Evans, who had been on eight or nine expeditions, fared no better: we were all in the same condition.
In the mornings there was two inches of frost on the *inside*
of the tent. A breeze would spring up and flap the tent, and the
frost dropped off in your face, like a nasty sort of schoolboy
prank. When the sun came up the tent was soon drenched, the
groundsheet filled with water and sleeping-bags were soaked.
But a sleeping-bag hung outside dried within an hour at this
altitude. The sun's rays were extraordinarily powerful in the
rarefied air.

A heavy snowfall in Camp II drove out Charles and me, and
we made tracks towards Camp I. At the foot of the gully we
gazed up at masses of new snow lodged on the slope of the
ridge we had to cross, in avalanche condition. The slope looked
unclimbable because it would not bear our weight. On the
40-degree incline I patted down the snow into ledges, yard by
yard, I mounted each ledge on my knees and stood up slowly.
Half of them collapsed, and with a sudden jolt I sank to the
waist. We spent several hours crawling up the gully in this
manner, expending an inordinate amount of energy.

On the ridge I gasped to Charles: "Oh, well, we've cracked it now. It's nothing but a doddle down this slope to Camp I."

Having gone about 150 feet down I heard a crack like a pistol shot. A split opened in the snow. I froze on the spot. Charles was behind and had not heard the sound. When I stopped he thought I was tired and resting. He charged up beside me. The slope emitted another sharp crack.

We looked at each other then turned and in spirit ran like athletes back up the slope to the ridge.

"That was a close shave," I muttered.

"Thank God it didn't go," said Charles.

The experience of nearly being swept down by an avalanche and the feeling of being trapped depressed us abnormally. We had no option but to return to Camp II. In a fit of despondency I spilt a pot of stew over the groundsheet. Next morning we were surprised to hear voices: Norman Hardie and George Band arrived, bringing the news that the slope had avalanched while a party was climbing it. The fixed ropes saved them.

Marker flags on canes were planted in the snow above Camp II: in bad visibility the route back could easily be lost. Marooned by nightfall or bad weather a climber could die 20 or 30 feet from his tent and not know it was there. Getting through the second icefall was hard work; we finished up in dead-ends, or astride blades of ice dividing crevasses, and had to look elsewhere. In the event, Camp III was pitched in the icefall. The platform chosen lay below an overhanging cliff which afforded protection from possible avalanches. On Kangchenjunga avalanches thundered all day. On an off-day at Base Camp George Band chalked a mark on his tent every time he heard an avalanche. The score averaged one every twenty minutes. Bearing in mind that he was within earshot of only one part of the mountain, the likelihood was that avalanches in motion somewhere on Kangchenjunga constituted a continual procession.

A spacious cavern excavated in the ice at Camp III saved tenting. The oxygen equipment was brought from Base Camp and stored here—we had more than twenty portable open-circuit sets and two closed-circuit sets. With the closed-circuit set you breathed pure oxygen, while the open set mixed oxygen with a much larger proportion of air from the atmosphere. The difference between the two was that the open-circuit system reduced the effects of altitude by about 1,000 feet, whereas the other had the remarkable effect of delivering to the user the vitality found at sea level.

Charles Evans and Norman Hardie donned the closed-circuit sets and explored in one day the route to the site of Camp IV and continued to a place where Camp V could be set up. This outstanding performance was made possible by breathing pure oxygen. On the descent the sets broke down, making them worse off than they had been when they started. A climber tends to lose acclimatisation after relying on pure oxygen to gain height. With an open circuit set, when the supply ran out, the pack could be dumped and as soon as you started downhill you felt better than you had going uphill, breathing the air-oxygen mixture through a mask. Charles and Norman swore that they would not use the closed-circuit method again.

The secret of acclimatisation was revealed after I returned to Base Camp for a rest. This was enjoyable enough but the benefit was felt in reascending through camps established on the mountain. I could now go up a two-day stage in one day without taxing myself. The climb from Base to Camp II was not at all arduous. Once I had regained Camps III and IV I discovered that I no longer puffed and panted getting out of a sleeping-bag and putting on boots; nor did I need a rest between the operations. The vigour with which one undertook camp chores and climbed with loads was still nowhere equal to an acclimatised performance in the valley. All the same it was a triumph of physical well-being.

The ascent to Camp IV at 23,500 feet was a piece of superb climbing on ice slabs. A drop of 3,000 feet was framed between your legs. Whenever a difficulty appeared, a fixed rope secured the position. The scenery was magnificent and on a scale that only the Himalaya portrayed. When I arrived in Camp IV

John Jackson and Tom MacKinnon were out conducting a heavily laden party to Camp V. Several sherpas had gone badly on this section. Charles Evans's man had dropped his pack down a snow-filled crevasse and spent half the day salvaging it. John Jackson had mislaid his goggles and was snow-blind. At the time the occupants of Camp IV were expressing great concern over the whereabouts of missing members of the party. They were presumably descending from Camp V. No fixed ropes had been placed on this section, so when contact was lost it was easy to worry and imagine the worst. Just as it was getting dark, John Jackson, in agony with snow-blindness, and Evans's sherpa stumbled into camp. The roll call was complete.

At Camp IV the weather changed. Instead of the fine mornings, there was snow and roaring winds lasting for three days. The tent sank lower and lower until there was no room inside to move. In a shrieking gale we shovelled snow off the sides two or three times a day. The mere thought of losing sight of the tent in these conditions made work outside a nervous experience.

Charles Evans had chosen his team as a dependable body of climbers and for an ability to get on with each other. In this he was entirely successful. Personal relations are an important factor in high altitude climbing, where the hardships and stresses are great. That one person might be a professor and another a labourer had no relevance to climbing a mountain. In Charles Evans we could not have had a better leader. He never told you what to do; in the nicest possible way he always asked if you would like to do something, and that was good enough for everyone. It was agreed that George Band and I would make the first assault. Norman Hardie and Tony Streather would form up as the second.

Approaching the site of Camp V the assault teams came across numerous objects lying in the snow: the caches of equipment made by John Jackson's teams had been swept down by an avalanche—and we were already laden with loads of 40 lb or more. By the time the extra items had been strapped to our packs most of us had close on 60 lb. Charles quickly realised that none of us would get up the last 500 feet. The slope was painfully steep and the altitude was 25,000 feet. Putting on an oxygen set he cut steps, demonstrating the justification and real value of the closed-circuit system.

Only the tips of tent poles were visible at the deserted Camp V. The party commenced digging, resting every three minutes or so from crippling exhaustion and clapping an oxygen mask over the face. Everyone was in such a bad state that next day, which was bad anyway, was voted for a rest. It was the coldest day at any time on the mountain. Two hours were taken to melt snow for drinks. Our bodily discomfort was extra-ordinary. I wore a pair of silk gloves under a pair of woollen ones, in turn under a pair of eiderdown muffs. Taking off the muffs to adjust an oxygen set I got the twinges in my fingers, which lasted a month. George Band removed his woollen gloves as well; he worked in his silk gloves for about 15 seconds to unscrew two valves. All his fingers were blistered.

The following day was mild. In good spirits a party of twelve climbed in Indian file towards the conspicuous snow gangway that forms a ramp slanting across the top part of the West Face of Kangchenjunga. The gangway is about 300 feet wide and rises 1,500 feet at an angle of 45 degrees. Charles Evans led at first and in due course was relieved by Neil Mather and Dawa Tenzing, the chief of sherpas. Band and I were to conserve our energy for the final assault. Hour after hour we plodded in steps cut by the vanguard. In a gully the slopes rose to an angle of 50 degrees. Here Dawa Tenzing seemed to go like a machine. Chop, chop, chop; snow chips flew from his swinging axe in an endless stream, skidding and tinkling down the slopes. The snow was in excellent condition and our hopes ran high.

When the cylinders of our open-circuit sets were empty a halt was called, late in the day, to take stock of the situation. The altitude was close to 27,000 feet. We had climbed more than half-way up the gangway. Then we noticed that a sherpa still had a considerable supply of oxygen left in his set. He had been climbing for several hours with the valve switched off! Why he hadn't dropped dead in his tracks will never be known. All we could think of was the difference this would make in digging out a shelf in the steep ramp on which to erect a tent. A rock was hit, so that the platform could not be made wider. A tent was put up and half of it flapped over the edge.

"Goodbye, George. Cheerio, Joe. Good luck!" The support group turned to descend, leaving George and me alone on a small ledge 1,300 feet below the summit. Somewhat disturbed by this cliff-hanging situation, we spent the evening knocking pegs into the bedrock to belay ourselves. If the tent fell down we would not.

Throughout the expedition I had had an insatiable appetite and consumed enormous quantities of food. At Base Camp a yak was chopped into steaks. I held out my plate and the cook (and what a cook he was!) filled it with delicious steaks. I ate four or five at once. At the intermediate camps I was in the habit of raising Base on the walkie-talkie to ask for more food.

"Camp IV calling Base. Do you read me. Please send up steaks. Over."

"This is Base calling Camp IV. Did we hear you right. Your request sounded like steaks. Over."

"Camp IV to Base. Steaks s-t-e-a-k-s are correct. Over."

The only time that I was sick on the expedition was when I had a pound of cheese and four Mars bars for breakfast.

At Camp VI George and I had to nourish ourselves with something less than a feast. We had orangeade and tea, asparagus soup, lamb's tongues from a tin and mashed potato. Thinking that it would be impossible to smoke at this altitude I had brought only five cigarettes. But I found that so long as I sat still I could enjoy smoking as much as ever, and wished that I had taken a full packet.

We drew lots for sleeping on the inside position and George teetered on the edge that night. We shared one oxygen bottle which was reserved to get some sleep. The mask became cold and wet from condensation and the bottle was kept inside the sleeping-bag to prevent the valve jamming. As soon as the oxygen was finished we woke up instantly. I felt entombed, lying in a sleeping bag, wearing huge boots and nudged by an oxygen bottle.

George and I set off to climb Kangchenjunga half an hour after daybreak. It was 25th May. George took the lead but after 200 feet he found that he was needing too much oxygen for the step-cutting effort. I took over and stayed in front for the rest of the climb. Photographs studied at Base had given me a good indication where to leave the gangway and strike up directly towards the summit. We traversed off too early and fetched up against perpendicular cliffs. We went back and I continued cutting steps up the gangway. I was cutting uphill steps in a straight line, which were smaller and fewer than downhill ones, and therefore less strenuous to shape. This economical procedure was regretted later. My rhythm was good and we gained height steadily. On the right I turned up a series of rock ribs and steps. The rock was rough, golden brown and firm. However, George preferred to clamber in snowy grooves at the side. My native instinct for rock had dulled good judgement. The rock climbing was quite difficult and a waste of effort compared with the snow grooves. After five hours of continuous climbing, ending in a little gully about 60 degrees steep, we pulled ourselves on to the crest of the West Ridge and sat down to rest. The position was superb. We munched a little food and were entranced by the scenery. By way of the ridge the summit was not more than 200 feet above us. Distances and difficulties are deceptive on high mountains, so that nothing is taken for granted. All we knew for certain was that our oxygen supply was low.

"We have only an hour left to reach the top or turn back," said George.

We shuffled along the ridge until a rock tower forced me to traverse the side. I came up below a steep wall. The only way I could see was a crack with an overhang in it. Turning up the oxygen supply rate to six litres a minute, which made an appreciable difference, I worked up the crack, banged in a peg and pulled over the bulge.

"Take some photos of me, George," I shouted. The shutter clicked. That was it. There was just a little snow comb and nothing beyond it. One expects to be overwhelmed by a terrific feeling of triumph at the top of a mountain, especially one as big as Kangchenjunga. Now we felt only relief at not having to step up yet again and also a great feeling of peace and tranquillity. After spending so long on a mountain one tends to lose sight of the fact that there is a top and that the point of the expedition is to get there.

We stood on a rock and the snow comb was only four or five feet higher. The snow could easily have been corniced. It was just as well that we had given an undertaking to the Nepalese authorities not to tread the very top. The mountain was sacred and Gods dwelt there.

The panorama was photographed. An ocean of cloud spread out on all sides and only the giants of the Nepal Himalaya stood out: Everest, Lhotse and Makalu.

My oxygen ran out soon after leaving the summit, George's a few minutes later. We dumped the sets and retraced our steps to the gangway. The widely spaced steps that I had cut on the way up sapped the last of our energy. It was practically dark when we tumbled into the tent at Camp VI, now occupied by Norman Hardie and Tony Streather. Sandwiched together, George and I gave them the news.

Within an hour my eyes began to prickle. During the rock climbing I had pushed up my goggles on to the forehead. They habitually steamed up and I had thought to myself: This is just rock, the sun won't affect my eyes. I was soon in torment. The pain could not have been worse if my eyelids had been poked back and red-hot iron filings poured into them. Water streamed down my face. I turned over and over in the night, unaware of the cold and tortured by the searing pain.

In the morning I was blind. I could see nothing. I groped down the gangway, played on the rope by George, and the occupants of Camp V came out to meet us with hearty congratulations. There was no medication and I continued to Camp IV. Two sympathisers pulled out my eyelids and stuffed them full of cocaine ointment. My eyes bulged like eggs but the ointment gave no relief. Feeling absolutely wretched I went down to Camp III and slept round the clock. Before normal vision was restored I had blurred images in duplicate and triplicate. Reaching for objects I sometimes found my hand grasping nothing.

Norman and Tony returned triumphant. They had found an easy way round the overhanging summit crack.

At Base Camp we learned that sherpa Pemi Dorje had died of pneumonia. On the day that the sherpas were burying him everyone was solemn. Incense was burnt and food offerings were scattered to the Gods. While the sherpas were excavating a tomb beneath a large rock one of the men who was levering a stone loose slipped and went somersaulting down the slope. Immediately all of the sherpas collapsed in hysterical laughter —their sense of humour never leaves them for long.

CHAPTER SIX

THE MUSTAGH TOWER

ONE SUNDAY EVENING in April, 1956, I was putting my feet up to relax when a knock sounded on the front door. A little earlier I had come home from Wales with Don Whillans feeling jubilant about the weekend's climbing. We had made a girdle traverse of Dinas Cromlech, crossing the walls of Cenotaph Corner at mid-height. I could hear my mother preparing the evening meal in the kitchen and there was this knock on the door. So I got up to answer it.

A tallish, well-built man, about 25 years old, with thick spectacles and a casual air stood on the doorstep.

"Hallo," he said, "I'm McNaught Davis"—there was a slight pause—"We've met before . . . at the Alpine Climbing Group. . . . We are going to the Mustagh Tower in a fortnight. . . . Would you like to join us?"

"Come in," I said.

We went into the living-room.

"Who is it, Joe?" my mother called.

"Oh, it's only someone who wants me to go to the Mustagh Tower."

"Where is that?"

"In the Karakorum."

"When, for Heaven's sake?"

"In two weeks' time, I think."

I closed the door and turned to my visitor.

"You did say in a fortnight?"

"Yes, that's right. Supplies and equipment aren't organised yet but they won't take long. I've just returned from Zanzibar . . . been working there for a year. . . . John Hartog in London has cleared permission with the Pakistan government, so all we have to do is buy food and gear and get our boat tickets. Are you game?"

In the past I had exchanged only a few words with Ian McNaught Davis, or "Mac" as he is known to everyone. We had met briefly at A.C.G. functions. This body was more an association than a club of proficient mountaineers; its members were dedicated to a high standard of climbing in the Alps and in more distant mountain ranges. Mac had been in the forefront of post-war university climbers, having made first or early guideless British ascents of routes like the Pear Buttress of Mont Blanc and the North Wall of the Cima Grande in the Dolomites. His reputation for apparent recklessness with motor cars was well known. As a raconteur he had no equal. He was one of those people who are slightly larger than life—a complete individualist who is capable of mixing successfully at any level in society without intruding—a sort of citizen of the world. His subsequent regular appearance on radio and television, sometimes with myself, earned him the unworthy comic-cuts name of "Mac the Telly"; it hardly suited his senior executive background in the computer industry.

John Hartog, an industrial chemist, and Mac had been corresponding over 5,000 miles about forming an expedition to climb the Mustagh Tower. More than any other this mountain had been universally recognised as impregnable since its discovery in 1892. R. L. G. Irving called it: "Nature's last stronghold—probably the most inaccessible of all great peaks, for its immense precipices show no weakness in its defences."

My own awareness of the mountain had been gained from references in Himalayan literature. Photographs taken from the famous "Golden Throne" viewpoint across the Baltoro glacier showed a huge obelisk nearly 24,000 feet high with terminal precipices of unwonted height and steepness. Mac told me that it had been John Hartog's ambition since the age of fourteen to climb the Mustagh Tower. He had collected just about every photograph ever taken of the mountain. This obsession with disproving the invincible image of the Tower had also driven him to make an exhaustive search for references in mountaineering literature. Altogether the information collected on the subject was very complete.

I needed no encouragement to jump at the invitation. The audacity of the scheme—even at this late hour and almost without organisation and planning on which months were normally spent—had the elements of a great adventure.

"What about money," I said.

"How much have you got?" Mac inquired.

"About eighty pounds."

"That will be fine. Send it to John Hartog when you can."

I found out later that Mac and John contributed £1,000 each.

Mac hurried away, saying as he went out: "I'll send your boat ticket in a couple of days . . . don't forget, we'll be leaving ten days after that."

It was all done as if he had called to arrange a weekend's climbing in Wales.

The only job that I was given was to buy some ex-army equipment to fit out the porters we would hire on arrival.

Having made none of the usual preparations the Londoners had no time to write begging letters. Soliciting free samples, food supplies and equipment is a universal practice of all mountaineering expeditions, but they had to pay for everything. The pair of them sat at telephones, ringing up provisioners like Selfridges to order 40 packets of tea, 30 tins of biscuits, unprecedented quantities of dried egg, and so on, asking for delivery to be made to Hartog's flat. The foodstuffs were packed in 30 waterproof cardboard boxes and stacked in the hall. For simplicity the contents of each box was identical—a regrettable plan because the monotony of the diet was later to turn us against half the food. When each box was full it was put in the bath, weighted with rocks and tested to see if it was still waterproof.

Somehow three tons of gear arrived at Liverpool docks on the day I joined Mac and John Hartog on the boat. It was my first meeting with John, who told me that a fourth member had been invited. He was the Scottish climber, Tom Patey, twenty-four years old and a unique figure in Scottish winter climbing. He would also be acting as medical officer. Still a house doctor, serving a year in a hospital to qualify, Patey had obtained special leave to join the expedition and was flying out to Karachi.

At Karachi we faced the gruelling journey across the Sind desert, that the superhuman Austrian climber, Hermann Buhl, was known to have endured in a luggage compartment. The temperature reached 120° F in this sultry and dry desert. Before we were through our estimation of Buhl had risen considerably. It was like being deported in a sandstorm with no form of protection for 36 hours. At every station where the train halted a wretched native entered to sweep out dirt and sand from the compartments. Our mouths were full of grit, .eating was a nauseating business of crunching food with grit and spitting out, and the only safe liquids to drink were soda water and lemonade. We cleaned our teeth in mineral water.

At Rawalpindi a mob of porters set upon us and carried off the baggage. Through mistaken generosity they were given three rupees each, instead of two annas—about 150 times too much! Even then they haggled for more because whatever sum they were paid it was always insufficient. We hired a horse and cart and drove through the streets looking for a place to sleep. By now a less patient Himalayan explorer would have been demanding to know who was responsible for the transit arrangements of the party. There was something pleasantly bizarre about our little expedition.

John found an hotel. We waited outside until he signalled that he had bargained with the owner over the price of lodgings. After that we were pestered by the horse and cart driver, who invariably caught us when we re-entered the hotel, shouting that he had been underpaid, robbed and what have you.

"I'll fix him," said Mac. He tipped an employee, who promptly threw the driver out when he came through the door.

Being in Pakistan, climbing in the Karakorum had several advantages over, say, Nepal. In Nepal a foreign expedition had to put down a large deposit of money, according to the size and importance of the objective mountain. Moreover, the Nepalese

government insisted that an army officer must accompany the
expedition, and that his wages and upkeep must be paid for.
There was no "fee" for climbing in the Karakorum and the
Pakistan army loaned men to expeditions as interpreters and
liaison officers without charge. The authorities regarded these
temporary transfers as excellent training and experience, and
obviously it was. The officer detailed to us was called Riaz.
He was extremely affable and devoted himself to our interests.

Another "perk" for expeditions visiting the Karakorum was
thumbing a lift from the Pakistan Air Force. Planes went up to
Skardu, the farthest point one could fly into the area. However,
the Air Force was usually reluctant to transport civilians
through what is generally recognised as the most dangerous air
corridor in the world. The authorities would co-operate if the
weather was perfect. We waited several days for the right
conditions, which did not materialise. They agreed to fly in
our baggage, leaving us to the mercy of a civilian airline flying
planes to Skardu.

The aircraft were Dakotas and no one made a secret of the
fact that their ceiling was 13,000 feet with a full load. The air
corridor along the Indus was interrupted by several passes of
the same altitude. The flight was so bumpy that I was dread-
fully air sick throughout the journey. I hardly knew whether to
regard this as a fortunate distraction from the terrors suffered
by my companions or not: in some places it looked as if the
wing of the plane was only ten yards from the wall of the ravine.
I felt so ill that I couldn't have cared less if we had hit it.

Skardu is a valley about 30 miles long and 10 miles wide with
a fringe of mountains rising to 20,000 feet on the horizon. We
booked into the government guest house where the charge was
only a few rupees a day. As leader, John Hartog was trying to
ensure that our running expenses remained consistent with a
shoe-string expedition. He ordered one chicken for the evening
meal, to serve five people including Riaz. Even before our
chokidah cook put it on the table John had announced that the
chicken must suffice for two meals. The chicken was small and
scraggy, like all the poultry in this neighbourhood. By the end

of the expedition Mac and I were eating two chickens a day each.

The following day we were rushed at by a horde of four or five hundred people who had come down from the surrounding hill villages on hearing the news that there was work to be had. They were standing outside clamouring for jobs. A condition laid down by the Himalayan Club was that all persons so engaged by expeditions must have a medical test for fitness. With such a great number to examine all Tom could do was squeeze their arms and legs to see if they had muscles. 120 men were selected and we commenced the trek into the interior.

The first obstacle was the Indus, 250 yards wide and flowing at a brisk pace. A ferry contraption called Alexander's Barge, resembling a huge punt, plied across the river. This floating platform was reputed to be the original built by Alexander the Great. When a plank rotted, it was taken out and replaced with another. The total replacements were said to be nowhere equal to reconstructing the vessel. Fully laden there was practically no freeboard and even this was full of gaping holes. To reach the far bank the vessel was towed upstream until it was on the inside of a bend. The shore lines were cast off and all on board prayed that the ferry would traverse the river on reaching the inside of the next bend on the opposite side. There were no paddles and deck hands made feeble attempts at steering with sticks. This hit or miss technique seemed to work quite well, although we were told that on some occasions the ferry had drifted 10 miles downstream before landing on one side or the other.

Miles of burning sand desert, drained incongruously by icy torrents, lay before us. Almost as soon as we started to cross this terrain the porters sat down, smoking, and did not look like getting up. We thought we had a strike on our hands. Twenty minutes later they stood up and carried their loads without halting for four hours. This was their system; walk 200 yards first thing in the morning, rest then start the day's march. The porters' performance was generally very good. Mindful of the expedition purse we had not engaged high-altitude porters. The plan was to watch for suitable candidates in the ranks of the Skardu men.

I came into the first camp-site to find that the porter who had been carrying my personal belongings had lit a fire and had boiling water ready. He wanted to know where the tea was packed and what would we like cooked for the evening meal. His name was Hussein, fifty-two years old, and clearly a man of initiative. There and then he was made chief porter, but I was lucky enough to retain him as my personal carrier. This, it transpired, was to be taken literally. Wading knee-deep across the endless succession of icy rivers, I had removed and replaced my boots so many times that I decided to try walking barefoot. The hot sand soon blistered my feet, so I reverted to hobbling in boots. Hussein noticed my suffering and hurried ahead of me. He took his load across a river then returned to wait for me. The first time this happened, I shuffled up to the bank, resigned but thinking about the discomfort of taking off my boots, when Hussein signalled that I was to jump on his back. He carried me across and after that I had no more rivers to wade.

On entering villages the entire population turned out for medication. The so-called sick and ailing formed long queues outside the tents, the object being to collect pills. There was nothing wrong with most of them. The malingerers pointed to their stomachs or heads, indicating a pain in one or the other. You popped a pill into their mouths and sent them away. They took it out, wrapped it precariously in a dirty rag and tucked it away somewhere safe until the need arose to swallow it for a genuine ailment.

The men in charge of a ferry of goatskin rafts on the Braldoh river extorted a princely sum from us. The operators, who in any case were paid by the government, knew that travellers could not pass upstream on the bank because big cliffs dropped straight into the water. The French expedition that arrived on the mountain after we did, decided to float down the river from this point on the return journey to Skardu. Their leader, Guido Magnone, also had a rubber dingy. He was sitting in it with a ciné camera, preparing to film his party's departure, and was held on a long painter from the bank by a porter. Someone shouted and the porter suddenly dropped the rope. Magnone floated away into the rapid current. He skimmed helplessly down the river for ten hours before landing at a village just above Skardu. In this time he covered a distance that normally occupied three days on the outward walk. We heard that a strange figure, clad only in swimming trunks, had emerged from the river and strolled into the village, almost frightening the population into hiding.

At the last village, Askolé, we engaged more porters, who were needed to carry food for the Skardu men. Beyond this point the porters would not be able to feed themselves in way-side villages.

A *maund* was the weight that the Askolé men would carry: about 80 lb. We had a 5 lb spring-balance, weighed sixteen units of food and put them in a sack. Referees on both sides agreed that the sack could be used to balance on the end of a pivoted stick for making up the loads. On the other end an empty bag was filled until it balanced the agreed load. After a few sacks had been measured in this manner I noticed that the natives were moving each new load along the stick, a little closer to the centre. We were losing 5 or 10 lb in each sack. As soon as the perpetrators of this deception looked away I pushed the master load somewhat closer to the centre point, so that the next sack contained about 90 lb. This went on all day, alternately swopping the weights and pushing them a little closer to the centre. Everyone had broad grins on their faces, as if nothing was happening. The root of the trouble was that in terms of payment for porterage and other "favours" these men had been spoiled by the mammoth Italian expedition to K2, which had passed through the valley two years before; 1,000 porters had been engaged and all of them had been given boots and many other luxuries by standards in the region. This expedition had cost more than £100,000.

On reaching the glacier zone we had a genuine strike to deal with. Riaz reported: "Mr Hartog, the men will not move without boots."

"Can nothing be done?" growled John.

"I have an idea," said Riaz cunningly.

He went out and spoke to two porters who were policemen by regular occupation. These men carried long thick sticks, out of habit I suppose, so that they could always be recognised as representatives of the law. In a flash one of them darted among the listless group of 150 porters, striking out in all directions with his stick. He was not beating them lightly. Blows rained upon anyone who came within range. The next thing was that all the porters grabbed their packs and ran for dear life up the glacier, and the strike was broken.

The Baltoro glacier is 36 miles long and we reached its snout on the tenth day. The scenery was now austere; barren ridges with a hint of snow caps peeping over the tops of the skyline. Miles of moraine rubble covered the ice on the lower part of the glacier. During the inward march it rained heavily and there was more trouble with the porters. Having no spare tents their lot was to huddle under rocks. We took pity on them and handed over the main groundsheet from our tent. Sixty bunched together under it. This act of kindness sparked off a fierce squabble because the remainder were jostling for positions under the groundsheet. After it had been taken off them everyone was happy again.

Urdukas was the last grassy oasis. Here all but six porters were paid off, leaving the expedition with six rupees and a few annas. We were now camped in a deep glacier avenue enclosed by soaring rock spires. The higher pinnacles were crusted in snow and ice while opposite there rose a gigantic, complex rock peak, resembling the Chamonix Grépon magnified at least three times. The Mustagh Tower lay hidden in the glacier recesses somewhere behind it.

The Baltoro glacier was like a tempestuous sea thrown up in mountainous waves and troughs, frozen and strewn with gravel and boulders. At this point it was five miles wide and we crossed it to reach the entrance of the tributary Mustagh glacier. After an incredibly tedious exercise in route finding and load ferrying, Base Camp was established on 25th May in the lower part of the Mustagh glacier. The plan was to approach the mountain from the west and attack its northern ridge. A short distance from Base we had to climb the Chagaran branch glacier, over an icefall with a vertical rise of 3,000 feet, into a snow basin above. Altogether the approach to the summit was no less than fourteen miles.

A camp that we placed in the icefall was a story-book setting for nightmares and works of the devil. You could almost feel the glacier moving. I lay awake at night listening to the terrific crunching and grinding of the ice, with intermittent crashes, and ice breaking in the bottom of satanic pits. At any moment it seemed that the frail slab on which the tent was pitched must slide into a void. None of the icefalls on Kangchenjunga had shown such activity and I was very glad to get out of the place.

The work of finding suitable emplacements for higher camps was slow and laborious. Our manpower resources were limited and of course the weather was a constant hindrance. More by personal inclination than design the party split into two pairs: John and Tom, Mac and myself. Tom used to go for walks on his own to relieve boredom. Mac and I invariably got up to some mischief, like rolling boulders down the slopes, or using the airbeds for toboggan runs. By the end of the expedition we had broken all the axes save one and the Liloes were in shreds. Eventually Camp II was set up below the 7,000-foot precipice of the West Face and about half a mile away from the ice slope leading to the col in the ridge that we intended to climb.

The ice slope was the first serious obstacle. Some 3,000 feet high, it looked about 40 degrees steep at the bottom, perhaps 50 degrees in the middle and only 30 degrees at the top. The first attempt ended in retreat; the second reached the upper section, about 600 feet below the col. The deep wet snow repulsed me. The clinometer read 61 degrees and that was enough to turn anyone. Next day Tom swarmed up the sticky snow curtain, declaring that it was "really great stuff". It was a conclusive demonstration why he was fêted as the best snow and ice man in Scotland.

1,000 feet of fixed ropes were draped down the upper section of the slope. A frozen pond on the col made a good level place for pitching tents. The ice could be chopped up and melted for water, which, compared with melting snow, saved a great deal of fuel.

At 20,000 feet we could now look up the ridge to the summit nearly 4,000 feet higher. A sense of utter futility crept over me. Could anyone climb this appallingly steep place? I was trained to avoid the snare of making hasty judgements. That appearances are deceptive are truer in mountaineering than most things. On one side plunged the West Face, perpendicular in the style of the Dolomites, only much larger; on the other the North Face shot down 7,000 feet to a glacier that was a gigantic staircase of ice cliffs. Everything was so steep that no appreciable quantity of snow could be seen on the rocks. The thunder of avalanches that I had lived with on Kangchenjunga was noticeably absent.

The four of us were thoroughly disheartened by the prospects but we were determined to put our noses to the rock of this fretwork ridge that trailed down so defiantly to the col.

In pairs, bit by bit, we edged up the ridge. Some of it was Grade V climbing by Alpine standards. Several easy-looking stretches raised our hopes, then dashed them on coming to grips with these places. They were so bad that we had to turn them on the West Face, traversing across atrociously loose rock. Ropes were fixed all the way up the ridge. We could then go down quickly and return to the highest point speedily the following day. It looked as if a further camp on the ridge would be necessary to make a bid for the summit. Before this could be found the weather deteriorated and we returned to Base Camp to recuperate.

"The Prengi are coming up the glacier," Riaz announced.

"Who are they?" I inquired.

"It is a party of Frenchmen," said Riaz.

We were very puzzled by this information. "How do you know that, Riaz?"

"Because the porters say they are coming. They are on the Baltoro now."

We were camped on the Mustagh glacier and could not understand how the porters could make such a claim. No one had come into our camp and none of us had left it.

"The French are coming up the Baltoro glacier," repeated Riaz, "and they are going to climb the Mustagh Tower. The porters say so."

A couple of days later the "Prengi" arrived: Guido Magnone, André Contamine, Paul Keller, François Florence and Robert Paragot. It was a bit like an off-day at the Olympic Games. No one could recall a situation when two parties were competing for the same Himalayan or Karakorum mountain at the same time. Especially one like the Mustagh Tower!

My impression was that the French had no idea how to tackle the mountain or where its weaknesses, if any, lay. On the other hand the French team was an extremely powerful one. John was the expert and he supplied them with details of a route that we had toyed with during our photographic studies. This was the southern or opposite ridge to ours. The French had already been round to this side of the mountain and had failed to detect a way on to the ridge. John's photographs, carefully preserved in camp, revealed a possible route tucked away behind a large rock buttress. This proved to be the key.

A messenger service for exchanging information and news was started between the two Base Camps. The French were installed an easy ten miles away on the Younghusband glacier.

One day Mac complained that he could not find a carving knife. We had brought five with us and none of them could be found. It was decided to send the porters off with loads so that we could examine their personal baggage. The missing knives were rooted out along with many other articles that we had forgotten existed. The porter who was acting as the messenger between camps was a particularly sly-looking fellow. One of his jackets was uncommonly bulky, and our suspicions were aroused on seeing the inside and outside pockets stitched up.

E

We unpicked them and pulled out his ill-gotten gains—French soap, soup packets and all manner of small articles purloined from the neighbours' camp. Confronting the man with the evidence, he promptly accused us of stealing.

A competitive spirit developed between Riaz and Ali Usman, the liaison officer attached to the French party. Now that they were on the same mountain, both wanted to reach the greatest height, which would give them the height record for a liaison officer. Hussein, our chief porter, entered into this to some extent. He was not going to be beaten by either of them. Both he and Riaz went to Camp III on the col, although they were poorly acclimatised and suffered from jarring headaches and sickness. Near the col Hussein was collapsing on the fixed ropes from fatigue and exhaustion. I wrestled with him to remove his pack but he refused to let me have it. His pride was such that he would rather die in the attempt than be humiliated by having to hand over his load to a sahib.

Tom Patey was always first to volunteer at Camp III to rush down to Base to fetch something that was needed urgently. Ordinarily it was nearly two days down and four days up. Tom would race to the bottom in a day and return in another two, looking as if he had been for a stroll round Loch Lomond. By contrast he hated cooking and flatly refused to pull his weight in this department. In national character Tom excluded porridge as a culinary chore and was always pleased to make it.

Mac and I were now in a position to attempt the summit. Camp III was amply provisioned and spare equipment had been dumped there. Nevertheless we set off with a small tent and restricted our survival gear, to economise on weight. The fixed ropes already hanging on the first 1,000 feet of the ridge were an insurance against the event of having to turn back in a storm.

Above the last rope the climbing continued as hard as ever. Worse still, the rock could be lifted out in handfuls. Just below a comparatively level section I tackled an overhang on the tip of a diamond-shaped buttress dropping away vertically for 3,000 feet. Pulling over the top, I ripped my down trousers. Afterwards the last part of the climb could be traced by down sticking to rocks all the way up.

The ridge eased temporarily but the crest was too narrow to stake out guylines. I felt that we ought to push higher, for there was still nearly 3,000 feet above. "Not a hope," said Mac, pointing towards the rearing crest, "only a fly could find a resting place up there." So we camped. The ridge was covered with boulders. Removing some of them a platform was cleared for the tent. We tied small boulders to the guylines and threw them down both sides of the ridge.

"We'll be blown straight off if the wind picks up," I remarked.

A calm morning, a clear sky washed blue and a blinding iridescence on the snow flutings of the surrounding peaks put us in high spirits. It was 6th July. After the usual frustrations of melting snow we made do with a cup of tea and half a cup of porridge each.

Wind-slab snow plastered the rocks for a while. Then a section of steeper and better snow gave us some delightful climbing up to a line of overhangs. Mac scratched his head, waiting for me to declare a verdict.

A band of rocks formed a continuous overhang extending from the West Face right round to the North Face. I messed about for an hour and could not find a way over the barrier. A revelation of this interlude was that I could do pull-ups, dangling freely on my arms, at an altitude of 23,000 feet. This had been impossible at lower altitudes on Kangchenjunga. The explanation had to be the light sacks we carried on the Tower. All we had was a camera, spare sweater, oddments of food and a couple of pegs—the sort of things carried in the Alps for a normal day's climbing.

I came down. "Sorry, Mac, it won't go. What about traversing below this lot on to the North Face?"

Mac had stiffened through inactivity on his perch. "Anything to keep moving," he murmured.

I went across the side of the ridge. It was typical North Face terrain: barren, steep, uncompromising and with an immediate sense of electrifying exposure. An ice wall followed the rock band. It was only 20 feet high and the angle eased off above. Mac located a good belay. I soon climbed the wall and got into a shallow gully about 55 degrees steep. The snow was unconsolidated and the next half-hour was extremely unpleasant. I ran out a full length of rope, floundered waist-deep in soft snow and tried unsuccessfully to swim out to rocks at the side. The snow was so thin at the edges that it would not support my weight. At the end of the rope there was no belay in sight. I had half expected the gully bed to avalanche. If Mac came off when he started up it we would be done for.

Shouting to each other we had a long discussion on questions of safety. Was it wise to go on? I tried to pass on the responsibility of making a decision to Mac. On reflection this was absurd because I was leading and he could not appreciate the precise situation from below. Quite properly Mac resisted taking the responsibility.

"Do you still want to go on?" I called down wearily.

"I'm ready whenever you say," shouted Mac.

That was how it was.

"Well, I'm ready now."

He did not question what I was using for a belay. He knew there was none.

Mac climbed beautifully and rested in the snow a few feet below me. I was vibrating with nervous tension. My thoughts were muddled by worries more intense than anything I had experienced in my entire climbing career. This desperately unhappy condition took hold of me and persisted all day. The first 1,500 feet of the ridge had taken merely three hours. The last 1,000 feet or so occupied eight hours. The ordeal left me feeling a mental wreck. Mac sank into a state of grim and probably dangerous determination. The technical difficulties were not formidable; it was simply that the nervous strain was sapping all our energy.

On the second run-out of rope I was still unable to gain the rocks. Again I brought up Mac without a belay. On the third run-out, no less than 400 feet of this suicidal snow, I broke through to bedrock and discovered a crack. I had never been so glad to see rock in all my life.

"For Christ's sake, let's rest a while," gasped Mac. We had reached a broken stretch. "I was just going to suggest the same thing," I said.

We made some snowballs. You punched a hole in the middle and filled it with jam. It was similar to a milk-shake and very refreshing.

The sky was like a plate of highly polished blue steel. We had a chance if the weather held. Behind us was a rock tower about 200 feet high. The rock was perfect for a change, and the holds were large and comforting. We thought that the top of it might be the summit. It wasn't. Another curve of ridge rose to another "summit". We trudged up this, thinking that the mountain was never going to relent. Both of us had reached the point of exhaustion when you promise yourself that if the "summit" ahead is not the real top, then you turn round and go back.

The second summit was not the top. Another tilted roof, headed up by another summit, gazed upon us callously.

We looked at each other, too tired to speak. I put my sack down and plodded a few yards along the ridge pole. Mac dropped his sack and followed.

The crown of rocks above was and was not the true summit. We had reached one of a pair of summits. Until now neither of us had realised that the mountain was double-headed. We were bitterly disappointed.

"Do you think it is higher over there, Mac?"

"Who can say? If we had a clinometer we might work it out. One thing is for certain. It's a good 200 yards or more."

It was also six o'clock, and there was an hour of daylight left. In any case we had burnt our boats so far as getting back to Camp III before nightfall. Looking down towards the glacier we could see one of the high French camps 3,000 feet below. We shouted and tried to attract their attention. We learnt later that the French had been playing bridge and were not expecting to be hailed from the summit!

We descended into the gap between the twin summits. I was suffering from pins and needles caused by lack of oxygen. I fell through a snow cornice and only just managed to support myself on my arms. You could look straight through the hole down to the glacier 7,000 feet below. If we tried to go any farther we would almost certainly have a serious accident. Although it was only 30 yards away the return climb back to the west top exacted a tremendous effort.

By the time that we had gone over the west top the valleys were in shadow. On reaching the sacks we had no choice but to bivouac. Hardly a word passed between us. Carrying the stones we needed to sit on finished us off completely. In the circumstances the bivouac that night was bearable. I had endured worse. The only precaution taken was to unfasten our boots. They were saturated and would freeze if we took them off. We put our feet in the sacks and tried to sleep. During the night it snowed a little, increasing our anxiety about getting down safely.

In the morning I found that I had made a bad mistake. For insulation I had sat on my gloves. Now they were frozen flat, like pieces of board, and impossible to put on. It was very cold and neither of us spoke. Without a word we tied on the rope and set off. The first remark that Mac made was prompted by an agonised expression on my face. I was wincing in pain.

"What's up, Joe?"

"My hands are sticking to the rock. As soon as I lower down on a hold the skin freezes to it."

"Hang on a minute, I've just remembered something," said Mac. He opened his sack and groped inside. He pulled out a pair of socks.

"I knew I'd brought something that wasn't necessary!" he exclaimed.

I pulled the socks over my hands. It was a fantastic stroke of luck and almost certainly saved me from severe frostbite.

Luck was something we could use now. The long rotten snow gully had frozen solid, allowing us to crampon happily in our former pothole steps. There was no danger but the pace was terribly slow. We had eaten no food since leaving Camp III at six-thirty the previous morning and the jam snowballs had been our only drink.

At the foot of the rock band we met John and Tom on the way up. We offered them our duvet trousers but they reckoned on having plenty of time to reach the summit because snow conditions were much better. Back in camp we spent the afternoon making countless brews. About two o'clock we saw our companions reach the west top. They succeeded in traversing to the other summit and attracted the attention of the French. Unfortunately they had to bivouac on the descent. John neglected to unlace his boots, with grave consequences.

In something of a shambles the party evacuated itself from the col. Mac and John were caught in a stone avalanche on the fixed ropes and had a miraculous escape. Said Mac afterwards: "The stones and ice particles were so dense that visibility was nil." They were attached to the ropes by snap-links. Thrown off their feet, they came to rest when the snap-links caught on the fixing pegs holding the ropes below them. Both their rucksack straps were severed by rocks and the loads fell to the bottom of the 3,000 ft slope. All the fixed ropes and items of supporting equipment were abandoned.

John Hartog was now in a bad way. His feet were bluish and not a pleasant sight. After rendering what aid he could, Tom was non-committal. John was transported on a stretcher made from tent poles. The Baltoro glacier soon put an end to this arrangement. We joined forces with the French team, which had reached the summit six days after ourselves. John travelled the rest of the way to Skardu on piggyback. He lost the ends of all his toes on one foot and the two smallest toes were amputated from the other.

CHAPTER SEVEN

CAVES AND TREASURE HUNTS

PRIMITIVE MAN, WE are told, began life in caves. Our early ancestors adapted them as crude shelters. Romantic hideouts of robbers and the persecuted belong to the same school of refuge. Something quite different are the caves commercialised for sightseers; they are usually picturesque and grandiose freaks of nature discovered in modern times. The sport of potholing has been developed in another division of caves—those eroded in limestone far underground. Then there are cave structures, partly or wholly artificial, excavated in antiquity as dwellings and uncovered by archaeologists.

In mountaineering a cave is only a miniature feature in the rock face or a large recess formed by a fallen capstone in a gully. Through a curious chain of events, but not the least through my own curiosity, my explorations branched into investigating a variety of caves in nearly all these classifications.

It began at home. A hair-raising escapade of the early Rock and Ice days on the mountain limestone of Derbyshire was making routes on the walls of Thor's Cave. The cave is situated about 200 feet above the river in the Manifold valley, a beauty spot adjacent to Dovedale. The river gorge is narrow and partially wooded, making it an ideal place for ancient settlements, and relics of early occupation have been discovered in the valley.

The hollow in the limestone tor measures 60 feet across and 50 feet high. It has two entrances, at right angles to each other, so that the cave is L-shaped. In the back and up to the right of the smaller of the two entrances is a slot known as the Window which opens into a steep gully with large and slightly overhanging walls. Having made a straightforward route on the outside face of the Window, on the right wall of the gully, I decided there was scope for another on the left wall.

Ron Moseley and Ray Greenall started up the right side route, bent on repeating my ascent. Lew Waghorn and I worked up the left side. It had been raining all day and greasy water was streaming down the rock. We had only one rope, insufficient for most requirements, which had to be doubled for artificial climbing. I pegged up an overhanging wall until the rope ran out at 70 feet. At this height the face was slightly less than vertical, with a hold on which I could place one foot. I banged in three pegs; two bent, gripping half an inch in the rock; the third went into a hole and rattled loose. I had to belay on them.

Lew came up nicely until he reached the last peg that I had put in, ten feet below the stance.

I cautioned him: "Be careful how you take that peg out, or you'll flip off."

"I can see that all right," he said, shifting his weight in another direction to relieve the strain on the peg. "I might have to leave it in," he added. We always tried to remove pegs. They were expensive and it was untidy to leave a rock-face bristling with artificial equipment.

Unfortunately there was no time for Lew to solve the problem. The peg came out of its own accord. Lew swung into the air, brandishing the peg like a dagger—a grim predicament on an overhanging wall.

In a forlorn gamble Lew tried swinging against the rock and stabbing the crack to replace the peg. "It won't work," he groaned painfully.

Then he attempted climbing up the rope. Three or four times he pulled himself up a yard or so and with failing strength dropped back exhausted. When this happened the jerk knocked me off the foothold. The rope was now tight enough to cut me in two and the strain on it forced out first one peg then another. I was left hanging on one, it was raining heavily and our spirits were falling fast.

"What are we going to do, Joe. I can't breathe."

"I'm going to lower you. If you don't get off the rope soon we shall both be gonners. I can't hold on much longer." With gripping the rope so long my hands were going numb. I was very worried in case I should let the rope slip.

Slipping the rope inch by inch, water squirted out as it ran through my hands, increasing the numbing effect. I twisted the rope round a wrist to act as a friction brake. The pain of it chafing my wrist was terrible. The rope bounced on my knuckles and disturbed the smoothness in paying out. We seemed to be on the brink of disaster.

When no more rope was left Lew dangled like a jack-knifed rag-doll on the end and about 8 feet out from the rock near the starting ledge in the gully. His body was revolving slowly and he appeared to be unconscious. Moseley and Greenall were watching morbidly from their climb. They could do nothing because they were cragbound as well.

I called to Moseley with some ill-humour: "If you think that you are in difficulty, I'll change places with you right now!"

The fact of the matter was that in this situation the chance of surviving was remote. I should have passed out from the strain of holding the rope. I was hanging from the waist on a rope loop attached to one loose peg, facing outwards, and with no other support.

After what seemed hours Lew revived and started swinging himself towards the ledge. He managed to reach it and the terrible weight on me was released.

I was not much better off because I dare not move while the slightest tug might dislodge the peg. I had been transfixed in this torturous position for half an hour. By all the rules I should have been lying dead at the bottom. If there was rigor mortis in the living then it might explain why I retained a grip on the rope.

Lew was another half-hour manœuvring a rope from the stranded Moseley party and taking it round to the top. Even when it had been lowered and I had tied on I found that he had dropped it on the wrong side of a nose of crumbling lime-stone. Rocks showered upon me, bounding off my head and feet. I swore at him but doubt if he heard what I was saying.

Below the undercut nose, in a stupidly exposed position, I saw that it was hopeless to climb in the line of the rope. When Lew understood the situation he had to pay out the rope so that I could climb a safer but very difficult crack. Climbing to the top without the moral comfort of a rope from above was the last thing that I wanted to do.

In darkness we had to set about rescuing Moseley. We left the cave in a complete shambles. Ropes and equipment were tossed aside and trampled in the mud.

Back in a little hut in the valley we ate a big meal. I relaxed in the hay, watching the candlelight shadows flickering on the rafters, thinking what a great life it was.

To my mind caves and roofs are synonymous. Their ascent involves the same climbing techniques. A roof is something more than an overhang. It is the horizontal distance between two vertical planes, like one tread of an inverted staircase. Working out under a roof and continuing the ascent on the outer plane of the rock-face is undeniably sensational but not unduly hazardous if the climber can securely place his pegs and other pieces of equipment.

Two of the extremes in scaling roofs in Britain lie in Malham Cove and on Kilnsey Crag, both under Penyghent in the Yorkshire Pennines. The surroundings are popular with walkers and tourists, so there is nothing secluded about the cliffs. They lie on the fringe of folds in wide, open tracts of moor and close to busy roads. Climbers first took a fancy to these limestone showpieces in the mid-1950s. The roof was becoming fashionable; our interest had been awakened by mechanised techniques employed for similar purposes in the Alps and the United States. Unlike the discovery of conventional new routes, say in Wales, these bulbous precipices were the scene of long sieges, where one party made progress beyond the farthest point reached by another, or returned on a series of weekends to press home its own attack.

The Rock and Ice laid the foundation work on the Great Overhang at Kilnsey, but in the event I did not make the first complete ascent. We first reconnoitred Malham Cove and Gordale Scar without doing any climbing. Early one afternoon a few of the party went for a walk across the moor to find Kilnsey. It was misty and outcropping rocks played tricks on the eyes. Then I thought that I could see a tree not far away. What was a tree doing on an empty moor? It seemed to get no closer. Gradually the perspective cleared. We were still nearly a mile away and it was the huge jutting chin of Kilnsey Crag. We went back and broke the news to our companions. I was very excited by what I had seen.

On the first attempt I spent five hours getting up to the roof on Kilnsey. It was more than 100 feet above the ground. During this time I was so engrossed with the technicalities that I had had no opportunity to study the roof overhead. Compared with the view from the ground, at close quarters I was astonished at its immensity. I was struck by the resemblance to a ballroom floor seen in a mirror on the ceiling. A quick inspection revealed some distant cracks into which pegs might be knocked. Not feeling up to it I descended.

On another occasion, with Don Roscoe and Don Whillans, I tried to force the roof at another point. A loose block barely ten feet from the top defeated me. I accidentally dropped a peg to the ground and later we measured the distance to the foot of the face where the climb began; it was 45 feet.

Ron Moseley returned and climbed part of this route, breaking out from a cave along a fault line that passed right across the roof. This was probably the epic of his life. He traversed 100 feet across the ceiling. The pegs were knocked into a knife-edged flake that tapered to nothing. After a blank section he came to another flake crack, square and two feet thick. He drove in wedges here and gradually convinced himself that he was prising the crack apart. Progress was five or six feet at a session. He became so frightened that he went back and lowered himself to the ground. By the following weekend Ron was composed again and ready to dismiss his fear as greatly exaggerating the difficulties. He returned to the farthest point, put in two more wedges and hurried down scared to death.

This went on for weeks until he had traversed 120 feet across the roof and victory was in sight. Fritz Sumner joined Moseley for the final ascent. They spent eleven hours in stirrups, lying horizontally under the roof, before securing a position on the wall above. They bored holes, fitted rawlplugs, screws and brackets. It was Moseley who crashed the psychological barrier and showed everyone that it could be done.

Shortly after returning from the Mustagh Tower I was approached by a BBC producer, Stanley Williamson, for advice on making a documentary film for television on climbing. The thought of being offered money to do something that bore no resemblance to work in my eyes was ecstasy! Williamson was charming, not at all like some of the overbearing news-hawks who had turned their attentions on me. He knew absolutely nothing about climbing (though is now a convert) and was prepared to put himself entirely in my hands. We studied my collection of photographs. I pointed out probable positions for cameras; the locations were agreed and we were in business.

Two days filming on gritstone were followed by a tour of Snowdonia, shooting on Suicide Wall and Kaisergebirge. The big event took place on Cloggy. The climbing party was Geoff Sutton, then the warden at White Hall, Gordon Mansell, a White Hall instructor, George Band, my summit companion on Kanchengjunga, and myself. The programme went off extremely well and finished with the rescue of a cragfast sheep that proved to be nearly the most exciting part of the day.

The Rock and Ice had been told by Mrs Williams at the Half-Way House that navvies used to sit on shovels and slide down the centre rack between the rails of the Snowdon Railway to Llanberis. We had done this for some years, using a stone of the right shape. It was fairly dangerous and bones had been broken by some who had tried it. The television climbers wanted to have a go.

After a demonstration, in which I drew attention to numerous projections that were liable to throw the rider off his stone, we started down, sitting on our chosen stones, legs apart and feet braced against the rails to break the momentum. Having had considerable practice I could reach speeds of 30 miles per hour. That was about four times faster than the train. I went gaily through Clogwyn station and down to Half-Way. The learners were nowhere in sight behind. I got off and popped into the café for a cup of tea. Then the head and shoulders of Geoff came into view through the grass. He couldn't stop and flashed out of sight. Gordon came along, stopped and let me go ahead. Below was a deep cutting on a bend. As I came out of it I saw Sutton struggling with his stone of more than a hundredweight, which had come off the rack. He just managed to get out of the way as I shot past. Immediately beyond was a gate. After I had gone through it I glanced back and noticed that the gate was swinging shut. I stopped. I could see both ends of the cutting and Gordon came out of the lower end like an express train. Geoff, who had just replaced his stone, had to pull it off in great haste. Then Gordon was making frantic motions with his arms towards the gate. I bawled at Geoff but he couldn't hear me. Geoff suddenly woke up and positively dived at the gate, opening it just as Gordon roared through. He must have already resigned himself to a serious crash. Lower down Gordon became involved with a flock of sheep that wandered across the line. It was not his day. He finished a short way above Llanberis riding on a split stone. He held it together until a hump in the track tossed him off in a somersault. He was covered in rust, and black and brown grease. Geoff arrived at the bottom without further incident. The non-appearance of George Band was due to coming off at a bend not far below the summit. He gashed his face, which had to be stitched. I don't think that any of them tried to descend Snowdon in this manner again.

One thing led to another. I was camping below the Grochan in the Llanberis pass. A man came up and said: "Is Joe Brown about this morning?" He was shown to my tent.

"I'm Tom Stobart. Your name was mentioned to me at the

hotel as someone who might be interested in making a film in the Dolomites."

I told him that I was very interested. Tom Stobart had been official photographer on the Everest expedition and he had made the film. He was also one of the pioneering climbers on gritstone in the 1930s.

"I've got a contract," he went on, "from the British Iron and Steel Federation who have commissioned me to make a film on safety for general release. The script is written—all I need are actors—two first-class climbers."

Don Roscoe happened to be standing nearest during this conversation.

"Well, I'm one of those," he said boldly.

"What about the pay?" I inquired.

"The budget is pretty small, I'm afraid. You can have £100 each and you'll have to pay your own fares and expenses out there. The location work will last about five weeks."

I conferred with Roscoe and we accepted. At the time we thought that the deal was a bargain. We regarded it as a free climbing holiday in the Alps, neither making nor losing money. In fact we were to find it otherwise, though through no fault of Tom Stobart.

In Cortina there was the usual crowd of technicians. An old guide called Chelso de Gasper, who had thirty-eight seasons behind him, had been engaged to supervise the climbing sequences. He was a marvellous man and it was a pleasure to share his company. He could still lead Grade V climbs without stirring a hair. The chief cameraman, Joe Amber, was equally aged and had never been on a rock-face in his life. Yet he was the only non-climber member of the film company, among many, who remained completely unperturbed by the airy ledges on which we left him to do his work.

The climax of the story was shot on the Spigolo Giallo or Yellow Edge. Coming down, the passage of a very steep ramp covered with stones was taken on the backside by the people in our safe-keeping. Chelso had just disappeared round a corner at the bottom when a flurry of stones swept down on some of the crew behind him. He heard their cries and reappeared rapidly. He warded off the stones with his hands. As they flew towards him he hit out and deflected them to another course. Roscoe and I were tremendously impressed by this, and afterwards there was not a mark on Chelso's hands.

On an off-day Roscoe and I attempted to climb the Cassin Route on the Cima Grande. This was just about the most famous climb in the Dolomites. We had very little in the way of protective clothing because the film-making did not require anything elaborate. So we started up this great face dressed as for a summer's day in the Llanberis Pass. I need hardly add that we didn't know where the route went. A thunderstorm hit us and lightning struck the mountain with such ferocity that we were thrown into a fit of spasms. The electric shocks were so powerful that but for belaying we should have been thrown clear off the face.

A foot of hail banked up on the tiny ledges. Water columns poured over the roofs into our faces. I slipped and recovered by a fluke. We double-roped and back-tracked to no avail.

"Bugger it, Don," I cried, "let's find a ledge to bivouac." We stripped off naked to wring out our saturated clothing, replacing it with woollen sweaters next to the skin. There was one dry match in the box and our cigarettes had been preserved in a polythene bag. Foodless, I chain-smoked and shivered violently all night. By morning we could hardly bend a limb.

Roping down, we were not fully aware, until an ascending party hooked in our rope, that there was no way back on to the rock after dropping over one roof. Later Chelso told us gravely that on the only previous attempt to descend the face the climber had been killed.

Hazard was shown in British cinemas as an allegory on care and safety in heavy industry. The parallels in mountaineering practice were well chosen and the total effect dramatised the dangers of imprecise actions, with a happy ending.

Tom Stobart formed a production company called T.V. Explorations with the well-known journalist, Ralph Izzard, formerly of the *Daily Mail*. Both had travelled widely all over the world. You only had to mention a place and sure enough one of them had been there and would reel off a string of exciting anecdotes. Together they either pre-sold or made on speculation films for television with Tom as photographer, producer and director and Ralph as script writer and the author of articles for newspapers and magazines. The commissions they sought were the essence of adventure, involving many skills.

In 1961 Tom invited me to go on a job in Persia. He put it to me: "Have you ever heard of the Cave of the Assassins?" I had and I hadn't. It was one of those mythical stories one associated with so many tales of lore concerning caves in that part of the world, like Aladdin's and flying carpets.

"Well, it seems there are several caves," he explained, "and one at least—probably more—has never been entered to my knowledge. There is a sheer cliff below it. That's where you come in."

"What can we hope to discover inside?" I queried.

"Anything of value belonging to former civilisations. Treasure, my boy!"

The hunt was on.

We flew to Tehran, a fine modern city with broad, tree-lined avenues, marble palaces and splendid gardens—a vivid contrast to the impoverished countryside beyond.

Tom bought supplies in the market, shopping as the grand master in the art of living off the land, H. W. Tilman, would have done. A huge trunk filled with herbs and a large Parmesan cheese were the basis of all our meals. Tom was a brilliant cook. Using these basic ingredients, he could produce a tasty meal from next to nothing. The cheese lasted several years. I went on two expeditions with Tom and after that time only a quarter of the cheese had been eaten. It was still there, in its plastic bag, sweating away. A few scrapings from the cheese and some herbs were served with a plate of steaming spaghetti; the result was delicious. At the time I had been under treatment at home for an ulcer. My doctor had given me a diet sheet and warned me to keep off a variety of foodstuffs, including spiced dishes and tomatoes. For two days in the Persian mountain our meals were tomatoes curried with herbs and cheese; luckily the ulcer never complained.

The Valley of the Assassins is locked in a remote corner of the Elburz mountains about 100 miles north-west of Tehran. The headwaters drain the western slopes of the Takht-e Sulaiman range (Solomon's Throne), which is crowned by Alamkuh (15,880 feet). Of interest to mountaineers, this part of the Elburz mountains, which spread around the shores of the Caspian Sea for 500 miles, was first visited by the Bornmüller brothers, two German botanists, who climbed Alamkuh in 1902. Farther east, the extinct volcano of Demavend (18,603 feet) is the highest point of the Elburz and this was climbed by Sir W. Taylor in 1836.

In medieval times a dissident religious sect had made its stronghold at Alamut in this impenetrable valley. A series of fortresses was built to reinforce the defences. Under the leadership of Hasan the sect supported the Ismaili doctrine in Cairo and waged guerilla resistance against the Seljuk regime in Persia. The Persian Ismailis were eventually cut off when they offered allegiance to the ideals of a deposed and subsequently murdered caliph in Cairo. A new blood line of leaders, called Imams, then flourished in the valley. It became a powerful branch of the Moslems, and the Aga Khan today, representing the same people in greater numbers in India and Pakistan, is the direct descendant of these Imams.

Hasan, the original "Old Man of the Mountain", was a fierce and fearless leader. About 1090 he introduced several changes in the Ismaili doctrine and practice, notably the adoption of "assassination" to deal with enemies. Assassination was carried out as a sacred religious duty. As grand master of the "Assassins", he presided over terrorist officers and directed the policies and activities of the sect. All attempts by the Seljuks to defeat the Assassins failed. High ranking victims were claimed and the Assassins' influence and activities spread as far as Cairo and Syria. Repercussions were even felt in Europe.

The Assassins were finally subdued in 1256 by the second Golden Horde led by the Mongol general Hulagu, a great grandson of Jenghiz Khan and a brother of Kublai Khan. Alamut was captured and the ruling grand master hanged.

The word "assassin" came from the phonetic sound of *hashishin*, a taker of hashish. The narcotic influence of eating hemp drugged the minds of the Assassins and kept them happy in their nefarious work. The word was brought to Europe by the Crusaders from Syria and it was first used to denote political and secret murder by Dante in the early fourteenth century.

None of the popular stories connected with Assassin practice are confirmed in Ismaili sources. The legend goes that the grand master first enticed those of his followers selected to commit murder into his castle, or to another dwelling place where it was alleged that the indoctrinations took place. A grand vizier, a sort of puppet figure with the status of a senior minister, who was completely under the spell of the grand master, was responsible for guiding recruits to the castle. He was also responsible for ensuring that a destiny no less than paradise was promised to them as an inducement—in case they had second thoughts before arriving. Shown into a tunnel, the grand master gave them hashish that produced a dream-like condition of erotic splendour. Then they were led along the tunnel, half a mile, to a garden full of beautiful girls, who fed them sherbet and pandered with favours to their drugged sensations. After a day in the garden they were taken before the grand master. He declared that they had experienced true paradise. If they served him well and laid down their lives for him they would find eternal paradise. Having ingratiated himself, the grand master took possession of their minds. He could pick out a candidate and order him to jump off a cliff. The man jumped without hesitation.

The tunnel could still be seen, but there was no sign of the building or garden. The castle was called Maimundiz. It consisted of five caves opening about 150 feet above the ground in an overhanging cliff nearly 1,000 feet high. The conglomerate rock was terrible to handle—quite the worst rock I had ever seen. It was more like soldified glacier moraine, all mud and gravel peppered with larger stones. A stone could be pulled out, and the face crumbled round the hole.

Hasan had erected masonry against the cliff and a ramp had linked the caves. Stones hurled from Hulagu's war machines had destroyed all means of access. The original approach to the first cave was so narrow that only one man could pass at a time. One guard armed with a spear was sufficient to defend the entrance. A bowman could not attack the position because both hands were needed to approach the entrance.

The Assassins' headquarters were at Alamut some fifteen miles higher up the valley. They stood on a huge pedestal, called the Rock of Alamut. The grand master had surrendered here. The Mongols brought him to Maimundiz and held a knife to his throat to force him to order his associates to capitulate.

Three of the five caves at Maimundiz were easily entered. We were concerned with the other two. They had probably not been entered since the invaders had overrun the valley.

Below the first cave I tried to climb a big corner. The rock was atrocious and I abandoned it 40 feet up. The rock below the second cave was surprisingly firm for 50 feet; then it overhung and I traversed into a chimney directly in line with the cave. The chimney was unbelievably rotten, with awkward constrictions in which piles of blocks and rubble had collected.

I was having to squeeze between these pinched sections, terrified that if the contents of a funnel sluiced out the least I would receive was a broken leg. There was nothing to be gained by having a rope lowered from the cliff top; it would hang away 50 feet from the face. If I could have had a second man on the rope it would have helped, but there was no one capable enough to follow. I was stuck in the chimney by myself, having gone through several boulder-filled constrictions. In the language of rock climbers, I was "gripped up". If ever there was a test to show that I could climb down anything that I had climbed up—a maxim in mountaineering—this was it. I got back to the ground sorely rattled.

Three days' climbing on this useless rock accustomed me to it. I decided to try the original route again where there was no danger of being trapped, only of falling off.

On reaching the overhanging portion I decided to bridge across the corner. In this position my hands and feet held the rock in place by pressure. As soon as I endeavoured to reach higher with an arm or leg the pressure was released and the rock crumbled. The way to deal with this problem was to test the embedded stones, sticking out in various degrees, by tapping them with a peg hammer. On receiving this treatment all the round ones dropped out. However some of them were the ends of long stones deeply buried in the dry mud; they sounded quite solid. I drilled holes in five of them and inserted bolts about half an inch long. Using the ringed heads of the bolts as holds I went up the overhanging section holding my breath. The upper section was a big V-shaped groove, much easier to bridge, and the last 20 feet was brickwork, 900 years old no less and the soundest part of the climb!

I squinted nervously into the opening. The cave floor was heaped with miniature Dolomite peaks of bat droppings. The party below attached a caving ladder to the rope and I pulled it up. This ladder was 150 feet long. I climbed it in about three minutes while the rest of the party took half an hour or more with a safety rope tied to them. I hoisted the delicate camera equipment into the cave and preparations were made for exploration and filming. When everything was ready we moved stealthily inside, talking to each other in whispers. Scrambling through side-passages a dislodged boulder sent a chilling reverberation through the caves and our hair stood on end.

The obvious indications of life-remains were old fires and bones. Tom Stobart found an arrowhead. Broken pottery was collected but none of it fitted to make a complete piece. Some pots were unearthed almost intact; only the tops were slightly chipped. One of them was glazed and this threw everyone into frenzied excitement. An expert told us that only three glazed pots of this period were known to exist. Later doubts were expressed about its authenticity. Of treasure there was none.

With the filming complete we were packing up to leave when a group of officials arrived. They had instructions forbidding us to remove anything from the caves. After a protracted argument we persuaded them that it was folly to return our keepsakes to the caves; in all probability they would never be seen again. We promised to take them to the museum in Tehran.

We found nothing of interest at Alamut and were disinclined to follow up a tip that one of the intermediate fortresses was worth a visit. Six months later a party of archaeologists went to this fortress and brought out the biggest hoard of gold ever discovered in Persia.

Since leaving Archie and returning from Kangchenjunga in 1955 I had been working on my own as a building repairer. Taking off to join expeditions in various parts of the world meant that I had to shut down for several months in the summer but I always managed to get plenty of work when I came back. My regular customers recognised that they got value for money. I had stopped undercutting prices and only a few people quibbled at the time. By working at a furious pace I kept costs down well below the average. The publicity I received from climbing adventures also helped with business. Customers were intrigued to find that the man putting in a new sash-cord or re-tiling the bathroom was also on the front page of their morning newspaper. Then I got married. I had to consider providing security for the long-term instead of saving small sums to pay for the next mountaineering adventure.

I had known Val quite a long time, and she used to come out with friends for walks in the hills and occasionally she climbed. She was a school teacher and of course the walking and climbing movement is strong in the ranks of education. We had what might be called a perfectly conventional church wedding, surrounded by relatives and friends. However, at the reception after the ceremony there did appear to be more reporters present than guests. Having survived this ordeal, when we booked into the Lakeland hotel for our honeymoon, like most newly-weds we thought that no one could tell that we were just married. The morning newspapers spoiled our secret. Our photographs appeared in nearly all of them, my wife and I standing together with a garland of rope coils round us.

Immediately on my return from Persia I began work at White Hall. For a year or more I had thought half-heartedly about working at a climbing centre. Then I heard that someone had left White Hall—the Derbyshire Education Committee's centre for outdoor pursuits. Eric Langmuir was warden at the time. We had a chat about the job and he seemed to be interested in my application. He approached Jack Longland (who was Director of Education) and the Committee, and I had the job offered to me. I was not qualified as a teacher but in outdoor activities it was thought that I could hold my own.

Val felt a little apprehensive because I had been my own boss for a long time and she didn't know how I would react to working for someone else again. But I was sure that there would be no problems.

As it happened I was invited to go to Persia with Tom Stobart, so I started at White Hall later than I should have done. This was in September, 1961. In Persia, Ralph Izzard had been talking about the possibility of making new archaeological discoveries at Petra in Jordan. The problems were again those of entering inaccessible dwellings, this time carved out of sandstone many centuries ago. Ralph Izzard had been there and described the situation as far more complex than the Valley of the Assassins. On the other hand the rock would be more reliable for climbing.

A few days after reporting for duty at White Hall I admitted to having promised to accompany T.V. Explorations on the Petra venture, which was planned for early spring in 1962. I asked for leave. Counting the weekends that I pledged to work before setting out, I was given two weeks' leave of absence.

After I had been at White Hall a week I received another invitation to visit Patagonia and climb in the Fitzroy area with an Irish expedition. I asked for three months' leave to coincide with the time of the expedition, but of course the request was refused. In fact I was offered trips on so many expeditions during this period that I could have been away almost continuously for two years.

Having agreed my leave for the Petra expedition I wrote to Tom Stobart: "We'll have to do the job in a fortnight, or I'll be taking the record for the shortest-lived instructor at White Hall." It meant that the film would have to be made in ten days. Tom thought that it could be done, adding to his reply: "Will you get a certificate to show that you are a Christian—otherwise we may be delayed through difficulties between the Arab and Israeli countries."

I went to a vicar in Buxton and knocked humbly on his door.

"Please, can you give me a certificate to say that I am a Christian."

He eyed me suspiciously: "Certainly not. How do I know that you are a Christian?"

"But . . ." I faltered, "I'm telling you, I am a Christian."

"That is not good enough," he lectured me. "I don't know who you are and your request is a very serious matter."

"Isn't my word good enough?" I asked.

"It is not that, my son. I must be able to see that you are a Christian before I can sign a certificate."

I departed, muttering to myself that it was only to be expected that the clergy would distrust the word of a stranger, even though one of the ten commandments was, Thou shalt not lie. . . . No wonder the church was losing attendances.

"What am I going to do, Val?" I moaned to my wife. "I'll never get into the country."

"I know," she said brightly, "go and see the vicar who married us in Manchester."

The vicar was not the man who married ur. Moreover, he pointed out that it would be unethical for him to give me a certificate, without really knowing whether I was a Christian. But after a bit of gentle persuasion I got what I wanted.

After all this trouble Tom sent another certificate in the post. I couldn't decipher the signature but it was headed: The

Manse—and an address that I knew did not exist. I wonder where he got it from? I travelled some days after the main party, flashing this certificate in the faces of officials, and was not asked any awkward questions. I joined my companions in Amman.

Petra is a ruined site situated about 150 miles south of Amman on the east side of the great rift valley of Wadi el-Araba. This rock valley extends from the Sea of Galilee in the north to the Gulf of Aqaba and the Red Sea to the south, a distance of 250 miles. Much of it lies below sea level and the Dead Sea occupies the central part of the valley. Petra is some 60 miles south of the Dead Sea.

We drove across the desert, empty for miles in all directions. A line of slim hills grew in the distance. We came to a village with a Beau Geste-like fort and camels and policemen all looking like extras on a film set. A mule train was hired and we walked down an open valley towards a barricade of sandstone cliffs. The land here was about 1,000 feet high. As we drew closer to the cliffs we could see carvings of no special interest in the rock. Suddenly the cliff was split by a huge crack about 20 feet wide with the walls closing in overhead. This was the entrance to Petra. At slight bends in the rift the sky was shut out. Resuming the walk into bright shafts of sunlight, a section of wall some 600 feet high would be lit up in an array of dazzling colours shown in the clean sandstone. A mile long, it was possible to drive a jeep through the rift. At the other end we emerged into the tapered end of a valley, the Wadi Musa. Immediately opposite rose a sandstone wall of 1,000 feet, revealing the most elaborate of the Petra carvings.

A magnificent architectural spectacle confronted us. It was called el-Hazne or "The Treasury of Pharaoh", hewn out of the cliff in chambers 40 feet deep in places. The façade, flush with the rock-face, was intricately carved and the relief work was recessed inside the cliff with equally beautiful workmanship. A series of buildings was carved in this manner, some with half columns of 100 feet, of perfect line and with the finest of chisel marks traceable on them. The Treasury had a large space cut out above the top of the building; a turret supporting a carved stone urn had been placed here. Over the decades the Arabs had shot the urn to pieces, hoping that it would crack and spill a fountain of gold. Other carvings were capped by the same kind of urn. We located one that seemed to offer a possibility of finding something; it was also situated in an ideal setting for picturesque film work.

At this point the cliff was dome-shaped, meeting the ground at 45 degrees. Yet the building had been carved in a vertical face by first excavating thousands of cubic yards of rock in front of it, leaving a courtyard enclosed on three sides. The face at the rear was 150 feet high and was flanked by relief-tooled side walls which extended into the valley. In an horizontal line across the face there were several openings to tombs.

Roping down from the top to reach the chambers was out of the question; the upper cliff overhanged badly. The face at the back of the courtyard below the entrances was unclimbable. Here was a problem as intricate as the carving itself.

The solution was to string a rope from one side wall to the other high above the courtyard and against the face. The distance and heights were too great for rope throwing tricks. I climbed the dome-shaped flank of both side walls, hammered in pegs at the highest points and attached ropes that were dropped into the courtyard below. When the ends were tied I could then pull in the ropes from the sides, stretching it in one piece across the façade at the height of the side walls. Using this long rope, I pulled a caving ladder across the face. Once this had been secured at the ends I slid along it, like crossing a circus high-wire, until I was level with the entrance to a tomb.

In this position, suspended high above the ground, I was still some fifteen feet away from the mouth of the opening. Originally the tomb entrances had been sealed with relief-decorated stones, the object being to give the impression that they were an integral part of the façade. The covering stones had been destroyed, doubtless by bombardment from below, but a fragment remained in the entrance to the one that I was trying to enter.

With a bunch of pegs tied to the end of a line I started to throw it like a grappling hook into the entrance, trying to make it catch behind the fragmented projection. When it held fast I pulled on the line and drew myself towards the opening. Almost within reach, the pegs broke loose and I swayed backwards into the air—an alarming sensation. The second attempt was successful. The tomb was dust and rubble; empty. By means of a rope I kept hold of the caving ladder while exploring inside, otherwise there would have been no way of getting out. As I stepped away on the ladder to leave the tomb I was thrown into a gigantic swing, returning almost to the entrance again, backwards and forwards in a sideways plane, until the rocking motion ceased.

Moving along the ladder to different points, I entered two more caves in this particular system by getting Tom to swing the ladder for me. I found nothing. We came to the conclusion that the Arabs must have robbed them by raising scaffolding. Half a dozen poles of about 100 feet could be made of bamboo; the original carvings had been done by working from bamboo scaffolding.

Farther away the hillside was honeycombed with caves that had probably served as normal dwelling places. Inter-communicating rooms had been carved in solid rock. One could only marvel at the patience and effort that must have gone into the construction. The hillside rooms were less elaborate than the big chambers near the tombs; their lavish carvings indicated some religious significance or they might have been occupied by chiefs.

Petra was the capital of the Nabataeans. This Arab race was famous for its unique pottery. They found a way to throw pots that has not been repeated since. A vessel thrown the same shape and thickness of a brandy glass had a flat projecting lip of two inches or more around the top. How this was done is a mystery. If the material was plastic enough to throw such a thin lip, then it must surely have been unsupportable and would collapse.

The carvings at Petra were worked between 500 B.C. and

A.D. 500. The city rose and fell roughly between these dates. Nabataean prosperity was at its height about the time of Christ when Petra was the major centre of caravan trade in the region. Roman occupation and influence in the area diminished the commercial importance of the centre and subsequent attacks by rival tribes pushed it into obscurity. That a religious significance lingered on was witnessed by the number of altars constructed throughout the city's history. Two impressive obelisks hewn from the rock were carved with the faces of Nabataean gods. Very little history was recorded in the language used by the tribe. There was only one tomb with writing on it. As a fortress and city combined the occupants could hold the formidable position from attack. But the Nabataeans were gentle people and the city was plundered on several occasions.

During our stay at Petra we were living in a tomb. On one side there was a ridge forming a sort of mantelpiece. Running my hands through the dust along the top I found three Roman coins. Behind the hill in which the tomb was carved lay a wadi. We noticed a square-cut cave high up in the opposite wall. It caught our attention because there was no façade; in fact there was no decoration at all, and but for the squareness of the opening it might have been a natural cave.

Once again the cliff above was protected by a big overhang. I climbed the face directly below the cave. A few feet from the entrance I had to drill a hole and insert an expansion bolt for direct aid. The floor was piled with bones and skulls and in a corner I saw some large broken pots. The remains of several hundred people were strewn in the cave. The pots were two feet high and an inch thick and would hold about three gallons.

The archaeologist in the party did not come up into the cave on this occasion. Fixing the rope, I slid down to show him one of the pots. He had no idea what it was. He had not seen its kind before. But he studied it for a while and declared it was medieval.

The archaeologist asked me to measure accurately the

dimensions of the cave. This was easier said than done. Many feet of dust covered the floor. I started digging to find the rock-bed. After removing a cubic yard I uncovered three skeletons. Their wrists were tied with coarse black string. One was clothed from head to foot in leather that was dry and brittle and just snapped when I tried to lift it. Cleaning dust away around the skeletons their outlines disintegrated. Another wore a bronze bangle. A thrill of pleasure at making this discovery swept over me. I rushed down to show it to the archaeologist.

"We must take care of this," he said thoughtfully. He took a cigarette box from his pocket and opened it for me to slide the bangle inside.

We found another unadorned cave that was easy to enter. It too contained skeletons, about twenty skulls with a matching number of bones.

"Will you come up?" I called to the archaeologist.

"What for?" he replied. "There can't be anything of interest up there. The cave is too accessible."

I went in with a torch to explore by myself. I found a small oil lamp standing on one of the skulls; a macabre touch. Marks of burning round the hole where the wick protruded were still visible.

Although we now expected to find nothing we were bound to inspect one of the urns on top of the big tombs. The urns were really huge. One was chosen more for its photogenic qualities than accessibility. The climb was unusually difficult. The urn stood on a cross whose arms extended to points. I had to hand traverse, dangling on my arms, along a projection to reach the base of the urn.

"It's going to be nasty," I called out. "A piece of the arm is cracked." I swung along it and the cracked piece moved.

The climb up the side of the urn to the brim was no easier. The rock was crumbling. The urn was empty.

Walking through a village all the Arabs lounging in the shadows had murderous looks on their faces. I could not make it out because they had been most hospitable on the inward journey. One of them stepped aggressively in my path and said, "Ramadan". I apologised and hastily extinguished the cigarette that I was smoking. Contrary to some of the fine things said about the religious month of Ramadan, fasting and abstaining from women and drink made the men dangerously irritable. There were more murders during this religious observance than in the rest of the year put together.

CHAPTER EIGHT

ESCAPES AND FAILURES IN THE ALPS

Taking part in an expedition is no substitute for a holiday. Most of the time Himalayan climbing is laborious and extremely fatiguing. A climber can feel good and enjoy the work one day and be struck down by illness and drained of energy the next. Above 22,000 feet, having reached peak form and fitness, human life deteriorates. Acclimatisation buys a climber more or less time to reach the goal but sooner or later he must come down to survive. Only an endless supply of oxygen would defeat the process. The weather is an equally serious drawback and even with plenty of oxygen it would precipitate the same outcome in the end. You can't win. Himalayan mountains are climbed in favourable circumstances but never "conquered".

In the Northern Hemisphere a big mountaineering expedition is usually finished by early summer. (Some parties go after the monsoon period but not many.) On returning home there is ample time to arrange a normal Alpine holiday.

On Kangchenjunga it had occurred to me that one might profit from the unique fitness gained by climbing in the Himalayas. There was good reason for thinking that after so much careful preparation and controlled exercise one should be supremely fit. Major routes in the Alps might then be climbed with little effort. In practice it did not quite work out this way.

I returned from Kangchenjunga lean and skinny, as one who has spent a year or two in a concentration camp. Underweight and feeling positively weak I went off to Chamonix with the Rock and Ice for my well-earned "holiday". The fallacy of the theory was not immediately apparent. In fact it was two or three years before I realised how much vitality was sapped from the body by high altitude climbing. Apart from that the technical standard of climbing in the Alps is much higher because altitude is not a serious drawback. Moreover, the weather is just as bad and plays havoc with the finest schemes.

The North Face of the Grands Charmoz was not too distant from the Montenvers. It was fairly serious in character and we could stroll to the bottom of the face in the late afternoon. The party was Don Whillans, Nat Allen, Eric Price and myself. Eric's previous Alpine experience amounted to one training climb on the tiny Aiguille de l'M. I think he must have regarded the choice of climb as belonging to the "all or nothing" school of mountaineering.

The face is approached by a number of converging ravines cutting through grassy slopes and moraines. A small glacier forms a crescent round the base of the lower wall, about 1,500 feet high, mainly rocks grooved by gullies of snow and ice. The wall supports a steep ice slope hanging in the middle of the face. At the top of this slope a large ice couloir splits the upper wall, whose vertical rocks taper to the fine conical pile that is so conspicuous in the panorama from the Montenvers hotel.

We slotted ourselves among some boulders at the foot of the face. So far Eric had found the preparations for a serious Alpine climb enjoyable, and as he had bivouacked in the boulders below Cloggy, there was nothing strange in the procedures that we were adopting. Eric eagerly awaited his first Alpine adventure. After supper it started to rain. It rained all night and by morning we were soaked. Bad as the weather was we were in a mood to climb. At first light we tied on the ropes and set to work.

There was no gradual approach above the bivouac place: typical North Face terrain rose straight up into a threatening sky. The first two or three pitches went through a waterfall, and the rocks were of Severe standard, then the climbing was easier. Our progress was remarkably good and we reached the edge of the ice slope in record time. The slope was a plain sheet of ice about 1,000 feet high. At an angle of 50 degrees it was not too steep. "Let's try moving together up it," proposed Don.

21. Camp III at 20,000 feet on the Mustagh Tower

22. Tom Patey   23. Ian McNaught Davis

24. The author in the Karakorum

25. French party in the Mustagh Tower area. *L. to R.:* Contamine, Paragot, Keller, Florence, Magnone, and porters

26. John Hartog, with frostbitten feet, being carried back to Skardu

27. Home from the Mustagh Tower

28. West (Yalung) Face of Kangchenjunga, showing the route of
ascent

29. Approaching Camp IV on Kangchenjunga

30. Erecting Camp VI, the last, on the Ramp, Kangchenjunga

31. George Band reaching the summit ridge of Kangchenjunga

The idea was to keep in hand the time saved getting up the lower wall. That would give us more time to cope with the upper rocks.

We put on crampons and stamped and crunched in a straight line up the slope. It was tiring work, painful on the ankles and leg muscles. The slope steepened as it neared the upper wall. The summit was smothered in cloud. I was in the lead at this point and could hear the others cursing behind. Soon it started snowing—wet clammy snow that quickly penetrated clothing and stiffened your limbs with cold.

A stance was cut in the ice and all of us shuffled on to it. Even then no suggestion was put forward that we ought to consider descending. Whillans and I were always optimistic that bad weather might clear, but it rarely did.

I stepped off the slope on to the icy rocks of a buttress. Visibility had closed to a few yards. Groping blindly upwards I came to a platform where the others joined me. We were perhaps only 600 feet from the summit. The rocks above were sheer and even more icy. After running out 30 feet of rope I was completely enveloped by cloud and could hardly see my feet. Snow was falling heavily and silently. Not a sound came from below. The quietness was uncanny. I thought, all you have to do is thump a hole in this filthy stuff, go up a few yards and repeat the process. But there was no hope of picking out the route ahead.

I cut some steps up an ice tongue; it appeared to go up the face a long way but soon petered out. Nose glued to the rock, I found something resembling a hand traverse, which crossed a wall and went round a corner, but I couldn't see where it led to. A little dismayed I retraced my steps.

We held a conference. Whillans was in favour of making a long horizontal traverse across the top of the ice slope to inspect the central couloir—if it could be found. Then the cloud blew off for long enough to see right across the face. Don took advantage of the break to carry out his promise and Nat Allen went with him. Whillans climbed easily across the steep ice slope, running out a full length of rope without stopping. He

F

sidled round a corner into the couloir. Eric Price and I watched
Nat follow him. Eventually they both disappeared.

The strain of standing bolt upright on the narrow platform
in the ice was beginning to tell. One felt like jumping off on to
some imaginary terrace where one could stretch out and forget
the pains of cramp. Half a packet of cigarettes later we saw Nat
returning across the slope. He got to within six feet of the
platform, having already called to us that avalanches were
booming down the couloir, when he lost his balance. He fell
over backwards, his arms flailing wildly in the air. There was
well over 100 feet of rope between him and Don. Unless he
could stop himself he would make a huge pendulum fall on the
slope. Worse still Don might not have a belay good enough to
hold him and would be pulled off. In any case Nat would
receive a terrible ripping on the ice. The action to save himself
resembled making uphill cartwheels on an escalator going
downwards. His crazy gymnastics seemed to go on for ages; they
probably lasted three or four seconds. On the platform a few
feet away we could do nothing but hope. He got his axe into a
little hole and steadied himself, then we fielded him on to the
platform. "Don't do that again, Nat. My nerves are shattered,"
said Price hoarsely. Don regained the platform without incident.

It was thumbs down for the North Face of the Grands
Charmoz. We had had enough. The party crept down the ice
slope, not daring to think about the consequences of a slip.
Eric Price was very subdued. On the lower rock face I heard
him suggesting nervously to Nat that he thought I must be
panicking. Why was I banging in one peg after another from
which to lower ourselves on the rope, and making no attempt
to retrieve the ones which were too poor to use? He knew how
particular I was about removing ironmongery from rocks in
Britain. At one point a peg fell out and clattered down the face.
I took another and planted it securely. "Hurry up," I said to
Nat, "fix the rope on that one and you go down and look for
the next rope off point." I heard Eric say to Nat: "Cripes, if
he's using two or three pegs at every stance he must be getting

very gripped." This amused me so much that I kept quiet.

In the Alps I had no illusions about being a purist. A safe and comfortable descent from a difficult climb in bad conditions called for plain and practical tactics. We had to get off the mountain quickly to avoid a second bivouac. Had our plight been worse, due say to nursing down an injured climber, more drastic measures could not have been taken. I was in complete control of the situation and so was Don. I believe that Eric realised later, without having it explained to him, why Don and I were thumping pegs into the rock as readily as we might knock nails into wood. It was better to be poorer through the loss of a dozen pegs—even if they did cost up to 7s 6d each— than a dead idealist.

In sleet and rain we stumbled wearily down the small glacier, away from the face. It was now too dark to find the correct route off the mountain, and for Eric this was the last straw. We searched for a way on to the Mer de Glace but always finished up on the edge of a precipice or in a blind ravine. Finally we went on a circuitous route across the foot of the Aiguille de l'M and got down to the Montenvers. We reached our tents in the valley in the early hours of morning.

To my knowledge Eric never climbed again in the Alps. I could hardly blame him. I don't think he blamed us. The ice slope had been particularly unnerving. We should not have gone up it moving together—even the great Hermann Buhl, when he climbed the face, had taken stances and belays on ice-pegs to overcome this section.

The miseries of the Charmoz climb reacted differently on Don and me. A failure of this kind was merely frustrating. We might have been frightened at the time but having regained the valley we felt only annoyance.

Now Don and I were anxious to look at the South-West Pillar of the Dru. This is the tall, narrow buttress at the right-hand side of the West Face. It is nearly 2,500 feet high and is particularly smooth. There was little doubt that it would prove to be a tougher nut to crack than the West Face. The Italian

climber Walter Bonatti and one or two others had attempted it
but the weather had defeated them.

We arrived below the West Face with enough bread to last a
week. I can't think why we brought up so many provisions
because it was not our intention to spend this amount of time
on the Pillar. The stone-raked couloir slanting up below the
face led to the foot of the pillar, a dangerous and difficult
entry at the best of times. As soon as we started up the couloir
so did the rain. Then the rain turned to snow, so we turned off
and scrambled on to the lower terraces of the West Face to
look for a bivouac place. The weather was really nasty. We
could not make up our minds whether to go down or sit the
night out in the hope of an improvement next morning.
Crouching under a large plastic sheet the debate went on in a
dilatory fashion. A warning cry and whining stones intruded
on our reverie. A party above us was retreating from the West
Face. They wanted to know if we would stay where we were,
to avoid the stones they were knocking down. This disturb-
ance brought us to the abrupt decision that we should go down.
Without further ado Don just chucked the rope over the edge
and we shot off down the couloir, dodging the stones and
regardless of the good advice the French party had given us.
This was just as well because we reached the glacier with ten
minutes to spare before pitch darkness came. We could only
suppose that the French were marooned on the ledge that we
had just left.

I had set out on our attempt to climb the South-West
Pillar wearing a pair of boots that a Chamonix equipment
specialist had wanted me to test. They had abnormally pointed
toes. I had found them excellent in every way for going uphill,
but going down they exhibited every fault imaginable. My feet
were rammed into the narrow toes and I was soon in agony. We
passed the slumbering Montenvers at 1 a.m. in driving rain.
I was stopping every three or four paces to rest my sore feet. On
reaching Chamonix I was hobbling and wishing that I could
walk on my hands. On opening the door of our two-man tent we
found it occupied by three people. Rain was drumming on the

canvas, so we threw ourselves inside and five of us spent the rest of the night there.

In 1955 there was an irregular cycle of good and bad weather. We had got off on the wrong foot from the start. When the sun was shining we were usually recuperating in the valley. Other people were hitting the right weather phase. When we were climbing the weather was bad and the lucky ones were resting. The bad spell that started when we set out to climb the South-West Pillar lasted five days. During this period Walter Bonatti was biding his time in the Charpoua hut on the other side of the mountain. As soon as the sky cleared he came over the Flammes de Pierre spur, roped down into the approach couloir and traversed on to the Pillar. In the next five days he climbed it solo. This incredible performance made Bonatti headline news and it remains one of the most brilliant exploits in the annals of mountaineering. Had we waited in Chamonix—had our attempt been timed a week later—Don and I would have been on the pillar with the Italian climber.

Some years later I plodded up the familiar track again towards the pillar. Morty was my companion. By now the pillar had been climbed several times. Whillans had already done it with Bonington, McInnes, Ross and two Austrians. Their ascent had been something of a nightmare and MacInnes had been an invalid with a cracked head.

Morty and I were fully aware of the struggle that faced us. The question was would we get a chance at all to start up the actual rocks of the pillar? When we reached the Rognon of the Dru, a mound of rock on the little glacier below the West Face, the snow cone at the foot of the couloir was black. This struck me as odd but registered nothing in particular. Crossing the crevasse at the bottom of the couloir was unusually difficult. I climbed a rock pitch above, which was covered with dust and debris. Then I heard the crash of falling stones. The couloir was humming with projectiles. It sounded as if the whole place was breaking up. I crouched down and put my rucksack on top of my head. Starting like the swish of escaping gas and finishing with a loud explosion the rocks burst all round me. A heavy sulphurous smell of broken rocks hung in the air. Fragments zipped over the edge of the platform in front of me and landed where Morty was standing above the snow cone. Glancing down I saw that Morty was not standing there any longer.

Having discharged several large salvoes the couloir was quiet again. I shouted: "Come on, Morty. Hurry up!" No reply. I shouted again. Silence. I thought, Oh God, he's been hit. I shouted myself hoarse. Still no reply. I was on the point of roping down to see how badly injured he was when a feeble voice called up: "Take in." Morty had escaped without a scratch.

In the couloir we were able to move on to a flank and avoid the firing line. The stones started coming down again. Hundreds of them. Dodging pieces ricocheting in all directions, we stole up into the narrow part of the couloir. Each fresh discharge was a little worse than the last. There was never a quiet period of more than five minutes. To make further progress it was necessary to cross to the other side, but this would be suicide. Although it was only 11.30 a.m. there was no choice but to bivouac on the bank of the couloir. The rest of the day was spent in idle speculation. We were completely pinned down by the cannonade.

Not the least of our worries was a great rock flake, about 50 feet high, sticking out over the bivouac ledge. All night long we grumbled to ourselves about this piece of rock. The warm air that was the main cause of the excessive stonefall might wreak some catalytic effect on the rock and if it fell we would be sliced neatly in two. We had the alternative of standing on one foothold each, a few yards away. The stones thundered all night, but by first light the falls had dwindled to thirty-minute intervals.

"Why don't you take a peep into the couloir?" suggested Morty. I poked my head round the corner. A flurry of stones swept by. I ducked exactly at the moment when they peppered the side of the corner. "You can bloody well take a look yourself," I said grievously. "No thanks," said Morty. "Come and have some tea."

Another thirty minutes went by. The couloir was dozing. "Come on, Morty," I said. "It's now or never." I began chipping steps in a thin ice tongue. We moved up the ice for about

150 feet. Morty stopped. "I don't feel very well. I think I'm going to be sick."

That was the end of another Alpine season.

At Whitsuntide 1958 the Rock and Ice held a camping meet at the foot of the Grochan cliff in the Llanberis pass. I was running down the slope to the roadside. My foot skidded on a pebble resting on one of the boulders on which I was hopping. I spun slowly through the air, landed awkwardly and shoved off again, expecting to come down more comfortably and stop myself. I hit the ground sharply. I felt a crack and knew instantly that I had broken a leg.

In a matter of moments two friends appeared. I was thinking how silly I must look. I had a broad grin on my face. "I've broken my leg," I said shyly. They would not believe me. "We know you and your pranks," said one. "You can't fool us."

Ray Greenall arrived. "I've broken it, Ray," I insisted, trying to suppress the urge to burst out laughing. "You are a liar, Brown. Come on, get up and stop this nonsense. I thought you were supposed to be taking photographs of Moseley having an epic up there." No one would believe me.

A small crowd gathered. I wanted to creep under a rock and hide. But I couldn't move. My leg was broken. Eventually Ray condescended to examine the leg. "It might be hurt," he conceded. "I'll carry you down to the road, but if you get off my back and run away I'll knock the living daylights out of you!"

Ray gave me a piggy-back to the bottom. I had now gone quite pale. My friends began to believe that I had a broken leg.

"You are not taking me to Bangor," I declared. "I might be kept there for months. I'll just get in the van and drive back to Manchester."

"Oh, you will, will you?" said Greenall. "Grab him, boys." They bundled me into the back of the van and propped me up with sleeping-bags and rucksacks.

In Manchester no one wanted to believe that I had travelled with a broken leg from North Wales without treatment. Having broken a leg before I was all too familiar with the procedure. I was out of action for three months. The plaster cast was removed about ten days before I was due to leave for the Alps. I was just about as unfit as anyone can be who is contemplating a climbing holiday. Normal walking had become an effort because the tendons had shrunk from inactivity. Nevertheless I was determined to go to Chamonix.

Don Whillans was in magnificent form. He had just done the South-West Pillar of the Dru. This he impressed upon me as the hardest climb of his career. I think he based this statement as much on the difficulties he had had shepherding a sorely pressed party as on the technical standard of the climb.

"What do you feel like doing, Joe," he inquired. "Anything you feel up to," I retorted. "Right, what about the West Face of the Petites Jorasses?" I thought a bit then said: "Isn't that harder than the South-West Pillar?" "It can't be," drawled Whillans. So Morty and I took his word for it.

Mindful of my condition Don promised to do all the leading. He decided to haul his own sack while Morty and I carried ours. The West Face of this splendid rock peak was a good example of an extreme modern rock climb. It was located on the Franco-Italian frontier quite close to the picture-postcard view of the North Face of the Grandes Jorasses and the scenery hereabouts was truly magnificent. A very strong French party had forced a route up the face at the end of the fine spell that Bonatti had used to make his daring climb on the Pillar of the Dru. It had been climbed about four times since.

The approach along the Mer de Glace and the Leschaux glacier was as long as any in the Mont Blanc range. This terrible walk did nothing but harm to my lately repaired leg. On the climb itself I was a physical wreck. I have never found a route so hard as this one. Because of this the face seemed endless. The climbing gave me little pleasure when it ought to have been pure joy. I could raise no enthusiasm for the work and there was nothing about the route that impressed me. I kept repeating to myself, where is the nice rock at a pleasant angle? All the rock was excellent granite but at a neck-craning angle. The tremendous effort needed to get up every inch of the way dominated my thoughts.

On reaching the crux of the climb, a long artificial section requiring many pegs, Don shouted down: "I'm not surprised they have the cheek to grade this A3. You can't get any pegs into the rock. There aren't any cracks. So when you get up here lean across the overhang a bit and you'll find a mass of jugs." Once again Whillans' genius had divined the means whereby the hardest pitch of a very serious climb could be tackled in a straightforward manner. Following Don's instructions I found the crux pitch comparatively simple.

We lost the correct route on the last 400 feet below the summit. Dusk was falling. Don kept running out one rope length after another up a long steep gangway. At the end of the top pitch on this section I arrived to find him belayed and sitting in a plastic bag. So Morty and I climbed in beside him and we spent the night there. Morty was sick during the night. He had a most unpleasant time. I was lying between the other two. Morty was so ill that he failed to notice that we had inadvertently dragged the sheet off him. In the morning he was very cold indeed.

We climbed to a point about 60 feet below the top. From here you could look down a couloir leading back to the glacier on the Chamonix side of the mountain. If we went to the summit it meant having to descend on the Italian side towards Courmayeur. Roping down the couloir was a hellish business. It was lined with ice, the rocks were loose, huge stones pelted through the air and several pitches were overhanging. I was never more glad to get off a mountain.

Faced with a painful crawl across miles of glaciers back to Chamonix I told Don and Morty to push ahead. I could manage on my own. They became specks in the distance. At one point I fell into a crevasse and felt terribly lonely. There was nothing to be gained by remaining in Chamonix while I was in this miserable condition, so three days later I went home.

Nineteen-sixty was a better year—at any rate in some respects. Whether I had been on an overseas expedition or not I was generally remiss in preparing for an Alpine holiday.

Many climbers went into special training several weeks before crossing the Channel. They tramped for miles over British hills, carrying heavy rucksacks (quite often filled with stones) and took in long easy rock climbs on the way. The object was to strengthen leg and shoulder muscles, which are strained by hut walks and rough scrambles to reach climbs in the Alps. Many preliminary Alpine exercises of this kind are harder and more strenuous than climbing to the top of any mountain in Britain. Once they had arrived in the Alps, climbers who took training seriously reinforced the process of gradual adjustment by first embarking on a programme of training climbs—a few short routes of moderate difficulty and altitude. The entire procedure was soundly based on the principles of acclimatisation.

I had never undertaken such preparations. I got off the train, so to speak, and in almost any kind of weather went straight in to attack some big route. It was not that we thought it clever or superior to act in this way; it was merely the impulse of enthusiasm. Consequently I had always found the first week's climbing in the Alps quite exhausting.

Playing a part in the documentary film *Hazard* had given me a taste for Dolomite climbing. These limestone towers were uniformly vertical and shades of difficulty often depended on the number of holds available or the degree of overhang. The quality of the rock was another factor; some of it was very bad. The similarity of climbing throughout the Dolomite region left little to choose between many hard routes, and it was often difficult to distinguish one from another although the mountains might be miles apart. Dolomite climbing had a character of its own; if one disliked it then it could be viewed with monotony and contempt.

In 1960 I decided to work up to the harder climbs gradually. I had a score to settle with the North Face of the Cima Grande, which had nearly done for Roscoe and myself. The party was mainly composed of people with whom I had begun to climb following the dispersal of the original Rock and Ice group— described in the next chapter. Present were Dennis Gray, Claud Davies, Trevor Jones, Les Brown and a couple of other lads.

On arrival in the Lavaredo area I renewed my acquaintance with the Yellow Edge. Everyone enjoyed this climb because it made no demand on our capacities. We then tackled the Cassin Route on the Cima Piccolissima. This was a shorter but harder climb. It faced south and caught the sun all day. This too was a delightful outing and we returned to the hut well satisfied.

Always excluding Don Whillans, anyone with whom I climbed automatically assumed that the rope I was leading would race away from the rest of the party. I preferred to climb in pairs so that the pace I wanted to move at would not be restricted by too many others on the rope. Speed was always a major asset in safe mountaineering. In the Dolomites I climbed with Dennis Gray while Les Brown and Trevor Jones formed a second rope that followed us. Right through the holiday Dennis and I invariably finished a climb in good time while Les Brown and Jones usually finished much later, having an epic on the final pitches as a storm broke and having to find their way down in the dark. This happened on the North Face of the Cima Grande, our next route, which gave me no trouble at all. The second pair narrowly escaped having to make a forced bivouac.

We now moved to the Tofana area close to Cortina. There we climbed the Pilastro di Rozes. This is 700 feet of steep slabs topped by a vertical then overhanging wall of similar height. Overhangs of ten feet and six feet started and finished the upper walls. We gained a considerable lead on the second rope, which reached the top of the slabs when I was going over the second overhang.

I had started to haul a sack up an overhanging chimney. Some way below Trevor Jones glanced up to see what we were doing. All he saw was a sack swinging 50 feet out in space. Trevor claimed afterwards that he just happened to look up at the moment I started pulling in the sack. He looked away quickly, blinking and shaking his head. That was a rucksack, he thought. No, it can't be. He looked up again. There was nothing to be seen but the huge impending face. By this time I had hauled the sack in. So he thought, it couldn't have been a rucksack, I'm seeing things.

When Trevor reached the ledge below the overhanging chimney we had just arrived at the top of the face. Trevor squinted up the chimney. My God, he said to himself, that must have been a rucksack I saw. Jones was paralysed with fear. Les Brown was leading and started to pull their sacks up the chimney. The sacks swung far out into space. Trevor had to cover his eyes because he could not bear to look at them. The shock froze him to the ledge. Les Brown shouted at him furiously but Trevor was unable to move. A weak voice called up: "I can't climb. I can't do it." Les couldn't hear him and continued screaming down for an explanation of the delay. Finally Trevor became more frightened of what Les might do to him than of the overhanging face. Once he started climbing he had no further bother.

As Dennis and I entered the hut a storm broke loose. The other pair were still on the face 300 feet from the top. Within a few minutes the mountain was plastered with snow. So when they eventually got down the story that Trevor told was terrifying in every detail.

After that we went to the Civetta area. Les Brown teamed up with Steve Read, who had a marvellous Alpine record. They set off at 2.30 a.m. to try the Solleder Route, one of the truly notable climbs in the Dolomites. It was not far short of 4,000 feet long and the difficulties were nearly continuous.

I was never much good at getting up in the morning. In the Dolomites 9.30 a.m. was my normal time for starting a climb—about the same as for a summer's day in Wales. On the morning in question Dennis and I resolved to try the North-West Face of the Torre di Valgrande. The first 1,000 feet was easy enough to climb unroped. At the foot of the first hard pitch we were surprised to see Les Brown and Read emerging at the top of it. They had been on the go for six or seven hours already. On reaching the Solleder Route the weather had looked unpromising, so they had come back to this lower peak. We were now climbing right on their heels.

The second of the steep pitches was the crux. I was just fishing for some holds to make a landing on the stance when

Les Brown was starting on the pitch above. He knocked down a stone the size of half a brick. Without warning it hit me in the middle of the head. I was stunned for a while. Then I realised that the tight-fitting hat I was wearing was filling up with blood. I was too frightened to remove it. There was so much blood slopping around under the hat that I was expecting to faint at any moment. The others were concerned that I might fall off through concussion. The blood started to leak through; suddenly my face and neck were streaming. Les rushed down, pulled off the hat and the contents gushed in a bloody mess all over us. It ran down an arm and one side of my anorak and dripped on to the rock. My thick black hair staunched the flow. I said that I felt well enough to continue.

We carried on behind the first pair. They pulled ahead of us a little. Higher up it started to rain heavily. There had been low cloud and a lot of mist all day. Now that we were fairly high on the peak, instead of taking the regular stances and stopping places, I was trying to save time by climbing through two or three at once before belaying. After doing this for a while I came to a crack. It was undoubtedly the correct line of the climb. It was full of water. The Gannex anorak that I was wearing protected me above the hips but my trousers were saturated. The water was drumming so hard on my hood that I could hear nothing else.

I wanted to avoid getting wet around the chest and arms so I left the correct route. There was a vague traverse line leading to a corner crack that ran up into a big groove in the face. The groove was dry. The noise of rushing water drowned my attempts to inform Dennis of what I was doing. Unknown to me I had already run out the 150 feet of rope between the pair of us. Dennis could tell by the movement of the rope that I was still climbing. He had to untie his belays in great haste. As I came to the end of the traverse and moved into the crack Dennis was forced to start climbing. He knew the position but I was still ignorant of it. Moreover, Dennis was in the firing line of stones dislodged by our companions above. While I was lay-backing up the crack Dennis was having to leap from sling to sling that I had left for protection on the face. Without the slings he could not have followed at the requisite pace. In that case one of us would have probably pulled off the other, which would have been unpleasant. I can't think why I believed that nothing was out of order for I was well accustomed to knowing when I had climbed the distance permitted by the rope interval. The pair of us were moving together on very hard rock in the pouring rain.

I came below an overhang. On the right, 20 feet away, I saw a big ledge that was on the correct route, but I decided to belay where I was to avoid getting wet. The two above were now climbing easier ground and crossing terraces banked up with finely balanced stones. As Dennis was coming up to me the rock dislodged by the others came crashing down all over the ledge. If I had continued on the correct line and crossed the ledge there was no doubt at all that we should have been badly injured.

We waited until the stonefall died down. I looked at my watch. It was after seven o'clock. I swore to myself: Christ, this is going to be a repetition of the Cima Grande of two years before. I put the watch away and sped off up the next pitch. Twenty minutes later I reached the top of the mountain. I looked at my watch again and it was one-fifteen! Down below I had looked at it upside down and had not bothered to read the figures. In spite of the delay through being hit on the head, and making a voluntary detour from the route, we had spent only five hours on the mountain. The normal time was about eight hours or more.

I had had just about enough of the Dolomites. The truth was that I was fed up with the similarity of the climbing. I longed to go to Chamonix and get to grips with some snow and ice. The architectural forms of the Chamonix granite were also vastly superior to the crumbling Dolomite chimneys and cracks.

We spent a fortnight in Chamonix and not a single route was climbed. The weather was breaking all records for summer rain and snowfall. The farthest we got was nearly to the foot of the South-East Face of the Fou with Robin Smith. This young Scotsman was superbly fit and the pace he set through the steep snow-covered rocks made the rest of us look like old ladies. Robin Smith asked me what I wanted to do. He said: "You give the word and we'll follow you wherever you go." I said, "Right", and turned to go down.

Flooding in the valley was so widespread that we could not pack up and leave immediately. On the day we went home the clouds parted for a few moments. All the peaks were completely white.

CHAPTER NINE

CLIMBS AT HOME—A CHANGING SCENE

Up to 1955 I had always climbed in nailed boots. Stockinged feet or rubber shoes were used when conditions made them advisable. A new moulded rubber sole had come on to the market; it was an important innovation. In a comparatively short time this rubber sole had been universally adopted on the continent—where even workmen took to wearing boots shod with it—and Britain quickly followed suit. This sole is called Vibram. It was actually developed just before the Second World War by the Italian climber Vitale Bramani but commercial production was delayed by the hostilities.

My attitude towards Vibrams was cautious at first. Indeed I went on climbing in nails long after my companions had been converted. Vibram soles are dangerously slippery on greasy surfaces and wet grass, whereas nails are unaffected. The use of moulded rubber soles on Kangchenjunga encouraged me to try them for British climbing.

The first hard climb I tried in Vibrams was Sunset Crack on Cloggy. This was in the autumn following my return from Kangchenjunga and subsequent benightments in rain and snow on the Dru and Charmoz. I was very tired and worn down to a frail reed of my usual self. I was certain that I could climb a route like Sunset Crack in any footwear, although over six months had passed since I had last done a route of this calibre.

Sunset Crack was chosen because it was familiar and not too difficult of its class. "I want to lead all the way up to try out these Vibrams," I said to Don. Whillans had been at ease in Vibrams for some time. He was willing to follow as second man because the climb led to the Pinnacle Face on top of the East Buttress of Cloggy where we had designs on making a new route.

My feet scraped wildly on the rock; I couldn't make the new boots stick on small holds at all. The edge of the soles were perfectly square but they rolled off nicks in the rock that I could stand on in nails. I pulled and heaved all the way to the top on my arms. The climb reduced me to a bag of nerves and I was unable to decide whether it was due to my poor physical condition or the boots. I certainly had no confidence in them. Don said that Vibrams, like any other kind of footwear, required practice before the technique for climbing in them was learnt. He was right.

On the terrace above Sunset Crack we looked at the imposing groove at the left side of the Pinnacle. We tossed a coin for the lead and I went in front. I climbed the groove for 60 feet and to within 20 feet of a triangular roof that blocked the exit. A large insecure rock stopped me from going higher. I could not get round it. "If I as much as breathe on this block, Don," I informed him, "it will come off. I'm coming back."

Don was not satisfied. We changed places and he climbed to the block. Not saying a word, he thumped it with his fist. Then he calmly lifted a sling over his head and dropped it round the rock.

"This will make a good runner," he called out casually. I was astonished by his coolness and felt a little silly. Don pulled himself straight over the block and went up below the roof. His position looked awkward and precarious. He spent a long time trying to flick another sling over a spike to the left; at last he got it on.

"I don't think this is much good, but I'll go across and have a look." All he meant was that he had done everything possible to safeguard the position and he was going to stick his neck out. He balanced across on mere ripples in the rock, curled his fingers over the spike and secured the sling. Ten feet higher he banged in a peg, moved round the roof and disappeared from sight. I knew instinctively that the climbing was very hard and he was now committed a long way up the face.

Presently a call from above told me that I could follow. In spite of Don's cavalier treatment of the block I handled it with the utmost care. (In fact a few months later the block disappeared.) The movement to the spike runner below the roof was desperately thin. After that I was climbing on nervous energy, leaning outwards on small undercut holds. Now a second over-hang heeled over in my face; I was convinced that I was going to fall off. "For God's sake, take the rope in—keep it tight!" I shrieked. But the rope remained in normal tension with an inch or two of slack as it should be. Either Don couldn't hear me or he was making me sweat for the honour of seconding *his* climb. More shouting brought no response. I clawed the rock, grappled with the overhang and finally got over it. On the slab above I was trembling. I was seized by an uncontrollable judder and my legs had become jelly. The rope tightened, I put every ounce of strength I had left into clinging to a thin crack and struggled up to the haven of grass at the top.

In a cynical voice Don said: "I reckon this will go down as *my* Cenotaph Corner." He was teasing me. It was quite an amusing thought and I was almost too weak to enjoy the joke. This was Taurus—not the hardest route by a long way that Whillans devised in his catalogue of frightening ascents.

The opposite kind of situation developed a few days later when I accidently wandered off route on the Grochan cliff when we were trying Ochre Grooves. The face was covered with little cubes of rock that snapped off as easily as breaking biscuits. A hold broke and I fell clear of the face. A sling no thicker than a piece of string hooked to a fragile thumb-nail of rock held me. For some reason I was climbing extremely well and the mediocre rock failed to deter me. Higher on the face a flake probably weighing several tons was resting on loose supports. I chimneyed up the crevice, hardly daring to breathe in case the whole flake came away. Then I had to stride across an overhang composed of something that resembled crumbling concrete. Don was impressed with the boldness of this lead and at the nerve and neck needed to do the climb. We christened it N'gombo, which seemed a fair description of the rock.

Climbs of this type, vertical or overhanging with friable holds and poor protection, undoubtedly gave others the impression that the Rock and Ice had a storehouse of equipment that supplied most of the answers to making new routes. It was almost as if the equipment was possessed with magical properties and that we were the sole possessors of it. In fact a lot of it was Stonehenge-like in design because we made many of the items ourselves.

One day I received a letter from a young climber in London, asking if he and his friend could borrow various items from my collection of equipment. He had been told that I had shelves and drawers filled with precious gear for artificial climbing; so would I mind loaning him some of it. The equipment was wanted, he said, for making an attempt on the girdle traverse of Dinas Cromlech.

This curious request re-awakened me to the idea of doing a traverse across the face of Dinas Cromlech. If it was practical, it would represent a major addition to climbing in Wales. A girdle would entail crossing the walls of Cenotaph Corner at mid-height. We weighed up the size of the task by making a preparatory study of the probable linkages between lines of existing routes on Dinas Cromlech. A girdle traverse had to cross a dozen routes at various levels between the top and bottom of the cliff. Provided that the girdle did not evade making the most of the best features of the cliff, we could see no problem in traversing between the known routes except at the huge gash of Cenotaph Corner in the centre of the cliff.

The walls of the Corner are about 80 feet wide, smooth and almost vertical for a height of nearly 150 feet. Looking round the outer edge of the left wall about 40 feet above the base of the Corner we realised that it would not be possible to go straight across at this level. A very delicate traverse led to a thin flake crack, which I climbed easily to a good spike runner. From this point I used tension on the rope to reach a lower horizontal break in the wall, which was surprisingly easy to cross and reach the middle of the Corner.

Far from being impossible, the crossing of the left wall provided us with a superb pitch of no exceptional difficulty. The climbing was usually enjoyable and we were looking forward to the rest of the climb.

Crossing the left wall in this manner involved about 70 feet of climbing. I then had to climb up the Corner to the point where it looked possible to go out across the right wall towards Cemetery Gates. I also climbed farther up the Corner and placed a runner on the chockstone below the niche. In this way the stance was protected by a rope fixed directly above, and the same rope would safeguard manœuvres on the right wall. By the time that I was ready to bring Don across the left wall I had done 100 feet of climbing.

Don made several attempts to lodge himself on the right wall. He came back saying that he was not happy about it. He refrained from taking tension on the top rope. We agreed that enough had been done for one day. We would come back on the next and try again to cross the right wall. Don went down to the bottom. When he got there, on an impulse I asked him to hold the rope tight so that I could have a shot at getting on to the right wall before going down myself. In tension from the pulley rope on the chockstone I leaned across the first blank section and succeeded in reaching the line of holds leading to Cemetery Gates. I had cracked it. I put in a peg to save our strength on the morrow and retraced my steps.

Such was the nature of the elaborate preparations and precautions we made for the girdle of Dinas Cromlech. Each stage was closely scrutinised beforehand and a technique appropriate to the problem was methodically applied. It took more nerve than sheer climbing ability to make the techniques work. Leaving the equipment in place we returned next morning and crossed the right wall without a lot of bother. This wall was impressively steep and the climbing very difficult, but our psychology and confidence in the techniques employed mastered the situation. The rest of the girdle was an anticlimax.

Had we relied too heavily on modern techniques, such as rope tension moves, and moral support from ropes arranged above and behind us, for crossing the Corner? One of the old guard thought so. He had watched us traverse the right wall and I overheard him in the pub that evening saying what he thought of the performance. "By Jove," he spluttered to someone else, "you should have seen it. Any of the old-timers could have done it with the gear that those young fellows were using."

That evening, as I was relaxing at home, McNaught Davis called inviting me to join the expedition to the Mustagh Tower.

Between 1956, when Don and I made the Cromlech Girdle, and 1959 members of the Rock and Ice produced a whole series of new routes on Cloggy. Towards the end of this period the Rock and Ice started to break up. Most of the driving forces in the club were getting married and moving out of the Manchester area. Other groups of climbers, appearing on the scene for the first time, either joined forces with people in the Rock and Ice or began making their own routes.

In the same period the number of people climbing was increasing dramatically. More and more young men and women, from all walks of life, were visiting the hills regularly and several strong groups of climbers emerged. It was no longer possible to go to Wales and know everyone who was there and what climbs they had done or were planning to do. Information about the early Rock and Ice routes was spreading. Some of the climbs were repeated and detailed descriptions were eventually published in climbing journals. Cloggy was still the yardstick by which advances in British rock climbing were measured. The remarkably fine summer of 1959 provided the opportunity for many young climbers to do some of the hardest routes on the cliff. It became quite common—as it is commonplace today— to go to Cloggy and see several teams all climbing on the hard routes and even trying new ones.

A new kind of restlessness was creeping into British and Alpine exploration. At home it was further accentuated by the shift of exploration from the central mountain areas to newly discovered cliffs beside the sea. The tempo of the pop-age had overtaken mountaineering but no one cared to admit it. It did not seem to matter any more that progressive work in rock climbing traditionally depended upon an ideal partner-relationship. The convenience—and sometimes necessity—of a constant partner was now being disregarded. The individual sought his pleasure in mountaineering from the variety that a number of widely-differing personalities could provide.

Old attitudes and long-held beliefs were blown aside by an explosion of ability that marked a sudden rise in the average standard of climbing practised in the country. This was previously taped at the Very Difficult or Severe grades. By the end of 1960 the Very Severe Grade had become commonplace. By 1961 Cenotaph Corner was being described as a "trade route".

After 1960 I made new climbs with upwards of thirty people. Most of them I would consider equal to myself, and several of them—on the grounds of age alone, for I was now nudging thirty—more advanced in outright daring. One advantage I held was my experience of this class of climbing. It now extended over a decade. Only Whillans and a handful of others could match it. The change of attitude towards companions was so decisive that I grew to regard the new people as equally reliable and well-adjusted to the rigours of mountaineering as my stable and staunchest companions in the old Rock and Ice.

Taurus was the last climb I made with Don Whillans on Cloggy. In fact it was the last new climb that he made on the cliff. Previous to this we had broken new ground by opening up the Far East Buttress with Woubits. The Far East is a huge broken area of rock, which is easily overlooked. High up on this section is a final 300 ft tower of vertical rock with two prominent grooves. The left-hand one was the most obvious and in fact is one of the finest lines on Cloggy. The start is over a small loose overhang, and we both had great difficulty in establishing ourselves in the groove above. The second pitch has a nasty looking groove with several bulges. Don started up it, none too happily. The climbing was hard and poorly protected. He dithered about in the groove for quite a long time, and finally moved left to a good spike on the left of the main overhang. The spike must have renewed his confidence for he shot up the next section and went out of sight into the main groove above the overhang. When it came to my turn I expected the section above the spike to be fairly easy; I tried climbing it too quickly and got into a muddled position on the move. This happened to be the crux of the climb and I had been completely misled by Don's reactions.

An unknown enthusiast christened the second route put up on the Far East as The Mostest. At the time (1957) it was thought to be the hardest climb on Cloggy. Whillans had made an attempt with Jack Sutherland but failed to find the entry on to the route. The main feature is a bottomless groove above a line of overhangs and the problem was how to get round the overhangs. The only line of weakness was up a crack formed by a pinnacle on the left. From the top of the pinnacle it was just possible to swing across the overhang on to the vertical wall above. Then a delicate diagonal traverse led across to a small ledge at the foot of the groove. On reaching this point I had used about 70 feet of rope and there seemed to be little chance of finding a stance before the overhang about 50 feet above. So I decided to take a stance on the foothold that I was standing on. "Come up," I shouted to Nat Allen, who was my second.

Nat reached the spike and looked at the overhang. Because of the diagonal line and lack of runners I couldn't give him any assistance from the rope.

"Looks too hard for my liking, Joe. Anyway, if I fall off I'll swing under the overhangs and you won't be able to help me from *that* stance."

Very wisely, Nat retreated. I decided there was nothing to be lost by trying to see how far I could continue. I untied from the belay and set off up the groove. At the overhang I placed a peg on the right wall and started to traverse left to get round it. The only position I could reach was a layback on the left edge. I quickly tried, but had to go back to the peg for a rest. I tried this move three times before I realised that I was not going to get any stronger, messing about and wearing myself out. I put a peg between my teeth and traversed across again. I could just reach a ledge above the overhang, so I placed the peg on the ledge and tried to knock it into what I hoped was a crack. By this time I was quite exhausted. Pulling hurriedly on the peg I levered myself on to the ledge. As soon as I moved up I realised that the peg was useless—it was just biting against the roughness of the rock at the back of the ledge, but it held and I didn't fall off.

A few feet higher I came to a ledge and the rope ran out. The last 50 feet looked fairly easy, so instead of unroping and soloing to the top, I decided to descend on the rope and recover the runners. The rope hung down the overhang and descending it I found myself about ten feet away from the back of the groove and had a desperate time swinging to and fro to reach the runners. I got down to Nat and we started to pull the ropes down. The first came easily but as the second was falling through the air it caught on a small spike and we couldn't move it. As it was now getting dark we left the rope and went off to the valley.

That evening we met McNaught Davis. He was straining to go out on Sunday and try something exciting. I said I would have to return to Cloggy to recover the rope abandoned on the Far East.

"Come along," I said. "The only way to get that rope back is to abseil down the cliff from the top. If you'd care to help I'm sure that roping down The Mostest will give you all the excitement you want. It's a terrific place. I've never seen anything like it."

"Go on," said Mac, "pull the other leg. Are you trying to tell me that roping down the Far East is going to scare me? If it's half as terrifying as flinging yourself down a wall in the Dolomites I shall be most surprised."

Mac accompanied us. Strolling up to Cloggy he mocked the idea that the Far East was more impressive, exposed and frightening—my words—than many situations in the Dolomites "I don't believe it," he insisted. It was very misty, close to raining, and the tension mounted as the shadowy figures of the party skirted the cliff and scrambled to the top of the Far East.

Nothing could be seen through the blanket of mist. "This is about the spot," I said. "Well," said Mac with a confident grin, "how are you going to demonstrate to us this shattering void?"

There was a large boulder poised on the edge of the precipice.

I pushed it over. Everyone listened intently for a few seconds. There was no sound at all. "Oh, it must have landed on some grass," concluded Nat. I started making the ropes fast in readiness for abseiling down the cliff. After what seemed minutes and just before I launched myself over the edge a loud boom rent the air. The boulder had landed. The expression on Mac's face was one of startled amazement.

Rumours that stiff competition motivated the actions of the Rock and Ice were totally unfounded. Yet it was widely believed to be true. Rumours spread because there were misunderstandings over "incidents" reported about first ascents. A possible route was sometimes examined by descending a fixed rope well before it was climbed in the orthodox manner. November was a good example. This is the conspicuous fault and very direct line up the cliff parallel to and left of Vember. It was tried as long ago as the 1930s by Colin Kirkus.

I had set my sights on November from the early days of the Rock and Ice. I had contemplated the ascent for several years and had already abseiled down it with Ron Moseley. Moseley began to show a genuine interest in November after this, and I heard later that he went back with someone else to have another look. Then unknown to me and shortly before I made the first ascent, he roped down with a pocketful of stones. He wedged them as inserted chockstones into the most difficult section of the climb, a crack in a blank wall. The idea was to make it easier to climb when he eventually tried it.

I went to try November with Morty. He and just about the entire membership of the Rock and Ice knew of Moseley's chockstone operation. No one had said a thing to me. Half-way up the route, approaching the crucial section where Moseley's handiwork would be revealed, Morty sang out: "Hey, Joe, Ronnie chockstoned the crack last week."

In my present position I could not quiz Morty as to what had been going on behind my back, I was too busy fighting my way up this very hard climb! But his curt announcement explained one thing. Morty was usually ebullient before starting a new route. On this occasion we had approached the cliff, roped up and climbed the initial pitch without Morty saying so much as a word of enthusiasm. I had thought it very strange. Morty had been reluctant to mention the chockstones to me in case he should have a row with Moseley for accompanying me on the climb. Morty might have been accused of taking advantage of the knowledge, especially by acting as my second. So he properly allowed me to tackle the climb in ignorance of the previous exercise—until I came face to face with the evidence. Then he saved his own face with me by divulging the information just as I was about to discover it for myself. Our relations with each other were sometimes as intricate as the climbs!

The chockstones were placed quite a long way apart. The last 80 feet of the crack are vertical, but fortunately supplied with good holds. So the technique was to climb a ten-foot section as quickly as possible, thread a sling round one of the chockstones and rest in the sling before continuing. The crack has almost parallel sides and Ronnie had had to hammer the stones in. One of them had split into two pieces, which was a bit unnerving at first—but the two halves jammed each other in the crack as well as a whole piece of rock. One of the difficulties of using aid for a long section on a climb is getting in the mood for free climbing again. On November the climbing is vertical but the holds are so good that it is almost possible to avoid using any aid at all. Near the top it looked more reasonable, so I planted a good peg and rested for a while. Then the last 20 feet went quite easily without further aid.

The climax of my climbing on the Far East Buttress of Cloggy during this period was the ascent of Woubits Left-Hand. This was an independent fault line to the left of Woubits, starting up the first pitch of the latter. I had noticed it previously but did not bother to look at it closely until 1959.

At the bottom Doug Verity, my second, was put off immediately by the repulsive steepness and beetling overhangs of the Far East. His anxiety was increased by my none too reassuring struggle to get up the first pitch, which was just as hard as I had found it with Whillans. Verity tried to follow but couldn't; I was stranded 120 feet up the cliff. Here we go again, I thought.

That day there were quite a lot of people climbing near by. Doug collected two of them, Jack Soper and Martin Boysen, both excellent climbers, who said they would have a go. Then it was decided that a rope of three would delay the proceedings, so Jack sportingly backed down and Boysen tied on to the end of the rope. I had not met Martin Boysen before but was aware of his reputation. He flashed up the first pitch of Woubits—a spectacular performance. I had my time cut out taking the rope in quickly enough. "Hi," he said on reaching the stance, "what comes next?"

On the left I went up a crack in a corner to an overhang. The climbing was hard and sustained and I surmounted the overhang on hand-jams. A few more moves brought me to a stance. Boysen did not follow at quite the same speed as before. Most of his training had been done on sandstone, which is good rock for learning to move on tiny holds—a quarter of an inch or so wide. Holdless cracks suitable for hand-jamming were still strange to him.

A smooth corner narrowing to a V-shaped exit remained; it was the most serious problem of all. I put in a peg and went up and down several times, trying to reach better holds. Easy ground was a few feet away. First one sequence of moves, up a few feet, down, then another sequence, up again, reverse, and so on. I explored all ways and felt sure that I was within an ace of making it. I kept rejecting the idea that I might need to bang in another peg. I got really exasperated and was very annoyed with myself. I could raise myself high enough, bridged across the V-shaped depression in the rock, but could not stay in the unnatural position long enough to unravel the final sequence of movements. So I took a peg, ding, ding, ding, and it was all over.

Martin came up quite neatly. "So that's it," he said. "Was it really necessary to put in that last peg?"

In the winter or early spring during the fifties I went to Scotland for six years running. These journeys were something of a pilgrimage until the habit was broken by the fall I had in Point Five Gully. I had always wanted to try this gully. It was unclimbed and had been declared unclimbable. It became an obsession with me. Snow conditions had to be just right and the years went by without Ben Nevis fulfilling my hopes.

These Scottish trips were full of incident. Someone in the party invariably had an accident or a lucky escape. If not, we were involved in rescuing someone else. Ben Nevis is and always will be notorious in these matters. On one of these occasions I went to Ben Nevis with my wife. We set off from Manchester with snow down to sea level. But a thaw had started and at Fort William there was no snow to be seen. The cloud base was low, the landscape grey and wet. Not even a tell-tale tongue of snow, indicating that winter conditions existed, greeted our critical gaze. It looked as if we had made the journey for nothing.

Walking up the long bleak glen to the hut we trod and slid in two inches of mud; the ground below was still frozen. The party was soon in ill humour. We were carrying enormous packs; Nat Allen, Nip Underwood and I had loads of about one cwt. while Val carried a sack of half this weight. The mud underfoot was so foul and the weight of the loads so depressing that we stopped every two or three hundred yards to rest. In these conditions you picked out a rock ahead before starting on the next stretch. Then you had a place on which to lower the rucksack when halting again. If a rucksack was dropped on the ground ten times the effort was needed to raise it on to your back again. We rested contless times and many hours went by before we reached the hut.

Being the property of the all-male Scottish Mountaineering Club, I understood that Val was barred from staying in the hut. She and I camped. Curtains of weeping rain drove through the glen without a break for several days. The tent leaked and, pitched on a slope, the sewn-in groundsheet collected nine inches of icy water at the bottom end. The wind ripped the fly sheet to pieces. Meanwhile Allen and Underwood were living like lords in the hut. Nat Allen was a stickler for abiding by club rules. No, he didn't think that Val ought to vacate the sodden tent and take refuge in the hut. On the fourth day I said, "To hell with the rules." Val and I moved into the hut.

Next day the rain stopped. It was a cold, dismal morning. The ceiling of dark clouds had increased rather than decreased in thickness but its general level was higher. We went to the foot of Tower Ridge to see what the conditions were like. The cloud drifted round us, intensifying the mystery and distorting the landmarks. Almost without warning we blundered into a slope of perfect snow. It was board-hard and as good as any I had seen in Scotland. Since we were all shod in nailed boots a toe step could be kicked without resorting to chipping holds with an axe. In this way we tramped up Tower Gully and Gardyloo Gully in rapid succession.

On the following day the snow was still good. We climbed Comb Gully, enjoying its wonderful ice pitches after the enforced idleness below. Next day, in worsening snow, we ascended Number Two Gully in one and a quarter hours from hut to summit. Descending by the easy Number Three Gully we started to reascend by Glover's Chimney, which was noted for its gigantic preliminary ice pitch of 150 feet. This lived up fully to its reputation and we felt very pleased with ourselves when we emerged on the Tower Ridge. On the ridge we were immediately aware of a sudden fall in temperature. Our wet boots had frozen solid; water running over the rocks from melting snow was now a film of ice, making everything very treacherous. We could not walk or climb any longer with flexed ankles and toes would not bend at all. Flat-footed we tramped round to the head of Number Three Gully again.

Impatient to get down I jumped over the snow lip at the top edge of the gully. Having gone down it earlier in the day I expected the snow to be even softer. The gully was about 55 degrees steep at the top, running out into a consistent slope of 40 degrees.

I landed on an old foothold. Instead of breaking it and sinking into the slope I bounced straight off into the air and next time landed face down on the slope with a bone-shaking thud.

In two hours the sudden change in temperature had frozen the gully, and the surface was like a tilted skating rink. I rocketed down the slope for 300 feet; so far as it was possible I was in control of the fall because I was the right way up, lying on my stomach with head facing up the slope. As I shot down I was trying to drive the pick of my axe into the glass-like surface of the slope to break the fall. All my weight was distributed over the axe shaft and was therefore exerted through the pick. The steel point made no impression on the slope whatsoever.

After 300 feet I was knocking up a fair rate of knots and the axe was merely bouncing on the surface. Then I hit a small soft spot. In a split second the pick buried itself with a terrible jolt; I clung to it. Now the pick had crushed its way into the hard stuff. It drove a crack into the ice below but I still continued to shoot down feet first. The encounter with the soft patch had slowed my pace and I was sure that my arm had been stretched six inches. There was a final flesh-and-bone tearing wrench and I stopped. I had barely caught my breath and was thinking of trying to raise myself to my feet when I was off again. The change in pressure from a condition of motion to one of standstill had dislodged the pick. I immediately applied the braking action again and came to a halt a few yards farther down. Altogether I had fallen 700 feet.

Feeling like an ape with arms trailing along the ground I inched my way cautiously to the bottom, 300 feet below, staggered across some scree and went over a hummock.

All this happened so quickly that the rest of the party had not even started down. They were still crossing the head of the gully when I arrived at the bottom. I traversed the hummock, which hid the mouth of the gully, and walked away. When my companions looked down there was no sign of me. On the far side of the hummock I could see into the middle and upper part of the gully but there was only one man in sight. I could just imagine what they were thinking. I tried to imagine that they might look upon it as a very fast controlled descent. But they knew better than that. I was feeling ashamed of myself. It did not occur to me that they might have missed my unplanned flight to the bottom or that something unpleasant might have happened to them, so I carried on to the hut.

Hours later no one had appeared. It was getting dusk. I pulled on my boots and went out to look for them. I met the rest of the party a few minutes above the hut. Nat was very angry with me for not having gone back earlier to help. Nip Underwood had done exactly the same trick as I. He had leapt over the lip and gone flying down the slope. Unfortunately he had landed spreadeagled with his head pointing down the slope, which prevented him from braking with his axe. Unchecked he went all the way to the bottom in this position. In the last 100 feet his axe—braced in both hands—had hit a rock sticking through the snow; he was thrown high into the air. This collision did more damage than the grating he received in falling the entire length of the gully. When I glanced up the gully from the far side of the hummock, Nip was already lying at the bottom in the concealed lower portion. He finished up with severe bruises and had taken a slice of skin off one side of his face. Although we were due to return home we had to remain in the hut for another two days until he was fit enough to hobble back to Fort William.

Ron Moseley and I spent a lot of time planning an attempt on Point Five Gully. I think we got as much pleasure out of anticipating the ascent as actually getting to grips with its frozen waterfalls and glistening overhangs. We even went to the trouble of making a paper model of a tiny two-man bivouac tent and drew up a specification for finished size and shape. Working from our plans Moseley's mother made the tent from strips of old barrage balloon material.

We proposed to pitch the tent close to the mouth of the gully late at night and start climbing at daybreak. On the first attempt our elaborate preparations included making up all perishables into small waterproof bundles—and our matches were sealed tightly with Sellotape in small bundles. We climbed to the bivouac site in darkness. Before we got there my trousers were soaked with condensation collected under a pair of waterproof trousers. The weather could hardly have been worse. The wind screamed across the precipice and spindrift blowing off the snow lashed our faces until they felt raw as uncooked meat.

On gaining the crest of Tower Ridge we were frozen stiff. It was useless to go any farther and neither of us fancied retreat in these conditions. There and then we put up the tent. Two axes formed an A-pole to shape the triangular entrance. There was one guyline to be tensioned by a rock for keeping the tent upright and retaining some of its shape.

We threw our sleeping-bags inside, unrolled them but even before we could position ourselves to wriggle in they filled with snow hurled into the tent by the wind. I pulled off my wringing wet trousers in the open and got into a sleeping-bag half full of snow. I might as well have laid down outside with nothing on. Moseley pottered about securing anything we left outside because our equipment might be blown away.

The storm raged all night. Lying in the tent was a real test of survival. We wriggled about trying to keep the blood circulating but it was impossible to drive away the jarring spasms of cramp. It was the worst night that I had ever spent on a mountain.

At daybreak the wind was still roaring. It sounded as if a giant was smacking the tent with a shovel. Starting to prepare breakfast Moseley discovered that the fuel container was full of paraffin. The stove was a petrol one. While he was weeping to himself about this unpardonable error I spent twenty minutes trying to open a bundle of matches wrapped in Sellotape. All our careful preparations for the bivouac were a failure.

With nothing hot to drink we made a half-hearted reconnaissance of the gully. Cascades of snow were pouring down the funnel. We took one look at it and scampered away.

Next day we went up to have another look. Powder snow was pouring down the gully, so I went along to join Don Whillans. He had set his heart on making a new route on the buttress of Carn Dearg and had been trying to climb this piece of rock without success for a couple of days.

Don was messing about under a line of overhangs, trying to find a way through.

"What's it like over on the right, Don?" I shouted.

"I tried there yesterday, but couldn't make head or tail of it."

Don's present position looked hopeless. I had a closer look at the point he had tried the day before and decided that it might go.

"Come down, Don, this groove should go with a bit of frigging."

We sorted out the fresh start with a sling for aid, then it led without much fuss to the overhang. I bridged out between the walls below it. The rock overhead impended for ten or twelve feet. With a sling round a chockstone I leaned away on the edge of a crack and hooked my chin over the top. One more big effort would see the overhang below my feet.

I looked at my watch. "I had better get down from here—it'll be dark in thirty minutes, so let's pack it in and come back tomorrow."

Next day Don climbed to the overhang and arranged the slings. We had agreed that he should do this and come down; then I would lead straight through and be fresh for the last move over the overhang. When he reached the overhang Don told me that he felt quite fit, so I told him to carry on. He shuffled up and grasped a big stalactite hanging down from the roof. Hugging it like a coconut tree climber he vanished over the top. When Don came to haul up the sacks I was amazed at the distance they swung away from the rock.

From below the next section of the climb resembled a huge corner, like Cenotaph. We anticipated that it must be extremely difficult. It was much taller than Cenotaph Corner but the back of it was split by a long chimney. I think Don must have felt that he had cheated me out of the overhanging pitch because he waved me forward and I stayed in front for the rest of the 800 ft climb. The chimney was relatively straightforward for 200 feet, then a series of nice grooves, somewhat harder, went up the cliff for another 300 feet. Then we were on top. It was Eastertime and there was plenty of snow on the Ben. We were very lucky in that we had a perfect day for this climb.

Our ascent had been watched from the hut. We heard a

G

shout just as Don's moment of triumph on the overhang was certain. "You English bastards." That was how the route came to be named Sassenach.

During the evening we were called out to help in a rescue on Tower Ridge. We were dead beat, but it sounded as though it might be a difficult operation and we couldn't refuse. We spent the night on a ledge near the top of the ridge and recovered the body next morning. It was a very unpleasant experience and we were glad that it was now the end of our holiday.

A Christmas week took us back to the Ben. The conditions were poor but there was a lot of snow. Morty, Nat Allen, Nip Underwood and I climbed Green Gully, said at the time to be the hardest gully on the Ben. We set off up the long ice pitch— normally avoided—at the foot of the gully at 2 p.m. and broke through the summit cornice at five.

The day after this we found ourselves standing at the entrance to Point Five Gully. In spite of the fresh snow, conditions were the most favourable that I had seen. Morty did not come with us. The first pitch measured 80 feet at an angle of 65 degrees. There was not much ice on the rocks. You could slam it with an axe and strike the rock beneath. I also noticed that the ice appeared to be formed in layers that were not bonded together. The texture of ice—there are many varieties—and the various conditions of its stability are a complex science that a climber can only learn the hard way—by trial and error and experience. I was now fairly proficient at judging the quality of ice for climbing and I could climb ice almost as well as rock. But the process of learning was never-ending.

After the first pitch the angle dropped back to 45 degrees; I went up this a short way, drove in two ice pegs for belaying and brought up Nat Allen. Nip Underwood remained at the bottom belayed to a rock spike.

Above me the ice reared up into a little ridge that curled over in a large bulge—all of 50 feet. Somewhere above it one might dig out another stance. I moved up to the overhanging portion of ice and began hacking big steps; I was quite happy with the situation and quietly confident. I could now see that in 20 feet I would find an excellent place for a stance. I banged home a couple of pegs right on the nose of the bulging ice. I jabbed my crampons into good footholds and got a yard higher. *Crack.* The front of the ice bulge disintegrated.

I peeled off backwards. From facing inwards to the bulge and leaning out with my back in space I tipped upside down in a flash. I saw both pegs come out; my next recollection was touching the ice where it was less than vertical. I missed Nat by a mile. My shoulder hit the ice below him and I just shot out into space. The next touch down point was 25 feet below Nip at the bottom of the gully. I had been going now for a good 150 feet, mainly through the air. Meanwhile Nat was making a flight through space as well. As soon as he had taken the shock of my fall through the rope, the stance on which he was belayed was so small that he couldn't brace himself to control the snaking rope. He was pulled on to the belay pegs, which shot out on receiving the vicious jerk.

In the air I went into a curled position, holding my axe in a braking position. I suppose this was due to habit. I landed head first in a patch of snow. The axe hit me in the mouth. It cut my lip—a minor thing. Curled up and spinning like a ball I rolled out of the hole that I had punched in the snow and went downhill another 50 feet. The moment after I left the hole Nat entered it. We just went down together about 50 feet apart.

Nat was falling like a rag doll. On the second bounce he went feet first into the snow and jack-knifed forward; this wrenched his legs badly before he pitched forward again into the air. Nip Underwood reported that Nat jack-knifed twice. It tore the ligaments in his legs. The fall was checked by Nip, who braked Nat, stopping me in turn.

Because I had been spinning so much I was trussed up in the rope and there was a final loop twisted round my neck. I was hanging on the slope and couldn't breathe. My tongue was sticking out and a queer rasping noise came from my throat. My arms were pinned to my sides, I felt as if I had no hands and all I could hear was Nat groaning.

I was on the verge of passing out when I sensed the rope

flipping about. Nat had realised that I was immobilised and was trying to loosen the mesh of bonds around me. As soon as I got the rope off and could breathe properly I recovered quickly. There was nothing wrong with me.

Nat was squirming in agony. Attaching a sling to his good leg we hooked the bad one on top of it. Then Nip and I dragged and lowered him along the rough approach slopes back to the hut. He was screaming with hot aches in his backside, which was terribly painful. There was not much that we could do. In the hut we broke open the first aid box and applied various remedies. None of them were any good. So we packed up and went down.

Nip and Morty divided Nat's gear and mine between them. I carried Nat for as long as I could and while I was resting my arms I let him hop. I'd carry him for 200 yards and put him down. I had not yet learnt how to improvise a cradle with the rope. All I knew was how to give someone a piggy back. Having put him down he hopped along on one leg, leaning on me until my arms had recovered. Then I picked him up and we continued until I had to rest again. This went on until we reached the bottom.

My wife was furious with me after this episode. "Joe Brown, you are a dud on ice!" To this day she still believes that I am a poor ice climber.

What is the truth of parting company with a companion who has been as close to you as the passion for climbing itself? Do you have a fight, go away and never speak to each other again? Well, I have heard of this happening. What is more likely is that you tire of each other's company. Old routines, no matter how memorable, become monotonous. You meet other people, they open new vistas of interest and the past is forgotten. None of this applied to Don Whillans and myself.

Our social habits, as distinct from climbing ones, took a different course. Our interests and outlook in climbing remained alike, but sometimes I liked to forget that I was a climber.

Don was a climber all the time. He is made that way. I would have been the last to have wanted to see him change. He would not then be Don Whillans.

Don was always more forceful in his approach to mountaineering than I. He could be aggressive to the point of distracting the most resolute and trusted companion. I think we both needed a change and we gradually drifted apart. In our turn marriage gave us new responsibilities that we had to cope with in our own ways. I believe that this would have been sufficient to break up our partnership in any case.

The Rock and Ice went to pieces because the overworked officials could not cope with indifference to club discipline any longer. Moseley as Secretary and Belshaw as Treasurer had carried the organisational burden for several years and when they appealed for reliefs no one would come forward. Quite rightly they threw in the sponge. They both got married and the club was suddenly no more.

The Rock and Ice was reformed some time later by Nat Allen and Dennis Gray. Whereas it is now a properly constituted club (it is called the Rock and Ice Climbing Club) and is composed of a fine body of climbers, the associations of the past belong more to history than to the present club.

From 1948 my progress in mountaineering had taken a traditional course in Wales. I had begun, like many others, by visiting Idwal, climbing its famous Slabs then graduating to the Holly Tree Wall and the steeper surrounding cliffs. These rocks had been climbed out by earlier generations; further exploration could only profit by filling in narrow gaps that were rarely satisfying. I had an appetite for bare walls of rock that had been hardly touched by human hand. I found them in the Llanberis Pass and on Snowdon. Like Idwal these cliffs are part of the central area of Snowdonia, where the mountains are highest and the weather the worst.

I soon got to know the central area very well, where Cloggy was the overriding attraction. It was natural to look for new routes on this cliff and our enthusiasm for climbing here was at first due entirely to the difficulties we had in getting out to the mountains. Having made up my mind what I wanted to do at the weekend, if the weather was bad we still tried our best to carry out the plan. A successful climb stimulated me immediately to think about the next. Instead of doing a new route and being satisfied with that for a while, it only satisfied me for a few days. I had the following week to think about it at work and prepare myself for the next new route at the weekend. Occasionally we made two routes in one weekend, but this did not happen often.

After a while my knowledge of Cloggy was so complete that the cliff was in danger of losing some of its charm. Every year it became easier to reach the mountains because more of us found it easier to buy motor cycles and second-hand cars. I doubted whether I would ever lose interest, but I got to the stage where I was quite happy to go up there and climb anything, or even just walk about. Although I was aware of several possible lines for more new routes there was nothing new to find on the cliff. It was only a matter of whether the footholds and handholds were there to make climbing possible. If I had done these routes I would certainly not have got to the top of a pitch and been surprised to find the next feature strange to me because I knew exactly what I would find. This was one of those things that made further exploration on Cloggy not as good as it might have been for someone with less perfect knowledge of the cliff.

Major climbing grounds were not unknown outside the central area but I had not paid much attention to them. The surroundings could be more like the setting of outcrops close to home. There was much to be said for climbing on even a small cliff at the head of a remote cwm, far away from crowds and under the bare crest of a tall mountain. Yet outlying and often lowlying places had been highly developed in the fifties—the long line of cliffs at Tremadoc had already become very popular with many climbers. Tremadoc was regarded as the perfect substitute for the central area when the weather was poor.

Situated well to the south of high mountains the Tremadoc cliffs were a few fields distant from and a few feet above the sea. Two miles of escarpment about 250 feet high were clothed in trees that concealed the true extent and quality of the rocks. Dense vegetation flourished on the slopes below the jungle entanglement of trees and buttresses, creepers and crazy flung rocks. Standing on the prow of a rock nose jutting through the trees one had a grand view of the estuary and open sea. A mile away was another kind of holiday world; souvenir shops, Welsh rock and ice cream stalls and a sandy shore lined with caravans.

When I first went there Tremadoc was as much a part of the popular Snowdonia climbing scene as Idwal and Cloggy. The cliffs grew on you and one of the main attractions was that climbing there involved so little. You just drove up, got out of the car and walked off the road on to the crag. The first wave of exploration had died away and I was told by Claud Davies that I should take an interest in the place. "Let's go down there," he said one day. "I'll show you a couple of grooves that haven't been climbed. You can say I'm wasting your time after you have seen them." I respected Claud's judgement, so we went.

The grooves were First Slip and Leg Slip; they got their names because my feet slipped off at the crux of the first. I had muddied them on soil thrown up from a bush that I tried to wrench away. The groove was very thin with small holds of the pinch-grip variety. Progress depended on friction between your feet and the rock. I was tied to a peg when they slipped off. We drove away three hours later having done both climbs.

One of the most distinctive features of Tremadoc is the Milestone Buttress—a superb 250 ft tower of rock with several large overhangs. It seemed just possible to climb an intricate route weaving in and out of the overhangs. The following week I went back with Trevor Jones to have a look at it.

The first pitch was covered with ivy. It stripped off easily and I dug out some good holds. On the second pitch, still having no plan for a route, I trended left until I came up against an overhang. The rock above it heeled over for another fifteen feet or so. There was not much hope trying to get up this part of the face. From a runner tied below the overhang I started traversing back to the right. Then the rope became tangled like a piece of knitting. I was hanging on just below an ochre-coloured slab. I untied and let the rope drop free. Trevor was horrified by this action; from the expression on his face you would have thought that it was he who was spreadeagled in the middle of the cliff without a rope! "Pull it in, Trevor," I chirped. "I'll traverse back and you can throw it up to me."

Reorganised I went back and climbed to the foot of the ochre slab. I stretched across it but couldn't stand in balance. There were no handholds to reach the next overhang. I banged in a peg and used that. A difficult little groove led up to another huge overhang. The only way round this was to the left, across a blank-looking slab, to a cave. I drove in another peg, to use tension from the rope. I got a good undercut hold and moved across. But before I knew what had happened I had both feet and both hands on the same hold. This is a right cock up, I thought. My position must have looked very sensational—a crowd of people had gathered below and I heard them gasp. But as soon as I moved up I reached a good hold and was soon at the cave. Trevor was too gripped up to follow. After having a good look at the rock above I roped off.

We returned to the cliff at the earliest opportunity. The news had leaked that I had a big route at Tremadoc to finish and we were accompanied to the buttress by a large group of spectators. Claud Davies came along as second man and Big Dave Thomas set up ciné equipment to shoot the scene.

Claud fell off while swinging on to the slab; a runner immediately above saved him from parting company with the rock. He regained his holds and managed to reach my stance. However, Trevor Jones was not so lucky. Claud had taken the runners off as he went past them. In a normal situation with three on a climb this might not matter. Now, when Trevor fell off, the rope was no longer pinned in running belays to the rock and he dangled far out in space. He stood no chance at all of getting back on to the rock. So we had to lower him to the ground where he abandoned the role of third man.

We were now at the highest point reached previously. The stance was a little cave. Here we were surrounded by overhangs

—if you fell off anywhere there was nothing but air below.

I traversed left, pulled across an overhang and went up a slab to a groove. I knocked in a large ring peg. The peg was six inches long and in the only crack available it gripped for about two inches; so I was very dubious about it. One wall of the groove was a fraction less than vertical, the other overhung noticeably. As soon as I had jammed myself across the groove I drove in another peg. Taking a bridging position across the walls was the only way possible for making progress, but the angle formed by them was most unfavourable for this technique. There was a constant tendency to fall out. The overhanging position of the groove did not relent. I fingered the top like a piano player; there was nothing on which to haul myself out. The final holds were buried under earth. I rammed my fingers into the stuff and tore it away. The position in which I was doing this was so strenuous that after a few seconds I had to reverse down the groove to rest on the last peg fifteen feet below. I went up and down three times before I dug out holds good enough to make the last breath-taking heave over the top. A roar of applause went up from the crowd. This was one of the new aspects of Welsh climbing that I could do without.

Talk of secret crags was another aspect of the changing scene in Snowdonia. It sounded a note of urgency among those whose main interest was exploration. Oneupmanship, a hint of competition and possible glory for the discoverer if he kept the secret long enough intensified the search for new pieces of rock. The country south of Snowdon was scoured. Although nothing as good as Cloggy was found, worth-while climbing sometimes came to light.

The most interesting thing to me about the exploration of these outlying crags was that the problems in climbing were new ones, because the rock features were different, and it made a pleasant change to the normal techniques on the high crags.

When the rumour that a spectacular cliff called Castell Cidwm came to my attention I was not exactly excited. I had never heard of the place and had no idea where it was situated.

Claud Davies and I made inquiries but learnt nothing. No one was saying anything. It was in the Quellyn area, on the west side of Snowdon, and that was all we knew. Hugh Banner was named as the discoverer; one could hardly walk up to him and say, "Tell me where your crag is." Then we heard that a certain well-known climber had fallen off the crag; he cut his hands and was taken to hospital. I thought, well, there must be something in this because the climber in question did not fall off easily.

My curiosity grew and the mystery deepened. Then Claud had a brain-wave. "Now I remember," he said. "When I was a boy of fourteen I had a holiday in the Quellyn valley. I recall scrambling beside a large broken crag at the bottom of the Elephant Mountain."

"But," I interrupted, "what good is a large broken crag? The slopes over there are covered with them."

He thought again. "It was ten years ago, of course. Wait . . . that was it . . . I remember a grassy gorge running up the side. One of the side walls was a face of clean rock."

"It doesn't sound a likely place to me," I retorted.

"No, well it was ten years ago and I was only a lad. I was probably mistaken. I couldn't have known what a good piece of rock looked like then."

"No harm done if we go there just to make sure," I suggested.

"All right, let's go," said Claud.

Coming up the road along the western flank of Snowdon the craggy step of Castell Cidwm was silhouetted at the base of the eastern skyline of the Elephant Mountain. Nothing could be more conspicuous. The cliff was 400 feet high and had a flat top; in Welsh mythology a chieftain had built his stronghold and lookout there. The rock face was certainly steep but very broken. Abundant quantities of grass and vegetation clung to it and it was the sort of place that would lure a botanist rather than a climber. Approaching by car the gully wall at the left side of the main mass was straight in front of us but we did not notice it. The large expanse of ungainly broken rocks forming the main frontage dominated our gaze.

"Nothing here," I grumbled, as we trundled through the heathery rocks at the bottom. Then we turned the corner and entered a broad gully down which a stream tumbled. Our eyes went up and were transfixed by a fantastic wall overlooking the stream. It had breadth and verticality and was bristling with a fringe of overhangs along the upper edge. We had found the secret crag of Castell Cidwm. Harry Smith was with us and we told Claud that there was nothing wrong with his idea of a good crag at the age of fourteen.

The first thing we noticed about the cliff was that natural faults—cracks, chimneys, grooves and the like—were almost totally absent. The steepness of the face was awe-inspiring and we were at a bit of a loss where to look for a breach in the defences. A shallow groove cleaved the right-hand side of the wall; it was hugged by overhangs but seemed the best place to start. We got up 60 feet then none of us could climb higher. I think we might have been feeling faint hearted; the cliff had an unnerving character and the rock, while good, was smooth and slaty in texture. It was not our day for pressing home an attack.

Harry Smith and I returned to complete the right-hand groove. The key to the second pitch was finding the right sequence of moves. The final overhang yielded using three pegs; the take-off was from a slab running with water. But for this we might have used two or even only one peg. Dwm seemed an appropriate generic name for the route.

In the next months I made two more first ascents on the crag—Vertigo and The Curver. At the time these seemed the only possible lines, because the walls between were lined with overhangs and looked really hard, so we turned our attention elsewhere. Now, only seven years later, there are nine climbs on this face.

CHAPTER TEN

THE PAMIRS AFFAIR

On a business trip to Houston, George Band met a Texas oil millionaire who was anxious to do some good in easing tension between East and West. He promised to donate $15,000 towards sponsoring a British expedition to Russia if the Soviet authorities would co-operate. George Band got in touch with Sir John (now Lord) Hunt in London. As it happened moves were already afoot in the Alpine Club for sending a private expedition to Russia. John Hunt had led such an expedition to the Caucasus in 1958 and the Russian hosts had made a return visit to Britain in 1960.

An application was submitted through diplomatic channels for a party to climb in the Pamirs. Simultaneously it was learnt that the Scottish Mountaineering Club had already made an independent request for the same purpose. Then the Russians proposed that the two parties should amalgamate and send a team of twelve climbers to Russia for two months; six Soviet climbers, they said, would join the British party on arrival.

The Scottish leader, Malcolm Slesser, having acted before the Alpine Club, had several meetings with Sir John. It was clear that there would be difficulties in choosing a team from the two parties. Hunt and Slesser took on the leadership and deputy leadership of the British side of the expedition. No one knew how the Russians would react to this.

Some of my best friends are Scottish and I have always noticed how touchy they are about nationalism. It is one of those things that I can't resist ribbing them about. So far as I am concerned the Scots are British but there is no denying that they have a way of refuting this. The final composition of the party, with eight of the twelve members ranking as Sassenachs or worse, aggravated the attitude that the Scots had got a raw deal.

Many months passed before the party was finalised. John Hunt had a reputation for considerable skill in picking a well-matched team to go on climbing expeditions. He did the best he could. Some people dropped out on account of business commitments, including George Band, and others drifted in and out for one reason or another.

The composition of the team was, England (with a New Zealand flavour): John Hunt, Derek Bull, Ralph Jones, George Lowe, Ian McNaught Davis, Wilfred Noyce, Ted Wrangham and myself. Scotland: Malcolm Slesser, Kenny Bryan, Dr Graeme Nicol and Robin Smith.

Hunt, Lowe and Noyce were Everest climbers while Mac, Wrangham and I had varied Himalayan experience. Bull and Jones had accompanied John Hunt to the Caucasus in 1958 and were familiar to some extent with Russian ways and habits in the mountains. Graeme Nicol acted as expedition doctor and, at twenty-three, Robin Smith was the youngest and most dynamic member of the party.

I was appointed as Ralph Jones' assistant; in turn he was assistant to Malcolm Slesser, who was in charge of organising equipment. This produced a situation in which I had nothing to do. As usual I was quite content to let them sort it out between themselves.

A meeting took place on Ben Nevis for members to acquaint themselves with each other. Robin Smith and I fell in together and made a new route on the mountain. He was regarded by most people as one of the top men on rock and ice in Scotland. Whereas I had been climbing much longer than Robin, I was profoundly impressed by the economy of his techniques. As an "over thirty" I had perhaps forgotten what it was like to be young and bursting with energy. He was quick and careful on difficult ground, yet he was completely reckless on easy terrain. Coming down Number Three Gully he started running, over-balanced and shot out of control. He broke the fall after 200 feet, crawling out of the avalanche debris that buried him with a sheepish grin on his face.

The Pamirs are boxed in the most southerly corner of the U.S.S.R., in the Republic of Tajikistan about 250 miles north-west of the Karakorum. The whole of the eastern half of the region, about 150 miles square, is filled by mountain ranges striking roughly east to west. The long broad valleys between them are the true "pamirs" that the native people regard as the roof of the world. In the north the ranges include the Trans-Alai and the Peter the Great, crowned by the highest mountains in the Soviet Union—Pik Kommunizma, formerly Mt Stalin (24,590 feet), and Pik Lenin (23,384 feet). The south-east side of the Communism Peak is skirted by the 50-mile Fedchenko glacier, the longest continental ice stream in the world. Our plan was to approach the area from the west, along the Garmo glacier. No European had been near these mountains since 1928.

I flew to Moscow with a number of the party in one of the more comical Ilyushin jets with drooping wings. When we touched down I am sure that we landed at twice the speed of any other jet that I had flown in. We *hit* the ground with a terrific wallop and began bouncing from side to side. As the plane yawed about it looked as if it might slide off the runway. Mac took up a position of driving a car out of control and gave us a loud and realistic death-defying commentary of screeches, squeals and crashing gears as he went through the motions of struggling to stop the runaway vehicle. Doubtless he had lived through the situation many times before!

Shaken by the nervous merriment of Mac's performance we stepped out feeling glad to be alive and were introduced to officials of the Physical Culture and Sports bureau. We drove to an hotel where we were informed that some of the key points in our plan for climbing in the Pamirs had been politely turned down by the Soviet authorities.

We had had designs on making a first ascent of the 9,000-foot South Face of Communism Peak. The direct route on this face, we learnt, had been "booked" by the Spartak Sports Society. Climbing in Russia was somewhat regimented. Various annual competitions were held with the equivalent of umpires and timekeepers in attendance to ensure that the "rules" were obeyed. Entrants for the "best climber of the year" took tests for style and speed in climbing. There was a competition for the "best traverse of the year". This might involve crossing a succession of 20 or 30 peaks, prepared beforehand by dumping cases of food at selected points. Thirty men working in half a dozen teams might spend a month slogging up and down individual peaks. When the supply chain had been established along the proposed traverse a detachment would start at one end and not come down until reaching the other, unless forced to retire by weather or accident. Strict training conditions and schedules were observed in competition work and no one was allowed to smoke or drink. The Russians were due for a shock when they saw some of our habits! The competition for the "major ascent of the year" in 1962 would undoubtedly be won by a team that got up the South Face of Communism Peak. It would be like climbing the North Wall of the Eiger with half as much again on top of it at a much greater altitude.

The main blow to our plans was the announcement that we would not be allowed to walk into the area. (An approach march into high mountains is a vital part of acclimatisation; it also provides gradual exercise leading to good physical fitness at high altitudes.) No reason was given. Anglo-Russian relations must have reached an all-time low at that moment.

I could not see the point of arguing with our Russian hosts. The bureau officials were powerless to intercede on our behalf. The decision had been made at high level and an appeal was outside the scope of the sporting authority. There were probably some military installations in the neighbourhood that Western eyes might report on returning home. Some of the British party refused to see it this way, which set something of a mood for the rest of our stay in Russia.

Another irritation—at least to independent people like climbers—was the closely guarded attentions paid to the party by Intourist officials. The expedition was treated like a trade delegation, a cultural exchange or even a body of sightseeing tourists, all of whom were placed in the care of the national tourist office.

We had to wait in Moscow for the completion of arrangements to travel into the interior. The guide allotted to us was a pretty girl of twenty-two. Her job was to keep us together and shepherd the party on tours round the Moscow sights. Descending from a bus the party deliberately split into several groups that strolled off in different directions. The poor girl was rushed off her feet chasing us. She spoke perfect English and poured out facts and statistics about the university, the museum, the Kremlin and so on with monotonous precision. By the time the guide had ushered us back to the hotel she was generally exhausted.

We joined our Russian companions by flying to Dushambe (formerly Stalinabad) 2,000 miles away. In the torrid heat this Asiatic city might have been Calcutta or Bombay, but without the dirt, squalor and flies. Streets and shops were spotless—a pleasant contrast to the uniform drabness of Moscow. The remote control of communism, coupled with virtually autonomous local government, had transformed the life and appearance of Dushambe in less than forty years. Indeed the delay in getting permits to travel in this region had been due to Moscow officials having to negotiate as if they were dealing with a foreign country.

In Dushambe we had to sort out our equipment for an airlift. Among other things we discovered that we had only about half the required number of ice-axes. This put us in a bit of a predicament and we had to borrow some from the Russians. On the other hand we had far too many snap-links. Robin Smith was very pleased when he found the box of snap-links—he was just like a child who had found a treasure trove.

Waiting for the aircraft, the whole party was taken on a visit to a school, which was evidently a model of its kind in the Soviet Union. In fact it was an orphanage. A special show was put on for us, with the children singing English songs. All the

32. Wedding day. Slim Sorrel in background

33. Scene at Petra

34. As an instructor at White Hall

35. Robin Smith in Russia,
wearing a chain of snap-
links

36. The Pamirs Expedition
unfrocked in a Moscow
hotel

37. Summit group on Communism Peak in the Pamirs

38. During television on Cloggy

39. During television on the Aiguille du Midi. Guido Magnone on the right.

40. Castell Cidwm. Left: *Dwm*. Right: *Tramgo*

41. First ascent of *Tramgo* on Castell Cidwm

42. First ascent of *The Mousetrap* on Anglesey

children over ten could speak English fluently. I was particularly struck by the children's happiness, and they were living
and learning in very pleasant surroundings. Clearly the
Russians place great importance on their children.

The Garmo glacier was only 200 miles away. The Russians
were straining at the leash, impatient to get to grips with the
mountains. The two youngest, Nicolai Alkhutov and Vladimir
Malakov, wanted to complete a programme of mountaineering
that would earn them their Master of Sport titles. The Master-
ship was the goal of all Russian climbers of merit. Both men
needed only one or two more notable ascents to gain the award.
The leader of the Russian group, Anatoli Ovchinnikov,
sportingly agreed to John Hunt retaining overall leadership
of the party, which solved one problem. He was a man whom
we felt instinctively that we could trust through thick and thin.
His companion Masters of Sport, Anatoli Sevastianov and
Nicolai Shalaev, looked equally fit and competent. The sixth
man was Eugene Gippenreiter, the interpreter. He had
managed our affairs in Moscow and was probably more
familiar with British mountaineering habits than any other
Russian. He had been to Britain twice on climbing and lecture
tours.

The Russians went by road with all the baggage to Tavil
Dara on the Garmo river. Banned from looking at the countryside we flew to Jirgatal, off the route, and continued by heli-
copter-lift to the Garmo valley. We had no firm plans for base
or mountain camps, having been assured that our Russian
companions knew the area sufficiently well to point out the best
places for staging an approach along the glacier.

As we climbed aboard the helicopters it was announced that
owing to the waterlogged ground we would be put down ten
miles lower in the valley than promised. We wanted to know
why marshy ground should interfere with a helicopter landing.
Then we were told that the altitude, about 10,000 feet, was near
ceiling for the machines; they needed a run to get airborne and
clearly this would not be possible if the ground was soggy. The

argument went on for some minutes, with everyone getting hot
under the collar. It was pretty silly, considering that the
objection to a walk of ten miles made no sense when we has
previously wanted to walk 100 miles into the area and had been
told that we couldn't!

The place we landed at was dry and dusty. It was a high
desert valley with plenty of trees and only a little grass. The
helicopters droned back and forth, bringing in equipment and
supplies, and stirred up clouds of mouth-choking dust that
penetrated everywhere.

There were no local porters for carrying loads. In a country
where everyone was supposed to be equal the Russians did not
approve of the capitalist practice of using native labour. They
said that it was merely three hours' walk to the place originally
intended as Base Camp and half that time to come down again.
A good man should be able to go up and down with a full load
twice a day.

We duly set off together but the Russians soon drew ahead.
Half-way up the British party was tottering. The Russians
passed us on their way down with Robin Smith in their midst.
He was the only one of us who could keep up the pace. He was
so obviously the youngest and liveliest of the British party that
he soon became the Russians' favourite. The parties toiled for
three days up and down endless piles of scree, shifting baggage
to the higher base. At this rate we calculated that it would take
several weeks to ferry everything on to the glacier. In that case
we would have to turn back and return home. Marching across
to the helicopter pilots with a bottle of whisky, John Hunt
persuaded them to make an air drop and so rid ourselves of
this crippling ferry work. No guarantee, they said, could be
given for the safety of those who flew in the machines or for the
condition of the boxes we intended to drop. I did not go on the
airlift operation but we all saw the results. It was done at maxi-
mum altitude and flying speed, about 100 feet above the ground
at 100 miles per hour. One slight error of judgement would have
been fatal. Some of the boxes exploded on impact and the
contents were strewn across the moraines and ice for several

hundred yards. Some of the tea, sugar and jam was lost but we managed to salvage most of the food.

On the first acclimatisation training climb only Robin Smith reached the top. The remainder, including myself, sat down completely debilitated half-way up and shouted after him that he was foolhardy to continue on his own. The Russians took a dim view of our take-it or leave-it attitude and must have thought that we were a bunch of old women. Mental and physical lethargy dampened our enthusiasm from the start. Much of it, I believe, was psychological—in comparing our fitness with that of the Russians.

The party divided into three groups, each containing four British and two Russian climbers. Mine included Malcolm Slesser, Mac, Kenny Bryan and the two Russian tyros, Alkhutov and Malakov. Each group had an objective peak to climb, as a preliminary exercise for a probable attack on Communism Peak. Ours was the closest to Base Camp, a striking ice wedge called Patriot Peak, about 20,000 feet high. Wilfred Noyce's group was to attempt the comparatively ambitious Garmo Peak (21,640 feet.) while John Hunt's had designs on a nameless unclimbed summit of 18,800 feet. These mountains enclosed one side of the tributary Vavilova glacier, on which we had no difficulty in establishing camps.

The glacier slopes leading to the foot of a big rock wall below the west ridge of Patriot Peak offered no resistance. A camp was placed near the foot of the wall and the next few days were spent in ferrying loads from Base. I was greatly disturbed by the slag-tip quality of the rock above us. In fact all the rock in the Pamirs is rubbish. The Russians have a pretty name for it that can be translated as "moving rock". The wall was broken by long ribs bristling with crumbling pillars. Now and then an avalanche swept down the gullies between the ribs in a cloud of white smoke.

Mac, Alkhutov and I made the first reconnaissance of the rock wall. We ploughed up one of the couloirs. After a few hundred feet I untied from the rope and decided to go down. I told Mac that in my opinion it was madness to climb in the prevailing conditions. The snow was unspeakably bad. But Mac resolved to continue for a short way. Alkhutov was determined to go on even if it killed him. About 1,000 feet higher Mac finally made him realise that it was a waste of time. Alkhutov had no wish to retreat for it was not in his character or training. Mac was beside himself with anger when they returned to camp.

The following day we went down to Base to pick up more stores while Slesser, Bryan and Vladimir Malakov took our places on the peeling rock wall. Overnight the snow had frozen much better, and by taking a more direct route they got to the top of the ridge where the site for another camp was mapped out.

On their return Mac gave his usual greeting to Vladimir: "Well done, Bloodymir! You mad, impetuous Russian dare-devil!"

Moving stores up the glacier, the Russians invariably charged passed us when we had flogged ourselves to a standstill. They flung a greeting without stopping and Mac replied by cocking a snook and shouting back, "up your hooter". As they receded at rocket pace into the distance Mac stood up and roared at the top of his voice, "balls to you". This happened so many times that the Russians stopped and inquired if we could translate.

Said one of them to Mac with the serious intention of ex-panding his English vocabulary: "What is this 'balls to you?' The other British climbers do not say these words to us."

"Oh, well, they wouldn't," said Mac, putting on a profes-sorial air. "The British can be very stuffy. You see, it is a very close English form of address, reserved for friends. You are our dearest friends, so we greet you as such."

The Russian roughly understood what Mac had said and told his companions.

"Tell you what," suggested Mac, "why don't you go up to Sir John Hunt and say to him, 'balls to you'. He'll appreciate it."

Murmuring the phrase over and over again to memorise it, the Russians departed. After that they charged past us as usual and hurled an equivalent Soviet greeting at us with much laughter.

Establishing a camp at the top of the rock wall was grim work. Mac likened it to climbing up a bookshelf that was 1,000 feet high. You could pull out pieces and slot them back in place at every step. More disgustingly loose rock on a high mountain I had never seen, and it was not far short of vertical. Even with infinite care and patience the movement of the rope sent down a continuous shower of rocks. One hardly knew which way to turn next. Fixed ropes were draped down the "library shelves" section. Without them it would have been impossible to take loads on to the ridge at the top where the camp was placed.

The unclimbed ridge west of Patriot Peak ran up into a gigantic cone-shaped buttress lying against the face of the mountain. We traversed across the foot of the buttress, since it could not be climbed direct, and went up some very steep snow slopes on the flank to its apex. A third camp was placed at this point. The climbing was now first-rate. Mac and I at last began to enjoy ourselves. With the two Russians we installed ourselves in the camp for an assault on the summit.

We were having to conform to the Russian system of returning to base on or before a prearranged "control date". If a party failed to reappear by this date all the mountaineering forces in the area would be marshalled for a rescue operation. It was not easy to cheat the system—apart from having Russian alpinists as companions—because food was rationed according to the duration of a planned excursion. We had wasted a lot of time getting established on the ridge. Even if the weather remained fine the food shortage would drive us back to report on the control date.

The four of us set out to climb 1,000 feet to regain the main ridge and study the final problems. The snow was extremely steep and again very rotten. During the months of July and August the weather in the Pamirs was generally so good that even at high altitudes snow would not freeze at night. It rotted to a depth of some four feet. On touching it, it collapsed like a precariously balanced pile of playing cards. One stone tossed on the snow automatically started an avalanche. We crept and slid in the awful stuff on to the ridge and went along the crest until another buttress stopped us. This appeared to go up to the summit, perhaps 1,500 feet above.

I turned to Mac. "I've had enough of this snow. I'm not going on. What about you?"

"My sentiments exactly," he retorted.

We made signs to the Russians. They were dumbfounded.

"Tell them it is far too dangerous," I hinted to Mac, who had a way of putting over our point of view.

The Russians didn't want to know. They indicated severely that we were lazy, malingerers and lacking in enthusiasm. I couldn't help but agree.

Mac turned on the Russians and announced: "Bugger you, Bloodymir. You can stuff your rotten Soviet snow up your Volga hooter!"

"We go to the top of the mountain," said Vladimir, waving in the direction of the summit. They made it perfectly clear that they were pushing on regardless of what we did.

"Farewell, Bloody-Smear. Boot off, Alkhutov. We'll watch you from here!"

Mac and I stayed on the ridge until they disappeared into the mist hovering above.

The descent to Camp III, then to Camp II, demanded all our tenacity. We managed to belay on numerous rock ribs. One held the rope fast while the other was played down to avalanche the snow ahead of him, clearing a groove in which the last man could slide with some assurance. We carried a few stones for starting avalanches over longer stretches of snow where the distance between the ribs was too great for the length of our ropes.

The Russians came back in the evening. They had not reached the top. They made no secret of the fact that they were very displeased with our behaviour.

"You are not pulling your weight and the weight it must be pulled by all climbers on the mountains," stated Vladimir with improving English. Mac was lounging in a corner of the tent, tucking into a good meal. He belched loudly.

From Camp II it was possible to shout down to Camp I.

Then we saw Slesser and Bryan who had come all the way from the glacier towards Camp II without a break. We told the Scots what had been going on, that the weather was bad higher up and, most of all, that we did not feel like climbing. We agreed to support the Russians in raising the height of Camp III. The Scots joined in this work and the Russians made their bid for the summit.

The Russians got back safely. They were not absolutely certain that they had reached the top. In dense cloud it had been impossible to tell. No trace of a previous ascent was found. It was Russian custom to leave evidence of an ascent in the form of a note in a bottle or tin on the summit. The Russians half expected to find a note that could be substituted for one of their own and brought down to prove their own ascent. Some time ago a Russian team had vanished without trace on Patriot Peak. It was thought that the party had gained the highest point by the south-west ridge and that an accident had occurred on the descent. In the end the Russians preferred to believe that they had arrived on a subsidiary top, leaving in doubt the success or failure of their own ascent and that of the previous party.

While evacuating the stage camps and removing equipment on Patriot Peak I was struck down by an acute attack of piles. I was totally incapacitated. We spent a few days in the lowest camp beside the Vavilova glacier, waiting for me to recover and the rest of the party to return. No one came until the third day. John Hunt and Graeme Nicol arrived looking all in, but this was not due to the hike across the glacier.

"There is terrible news," Hunt said gravely. "Wilf and Robin are dead".

Wilfred Noyce and Robin Smith were roped together, having changed places with their Russian companions on the descent of Garmo Peak after a most successful climb. The snow might have balled up under their crampons, causing one of them to slip. The accident soon came to the notice of other expedition members, although the Russian pair, who were somewhat above and behind the Britishers, were not aware immediately that anything had happened. Bull and Wrangham had seen Wilf and Robin fall 4,000 feet to the glacier below. The bodies had been recovered and buried at the foot of the mountain.

I wanted to weep. Something had been removed violently and without warning from the lives of each of us. It was disturbing enough when the death of a climbing companion was brought as news in home surroundings. Here we were isolated in one of the most foreign and inhospitable corners of the world. The sorrow of sudden death was heightened by the time in weeks that we had spent together as a team. The tragedy involved all of us as much as if we had been tied individually to the Noyce-Smith rope.

John Hunt put it to us that each member of the expedition must decide for himself whether to stay or return home. But he felt that the expedition would have failed in its main object, which was to improve East-West relations, if we all turned back at this stage. The Russians felt the same way but all agreed that if it had been a normal expedition, say to the Himalaya, then all of us could be expected in the circumstances to retire and return home.

As leader and as a figure working in public life John's position was clear; compassionately, politically and dutifully he had to go back and answer the questions posed by public curiosity and the press. The worst job was visiting the relatives. I didn't envy his lot. Those who had seen the accident or who had assisted in the recovery and burial operation were heartily sick of the Pamirs.

The great Spartak expedition was now in the region. Thirty bronze-tanned men had assembled at Base. The serious expression on their faces betrayed the concern they felt for our well-being. Activity up and down the Garmo glacier highway doubled as the machine of Russian mountaineering revved up for an assault on Communism Peak. It was under the direction of the almost legendary figure and doyen of Soviet alpinism, Vitale Abalakov. He commanded loyalty and discipline over his men as of a general.

All the parties were now returning to Base Camp. Because I was still suffering from the effect of piles, Bryan and Slesser had gone ahead and Mac and I were following more slowly. Almost before we reached the glacier the first two had disappeared from sight. The séracs and crevasses on the glacier were frightening in their complexity, and it was very tiring moving through them. We sat down to rest and have a smoke. Two of Abalakov's team came across us and stopped to talk.

"Have a fag," said Mac. "Relax. Take a rest. There's no one watching." The Russians looked round nervously, glad of the invitation, and smoked the cigarettes. They made us promise not to divulge to anyone that they had been smoking because this was against the rules.

We told them about the accident and they were badly shocked to hear the news. Mac excused our present sloth by referring to my illness—it was true enough that I was still unwell. The Russians offered to walk down the glacier with us, but we said we would hold them back. Eventually they left and we set off in the same direction.

The crevasses were still a maze. We decided to cross a moraine to the other side of the glacier and look for a better route. This was a real stroke of luck. We found a long level lane, and as Mac said, you could have driven a car down it. Our pace gradually increased and I began to feel much better. We rested every half hour, smoked and continued. A few hundred yards short of the camp we flopped down for the last time.

Then we were surprised to see two figures in the distance coming down the glacier towards us. We were even more surprised when we recognised them as the Russians whom we had met earlier in the day. The Russians bounded into view and stopped dead. Four hours earlier they had come across us in exactly the same position—flat on our backs and smoking!

The Russians told us that Malcolm Slesser and Kenny Byran were at least half an hour behind. By this time I had recovered completely. We scrambled to our feet and set off at a brisk pace. I drew ahead of the others and when Mac arrived in camp a couple of minutes later he was whooping with joy,

shouting "We've done it, we've done it". At long last we were
fit enough to hold our own with the Russians. Mac explained
that the Russians had been very impressed with us getting
ahead of them. One of them put it to Mac: "If Joe is like this
when he is not well, what is he like when he is really fit?"

In the following days six of us decided to stay in the Pamirs:
Malcolm Slesser, Kenny Bryan, Graeme Nicol, Ralph Jones,
Mac and myself.

We agreed with our Russian companions to make a bid for
Communism Peak. Short of time and with virtually no knowledge of the problems ahead, the six of us were pressed into the
Russian system for scaling big mountains. Very little food was
carried. Each camp was more or less uprooted and taken on
our backs to the next site ahead. No supporting relay group was
used to build up camps. This modified "sports plan" entailed
walking 25 miles through a vertical distance of 14,000 feet on
some of the roughest glacier terrain in the world, and climbing
vast ice slopes and ridges, all in fifteen days. Ten days were
allowed for ascent and five for descent. Nothing mattered except
keeping up to the daily climbing schedule and reaching the top.

Malcolm Slesser tried to accustom himself to the rigours of
the routine. He made a real effort to play the game and set an
example. At the other end of the scale Mac and I strolled into
camps at a late hour, having dawdled on the way, and came in
for a lot of hard remarks. The Russians tried to scare us out of
the habit of working between camps on our own by overstating
the stonefall danger after midday. When various ruses failed
they wrote us off as "decadent western layabouts". Trailing
behind the others, even our route finding was criticised. Mac
and I could see no point in getting from one camp to the next in
the shortest possible time and spending the rest of the day
sweltering in a humid tent. The whole day for a walk could be
enjoyed if taken leisurely.

The approach along the glacier finished in deep snow. We
arrived at the foot of a broad scoop in a face over 4,000 feet
high, called the Georgian Couloir. Then Slesser and Bryan fell

ill. Bryan was very sick with a combination of food poisoning and dysentry. It was advisable for Bryan to descend and Ralph Jones volunteered to go with him. The Russians decided that they would go to the top of the couloir and wait for us there. The Spartak expedition was already camped on the plateau at the top, so we arranged to rendezvous there.

All day we watched the Russians creeping up the gigantic couloir, gaining height steadily. By midday they were half-way up. Between watching the Russians and resting some time was spent in an argument that arose from Mac and I refusing to carry oxygen cylinders up the couloir, according to the "rules". Oxygen was not essential on the mountain. Considering that we were carrying all our equipment for making camps progressively as we moved higher, the additional weight was the difference between an uneasy peace and rebellion.

Next morning Slesser declared himself well enough to climb. We started up the couloir as a rope of four. The climbing was on steep snow and ice and continuously interesting. It was steep enough to warrant the cutting of handholds. Even the great loads dragging on our backs felt lighter. At the half-way stage we rested and had a snack. We were surprised to find evidence of a Russian camp in a crevasse. We thought that they had reached the top in one day. Mac and I dropped the oxygen bottles in the crevasse and everyone was too tired to argue again.

Then we saw the Russians merely 600 feet above. What had held them back? The couloir at this point was about 300 yards wide. Its bed was grooved by a number of subsidiary gullies and ribs. The Russians had gone up some 500 feet of steep snow to the edge of a long ice passage leading through the complex. We gazed at the gleaming sheet of ice, about 700 feet high. Somewhat taken aback, I expressed the opinion that the slope looked all of sixty degrees.

Now we split into two ropes of two. I led off with Mac. Fifty feet up the ice I spotted a rope hanging down the slope. It was no ordinary fixed rope. Normally a fixed rope is fairly thick and comforting to hold—otherwise there is no point having it for support. The Russians had fixed a 400 feet length of cord about ¼ inch in diameter. I pulled on it. The rope was hanging freely for as far as I could see up the slope. A rope of this length was usually fixed at intermediate points not more than 100 feet apart. This strengthened it, reduced lateral movement and avoided undue stretch. This single length of thin rope, with no visible means of support, and lying down an ice slope of sixty degrees, turned my stomach over. Two climbers or more could work up a normal fixed rope in perfect safety. But this would not be feasible with the Russian rope.

Mac joined me at the end of the rope. "Typical Russian roulette stuff," he commented sourly.

"There is only one thing to do," I said.

"I know, I know." We both started untying the climbing rope. "Make it as quick as you can," said Mac.

I went straight up solo on the fixed rope, hand over hand, and eventually hauled myself on to the rib where the upper end was anchored. The anchor consisted of one standard peg driven into the rock. A second peg had been placed somewhat lower down to direct the line of the rope on to the ice slope. I murmured something about the bloody Russians to myself. The upper peg had already been pulled into a dangerous downward angle by the strain put on the overworked rope.

I stationed myself beside the peg. Some time later there was still no sign of Mac appearing from below. I continued up the slope, cutting steps to the top of the couloir. I sat there for another hour or more, nibbling at a tin of meat. Then a lot of shouting drifted up. Mac appeared. It transpired that Slesser and Nicol had rejected the idea of soloing up the rope because if a grip on it was lost, death would be certain. Their concern was understandable. Graeme Nicol was suffering from the effects of altitude and Slesser had barely recovered from his illness. Mac had been delayed by coaxing them on. Their progress was extremely slow. They had secured themselves to the rope by a system of prussik slings.

I lowered a rope down the top part of the slope to assist them. Slesser came up last looking wretchedly ill and all in. I took his pack and carried it on to the plateau. The Russian camp was still thirty minutes away. In the present condition of the party, even crossing level ground, the distance could have been thirty miles. The light was fading rapidly so we camped at the top of the couloir.

Above the Spartak camp rose a huge slope broken by short ice cliffs to the final ridge of the mountain. That morning we saw an army of ant-like figures swarming about the slope. Gradually it moved downwards. We guessed that something was wrong. Abalakov's son was seriously ill; his breathing was bad, pneumonia was suspected and he was falling into a coma. Graeme Nicol inspected him and advised the Russians to get him off the mountain without delay. A stretcher party was formed and the Spartak climbers departed.

Two nights were spent in the Spartak camp on the saddle between Communism Peak and Molotov Peak. The altitude was about 21,000 feet. Graeme Nicol now showed signs of sinking into a stupor. He responded sluggishly to conversational suggestions and commands. He seemed unable to collect his thoughts and act in a logical manner. If he was asked to step outside the tent to scoop up snow in a billy-can he replied hesitantly: "Where do I get it from?" A lilo propped across a tent door to keep out draughts caused him to say: "I can't reach the snow because something is in the way." Slesser too was finding it difficult to co-ordinate his thoughts. Such are the effects of altitude and I have often wondered if I could be bothered to continue climbing if I was affected in the same way.

Starting up the big slope the Russians steamed off in characteristic fashion. With two semi-invalids we soon fell back. The weather was bad and occasional clearings in the mist revealed nothing except an endless expanse of snow tilted at forty degrees. Sometimes we saw a reassuring footprint. After nearly four hours of trudging up the slope Graeme Nicol was grey with fatigue and sagging at the knees. Mac and I split his load between us. Soon we broke through the cloud. Scanning the wastes there was no sign of the Russian camp. We groaned to ourselves that none of us could continue to the summit ridge.

The Russians were remorseless but how could they have gone that far in a day? A little higher we found a solitary pole sticking in the snow. Next to it was a hole about two feet in diameter. There were marks of trampling feet all around. I bobbed down and looked inside. Well underground I was greeted by our Russian companions with a salute from cups of tea and the waving of hard biscuits. I shouted to the others to come in.

The "camp" was an ice cave about 12 feet square and barely high enough to sit up in. The atmosphere was claustrophobic. The sides of the compartment were solid ice and the pressure from above was making them bend inwards.

The evening meal was dehydrated curry—an unpalatable dish at the best of times. We had nothing else. I spent most of the night retching with my head stuck in the cave entrance. I hadn't the will-power to go outside.

Having been sick all night it was now my turn to be laid low. The prospect that morning of steeling myself to make the final effort was horrifying. I was feeling absolutely wretched.

"I can't do it," I said to Mac. "I haven't got an ounce of strength left. You go on with the others."

"Well, if you're not going, nor am I," he declared.

"I haven't got the breath to argue with you. Clear off and don't be silly." But Mac wouldn't go.

I lay back thinking that I had reached my last resting place. I was entombed in an ice cave, with the walls closing in every day, at the top of the highest mountain in Russia.

A few minutes later: "Are you coming, Joe?" demanded the callously impatient McNaught Davis.

"I'll come outside and have a look round."

"See," he said, pointing towards the invisible summit, "we'll soon trot up that lot."

Malcolm had made a remarkably good recovery and set off at a cracking pace with Nicol trailing behind him. Mac and I plodded below them while the Russians were doing their usual track performance.

The long slope soon ran out on to the ridge. Alternate crests of snow and rock with an exposed face sweeping down on both sides for 6,000 feet revived my interest. The climbing was really pleasant. Once on the ridge I forgot about my weakness and empty stomach. We went into the lead. The Russians were about 200 yards ahead and we caught them up.

"We are waiting for you," said one of them.

"That's nice," retorted Mac, lighting a cigarette.

"You go to the lead now," said the Russian. "You make steps in snow."

"Better do what he says," said Mac, "otherwise if we ever get back they will sentence us to the salt mines." He turned on the Russian spokesman: "Yes, all right, you galloping Georgian revolutionary, we'll do your work for you!"

We waded ahead in deep snow with no idea where the summit was. "The cunning bastards must have known it would be like this up here," remarked Mac. All the same it was pleasant to be in front again.

Slesser and Nicol dropped a long way behind. In due course the Russians took a turn at leading again. Then they stopped to have a "party meeting".

Lighting up a cigarette, Mac said: "If I'd known I would have brought a book to read."

"Please, you listen to us," said Eugene Gippenreiter, the Russian spokesman. "Anatoli Ovchinnikov, our leader, will now speak."

Anatoli said: "In the Soviet Union all peoples go to the summit. The peoples who not reach the summit make the climb a failure. Success of the expedition is the success of each individual who reaches the top. Peoples who not reach the top are not a success. You understand?"

"Yes, we know all that," replied Mac. "What have you got in mind?"

"So now we climb like mountains climbed in Russia. The strong will go in front and the weak will stay behind. The strongest of the weak will go to the very back—bring up the rear, as you say—and will force the weakest to keep up. This way we make sure our expedition is a success to every peoples."

The British outlook was that only one man, but usually two

as a roped party, had to reach the top of a big mountain for the expedition to be declared successful.

"So now Joe Brown will go with this young climber. He is very fit." He motioned me towards their best man. "You," he said to Mac, "will come with me."

The Russian youth that I had been paired with took the lead and went up like a rocket. We were now over 24,000 feet and I wouldn't dream of setting this pace at half the height. God knows where the summit is, I gasped to myself. False top followed false top. 400 feet away, 4,000 feet away, I didn't know or care. The Russian went flying up some rocks. The pace seemed to increase. Mac was right. They were all bloody mad. I was determined that the rope between us should not be pulled tight. My heart pounded and my lungs were ready to burst. I thought of Snowdon. Where was Snowdon? Oh yes, that Welsh hill with Cloggy in its side. Who ever went up Cloggy at this speed? Glasses steaming up again. Where is the top of this mountain? No you don't. I let out a spare loop of rope that I had gathered in in a moment of advantage. Another little rock buttress. Is that the fourth or fifth? Doesn't matter. That's funny. Nothing beyond the top of this one. The Russian toppled on to his back, gasping, big eyes bulging in his head. I did the same. I lay quite still and there was only the sound of my body gulping in the oxygen-starved air.

A little later Mac, his partner and the other two Russians came on the scene. There was rejoicing. Hands were shaken and backs were slapped. The chairman called the meeting to order. He made a short speech. British and Russian flags were produced and flown from ice axes. Then he made a presentation of badges brought in secret all the way from Moscow. Just as I was thinking of reminding Mac that we ought to start down, Slesser and Nicol popped up from nowhere. Everyone was surprised and pleased to see them. The summit ceremony was repeated for their benefit. The Russians could now claim unqualified success for the expedition.

Descending the ice slope above the Spartak camp the angle was steep enough to require belays. I was searching for old axe holes which had been filled in by drifting snow. I spotted what I thought was a good one, took a step towards it and the snow just gave way. I had a brief glimpse of flashing ice walls and came to a stop jammed in a constriction of the crevasse. My first feelings were of rising panic, thinking that I would suffocate with the snow that had fallen on top of me. Moving a little dislodged the snow and I could see the rope going up the green shiny walls to the hole in the snow above. The rope was suddenly drawn tight and I couldn't breathe, so I had to shout to Mac to slack off. After a desperate struggle I shifted the wedged rucksack which was holding me into the crevasse. With fear driving me on I bridged up to the surface. The effort of getting out was so great that I could only gasp for the next twenty minutes. The Russians came by, stopped, glanced into the hole, smiled and carried on.

Next day, descending the Georgian Couloir, we nearly had a disaster on the fixed rope. Mac went down first and his crampons worked loose. He slipped off and all his weight came on the rope. The supporting pegs hardly seemed strong enough to hold his weight, and had they come out the rest of the party would have been dragged down with him. After a lot of crazy antics and cursing Mac sorted himself out and the rest of the descent went smoothly.

The chief concern was to recover as much of our property as possible. The long trail down the glacier was littered with valuable equipment dumps. The problem was how to transport the material. Twelve men and helicopters had brought it up; there were four men left to take it down. To make matters worse some of the equipment lay in places well away from the shortest route to base. At one camp I collected five tents in addition to my personal gear. I abandoned several hundred pegs and new perlon ropes that had never been uncoiled. Any member of the Rock and Ice would have walked for days to collect the stuff we left on the glacier.

Base Camp was empty. Next day Bryan and Jones arrived with the mail. We moved down to the lower Base Camp among the trees that grew out of dust. The party was stuck here a

H

fortnight. No transport arrangements had been made for our evacuation from the area.

A lot of bridge was played. The Russians could now break training. Crates of whisky were demolished at big drinking sessions that reduced us to something less than gentlemen. At one of them Anatoli Ovchinnikov, the leader of the Russian group, was regaling the company with his battle experiences during the war. In the middle of a bayonet charge Slesser poured a glass of whisky over him. The Russian stood up furiously and ranted like a madman. No one blamed him. We could not understand why Slesser had done it. Anatoli was restrained by his companions and taken out of the tent screaming, "me no like, me no like". There was no doubt in my mind that he was referring to Slesser. Yet later his words were construed as meaning a dislike for whisky.

The Russians had a case of rifles. One of the pieces was fitted with telescopic sights. We practised a lot with these guns. All of us received black eyes from the one with telescopic sights. They were set too far back and the recoil smashed the eyepiece into your face.

Taking stock of the equipment that we had managed to bring off the mountain, it would cost a fortune in excess baggage to get it home. It occurred to us that if we could sell it to the Russians the money would be just as good. The only inferior thing about the Russians was their equipment. It was antiquated by comparison with ours, which was the best in the world. We could have sold many articles at a huge profit but were satisfied if we recovered the original cost.

A sale was held. The Russians had astonishing sums of money. In an area where there was nothing to be bought for scores of miles in any direction, every man had hundreds of roubles in his pocket. We sold everything except a pile of camping gas cylinders. There were hundreds of spare cartridges. It was fairly obvious that we would not take them back to Britain. So no one made an offer because they could be picked up for nothing after we had gone.

We were desperately short of ideas for amusement. Mac

remembered how on the glacier Slesser had nearly blown himself to bits with a gas cartridge. He and I built a fire and started throwing them on it. One at a time was lobbed because this caper was pretty dangerous for bystanders. In ten seconds it went off with a terrific bang. A few seconds later you heard the tinkle of the cylinder landing two or three hundred yards away. We had "fired" about twenty of them before the Russians ran up angrily, saying that it was very dangerous having these cans flying through the air. "They are not frightened of falling stones and ice," said Mac innocently, "so why should a little can bother them?" The Russians bought the lot without more ado.

The helicopters arrived and took us to Dushambe. Visits were made to Samarkand and Tashkent. About 750 years ago Jenghiz Khan had massacred three-quarters of the half a million population of the fabled city of Samarkand and today the citizens number barely 150,000.

Mac had assumed the role of James Bond. He was passing secret messages instead of coming straight out with a piece of information. The Intourist guide stationed at our hotel spoke English with a public school accent. He was really smooth, almost too good to be true. To Mac he was "our man in Samarkand". Mac was irrepressible. If it had not been for his company in the Pamirs I would have gone home with John Hunt.

On the way to Moscow we had to change aircraft. Slesser had been taking photographs. In the airport café he unconsciously started to adjust his camera, as tourists are prone to do. Leaving the room and walking down the stairs a man stepped out of the shadows and tapped him on the shoulders.

"Come with me, please."

"Where?" said Slesser, startled.

"The police station."

That's the end of him, I thought.

"Whatever for?"

"You have been reported for taking photographs from the aircraft. You must come with me and sign a statement."

The statement was in Russian and he refused to sign. Slesser gave them the film and he was released. He would have been in serious trouble if he had signed the statement or if the film had been developed before the connecting aircraft flew off. Mac was busily telling us that he would have to report "Double O so-and-so" to "M" when he got back to London. "Getting too old for the game," said Mac. "He's past it now."

We nearly missed a reception held for us at the British embassy in Moscow because our trousers were taken away from the hotel room at the last moment for pressing. The party paced up and down in its shirts, unable to leave the room, as the hours ticked by. The room service was bad and the food prepared for us at the reception had been eaten by the time we got there.

In the main lounge at Moscow airport the aisles were thronged with men dressed in blue raincoats with turned up collars.

"Keep an eye on them," said Mac intuitively. "They are the men from SMERSH."

We were hanging about near the Customs Office, trying to look inconspicuous. The Russian posted to watch us had gone on an errand. An Englishman came up and started chatting. He was very agitated.

"I say, old man, could you possibly take some film out for me?" He was talking to me. I thought, Christ, what a thing to ask.

"He's our man in Moscow," I said, nodding to Mac. "Ask him."

"It's nothing really, just a small package."

Mac butted in: "Don't you know that we are not supposed to smuggle out 'packages'?"

"It is not like that at all," the man whispered nervously. He started fingering an anorak folded on my arm. His eyes were darting all over the place.

"This is a jolly nice anorak you have. Can I have a look at it?" He pulled it off my arm. He was in a terrible state of nerves. I imagined that everyone in the room was looking at us and wondering what was going on. I could see the men from

SMERSH closing in, hands in pockets, faces hard as stone.

"Keep your voice down," ordered Mac. "What the hell do you want?"

The man started pulling a huge Kodak film box out of his pocket. It was jammed inside and he was struggling to tear it loose. He's crazy, I thought. The yellow box was bright as a beacon. He stuffed it into the anorak and shoved it back to me. I had to take it in case the box dropped out and fell on the floor where everyone would see it.

"Look here," I said, "this bulge will be seen a mile away. I'll spend the next ten or fifteen years in prison."

"They will never suspect you," he said in a conciliatory tone.

Before I could remonstrate further our Russian "guard" returned. The man slipped away. I was scared stiff.

"Don't worry," purred Mac. "I've got my finger on the trigger." He was trying to sound cheerful. But we were not playing games now.

The Russian said: "There is a delay. The plane is late. I will see if you can leave your luggage here."

I did not know what to do. I was convinced that we would be caught. Folding the anorak around the box I put it down carefully among the luggage. If someone picked it up the box would certainly fall out.

He returned, saying that we would have to shift the luggage. The Russian started to assist us. I almost shouldered him out of the way to grab the anorak.

We boarded the plane without trouble. We were wearing all the clothing and equipment that we possibly could to save on excess baggage charges. For instance, each person wore sixty snap-links! We looked like balloon men and on the scales we would have tipped fifteen stones. Once inside the aircraft the party stripped, filling up the compartment. The yellow box was lost among the loot.

As soon as we stepped off the plane at London airport a man came up to me for the film. He said it was a newsreel.

"Ah, well," said Mac with satisfaction, "that's another mission accomplished. 'M' will be pleased."

CHAPTER ELEVEN

THE SIXTIES—TOWARDS THE SEA

My main job at White Hall was taking young lads climbing. At first, when you try to teach people, you tend to teach what you already know, which in my case was more or less instinctive. To be able to explain to someone how to do a particular climb or apply a particular technique, you have to know exactly how you do it yourself. So I had to analyse my own approach to climbing. Because of this I became much more critical of my own climbing and I am sure this improved my own technique.

One of the handicaps of teaching, so far as I was concerned, was having to give talks on climbing. At first I really disliked this part of the work, but after a while I suppose I got used to it and it didn't bother me.

One of the advantages of White Hall over most centres is its ideal position. A lot of the climbing is on gritstone which is much better than Welsh or Lakeland volcanic rock for teaching beginners how to climb. For one thing you can look after parties much more easily because the crags are small, but the main point is that you can teach particular techniques more easily. For instance, if a lad isn't too good at jamming or lay-backing, then on gritstone you can find a climb which has to be tackled by these techniques. Whereas on larger crags it is nearly always possible to do a pitch by several methods.

From the instructor's point of view the position of White Hall is ideal. Instead of having to concentrate on one particular mountain area, courses from White Hall go all over the country —Wales, the Lakes, Scotland. This is more varied than most centres and it helps to keep the instructors interested in the job.

Living in a centre is sometimes rather like being on an expedition, with the close community life and always being surrounded by climbers. I would never like to be the warden of

a climbing centre. Most instructors go there more or less
expecting it to be a free and easy job and it must be very
difficult for the warden to maintain a friendly atmosphere as
well as getting people to do their work.

The opportunities for doing new things at White Hall were
tremendous. I had been climbing for nearly fifteen years on
gritstone, so it wasn't really a novelty for me, but I took up
canoeing. There are some splendid rivers near the centre, all
suitable for this exercise. In some respects canoeing is similar
to climbing. It demands high technical skill and involves a
certain degree of danger and competition. Even rivers are
graded I to VI, as routes are in climbing!

In the winter of 1963 I went to the Cairngorms with a White
Hall party for skiing. We stayed at Glenmore Lodge where Eric
Langmuir was now the warden. There I met Tom Patey again;
I had not climbed with Tom since our expedition to the
Mustagh Tower seven years previously. We celebrated the
reunion in Scotland by climbing together and before I returned
to Derbyshire we had made plans to go to the Alps the following
summer.

July arrived and Tom drove up in his little car to collect me.
At the last moment he had written to say that five of us would
be travelling together. I wondered how we were all going to
manage because we were planning to stay a month in the Alps
and my gear alone must have weighed close to one cwt. Everyone else had the same amount of luggage and the vehicle was
crammed full inside to the roof. I sat with a guitar and banjo
on my knee and off we went.

In Chamonix the same old story was being told. Everyone
was walking round moaning that it was the worst season ever.
In fact the fortnight previous to our arrival had been reasonably
fine and we learnt that there had been several ascents of the
Frendo Spur of the Aiguille du Midi. So we decided to try this
as our first route. There was some merit in not having to rise
too early for the climb because we could walk to the cable railway just outside the town and catch the first car to the Plan de
l'Aiguille station at 5.30 a.m. After that an hour of walking and

scrambling up the glacier brought us to the foot of the spur.

Looking at the spur from below you get the impression that for three parts of the climb the route is on rock, about 2,500 feet. Then there is a snow ridge that merges into a very steep ice slope. It seemed that the ice slope would be about two rope lengths before it finished against the last rock buttress, which also looked about one or two pitches long.

Tom and I had brought along two novices who had never climbed in the Alps. The lower part of the spur was pleasant climbing and if we had been on our own we would have gone up the rocks unroped. With two novices we had to rope up and move somewhat slower than the pace I would have liked to set. On reaching the snow ridge I discovered that I had forgotten my crampons; although we could kick steps in the snow for a pitch or two, higher up a pair of crampons would have been of great assistance on the ice.

"Oh, never mind," said Tom. "I shan't bother with mine in that case." Tom led off up the snow and ice. He was so confident on snow and ice that when we climbed together he automatically took the lead on this type of terrain while I usually went to the front on difficult rock pitches. He was perfectly happy to cut steps in ice all day long.

After another pitch we arrived at the ice. We told the novices to put on their crampons, just to be on the safe side. We could still see traces of steps made by a previous party but they were nearly obliterated and not of much use. Tom cut new steps in a straight line and I enlarged them. The slope went up for 800 or 900 feet—very much more than we had estimated. The top of it was very steep.

Tom's second was standing at the top of the slope watching him trying to reach the rock above. Wearing crampons, the second was now very tired from standing in small holds on the front spikes. Suddenly the second's legs started to shake violently. None of us was belayed so I had to work furiously to cut a stance before we were all dragged down. As soon as I had done this and put in an ice-peg on which we could tie ourselves to the slope my second also began to shake. So I had to indulge in another flurry of activity and make another platform to stand on.

Meanwhile Tom had his own troubles. He was struggling to get up an icy crack and finally pulled on to a good stance. I had a few minutes to look round and shouted up that the rock buttress looked all of 600 feet. "Yes," said Tom, "our calculations were a bit out."

It was soon apparent that the correct line up the buttress was buried under ice; you could see the cracks one was supposed to climb about six inches underneath the ice layer. Tom and I explored alternatives and we became separated. I climbed a fairly difficult crack then went along a hand traverse into a vertical crack. This was full of loose rock and I spent some time pulling it out. Tom's second couldn't get up this pitch so they went off to the right on to another part of the cliff. The next pitch was easy and I found a pleasantly exposed hand traverse rising to the summit ridge. Sitting on top we were able to shout directions at Tom who arrived a little later. The weather was marvellous, and with no danger of having to bivouac the Frendo Spur was a most satisfying start to the season.

One of the good things about climbing with Tom is that he is a fanatic about planning. During the winter, in preparation for an Alpine holiday, he studies guidebooks and magazines, extracting information and memorising projected climbs in infinite detail. He probably knows more about possible new routes in the Alps than anyone else I know. If you want to know where a new route might be found on a particular face, then Tom is the man to go to.

Tom had been studying the Gréloz-Roch route on the West Face of the Aiguille du Plan. It went more or less up the centre of the face to within 600 feet or so of the top, then traversed to one side for a long way. "Looks like a good wall at the top of the route," said Tom, "so what about trying to straighten it out."

We used the cable railway again to approach the face. The lower section was no trouble at all and we duly arrived at the point where the detour started on the right. There was not much hope of climbing straight up, so we moved left to where a traverse looked possible. It was a bit like the Red Slab on Cloggy. Tom had a shot at it and came back. I went up and found a peg in position—someone had been here before. A little farther I found another peg with a piece of string attached to it. This suggested that the owner had roped off from this point. I managed to get up the pitch, which was very delicate. A shattered chimney above led to a terrace. Now there was a sheer smooth wall looking quite unclimbable except by artificial means. This worried me because we had not come prepared for artificial climbing. We had five pegs between us.

When we started up the wall it gave five or six pitches of continuously even climbing in a magnificent position, about Grade 5, and we did not have to use artificial methods. It had begun to rain and at the top of the wall we were climbing in snow. A couloir about 150 feet high led to the summit. The snow in the couloir was weird stuff—it made me feel creepy. Tom would stake his life on almost any kind of snow. No matter what its condition might be he does not regard any snow as bad. One of the unnerving things about climbing with him is that when the rock difficulties are finished, on snow he was liable to unrope and climb it solo. This he now did in the summit couloir. I always felt a bit upset about this practice and I followed him cautiously, boring holes armpit deep into the rotten stuff.

Descending by the normal route to the Requin hut Tom bounded down the glacier and started avalanches all over the slope. I was fully expecting to be buried on the way down.

In the hut the warden's daughter recognised me from a television programme I had taken part in, so we were invited into the kitchen and treated royally. I had badly blistered feet and she doctored them for me so well that we were able to continue down to Chamonix twenty minutes later.

Tom went off to Zermatt with the novices to climb the Matterhorn. I was not very keen on doing this. In the British camp at Chamonix I met Des Hadlum. "I still haven't done the South-West Pillar of the Dru," I told him. He agreed without hesitation to accompany me. Des is one of the most dependable climbers imaginable. He can't be ruffled. I could not have had a more able and willing companion. If you stopped for a meal or to bivouac Des had everything arranged neatly and the stove hissing with soup on the boil in no time at all.

We bivouacked near the Rognon where we noticed another party settling down for the night. We broke camp at 5 a.m. Going up the snow cone close to the couloir we noticed a large piece of bone which we thought must have been dropped by a bird. In the couloir itself we were amazed by the absence of falling stones; in fact only one stonefall occurred all day. Two rope lengths farther up we came across some gear scattered all over the place and saw a great smear of blood. It was then pretty obvious what had happened. The party on the Rognon was a rescue team. As we climbed higher up the couloir some people appeared and started shouting at us in French. Neither of us understood what they were trying to say. Higher still we discovered more abandoned equipment but we didn't feel like picking it up. Then a helicopter flew in, landed on the Rognon and more people got out. Looking up at the West Face we now saw tiny figures traversing on to the wall from the North Face.

Up on the pillar we climbed a line of terrific cracks, so obvious that I did not bother to check if it was the correct route. It led under some very large overhangs where I realised that we would have to descend and search for the proper route more carefully. Eventually we reached the first Bonatti bivouac place. Sitting down for a bite to eat I checked the route description that we had brought and found that a page was missing. The printed description, which I had torn from a journal, finished at the point we had just reached. Well, worse things could happen on a climb.

The helicopter came right up close to us. You could plainly see the people in the cabin. The machine buzzed round us all day. It was really off-putting—not that it frightened us—you simply couldn't shout to each other over the roar of the engine and communication on the rock face became quite difficult. Mist rolled in and we thought we were in for bad weather. But the helicopter still flew close to the pillar and from this we gathered that the mist could only be a thin cap on the mountain.

We carried on climbing until a large wall blocked the way. I was not too sure of the best direction to take because various ways are possible on several parts of the pillar. I went up the wall beside a line of pegs. The wall was so foreshortened that I was deceived into thinking that I might get up it in two pitches. I ran out of rope and had to take a stance in stirrups. The next 50 feet was climbing on rotten wooden wedges in a crack. The position was superb but any one of the wedges was liable to pop out without warning. Then the pegs just ended in a blank wall. For a minute I thought I had gone up a blind alley. Looking round a corner to the right I saw a piece of rope hanging there. I made a tension move to this point, went up a little then moved in the same manner again to the right, and found myself above the wall. There were some fairly easy slabs above but in the mist it was hard to make out the route. All I could see were these slabs steepening into walls then overhangs about 150 feet above.

I set off towards the overhangs, hoping to find some sign of the route. Fortunately I moved in the right direction, over to the left, where the climbing was magnificent. After a corner I entered a superb layback crack with a wedge in it. I still had the diagram from the dissected route description, and checking this I was surprised to find how far up the climb we had come. Up to this point we had climbed with our sacks on, whereas we normally hauled them up on ropes.

Above the layback crack was a series of little chimneys. Although these were easier than the lower pitches the sacks on our backs wedged inside them and made the climbing really exhausting. We were now either too tired or lazy to change over and start sack hauling. The rocks became progressively easier and across a shoulder we could hear lots of people chattering as they went down the normal route. We could have crossed the shoulder easily and joined them but a splendid ledge on which we had arrived persuaded us to lie down and rest. There we spent the night.

Next morning we scrambled to the summit where we found a rucksack with gear strewn round it. We thought it must have some connection with the rescue operation in progress. On the descent I moved slightly away from the correct line for about 300 feet, returning to the proper route on the shoulder. We heard later that the owner of the rucksack lying on the summit had fallen down the ordinary route and that "he was sort of spread out all over it"—in the 300 feet section which I had unconsciously avoided.

Traversing towards the Flammes de Pierre we looked down the approach couloir of the normal route and saw a body lying in the bed with a rope beside it. This corpse was a guide who had been roping down the face on a bad sling which broke. All told there were three bodies from separate accidents on the Dru at this time. We were feeling a bit sick. "I want to get off this mountain," Des said glumly. We rushed down the couloir to the glacier and made another route-finding error. We finished having to rope down over a 120 feet overhang on to the glacier. Pulling the rope down after us it jammed. I couldn't see any way of climbing back up and we were in a filthy temper. "What a bloody stupid thing to do right at the end," I fumed. We stretched the rope out far to one side and the springy tension set up in it freed it from the rock.

Tom returned from Zermatt and the next thing he had lined up was a new route on the Pic Sans Nom, a peak between the Aiguille Verte and the Dru. We bivouacked near the bottom of the North Face. We had such a comfortable night that it was 7 a.m. before we got away. The first 1,000 feet was nice climbing up an overhanging ice cliff. The top of it was crumbling and looked really nasty. Tom went straight at the cliff, intent on climbing it direct. The ice was so rotten that even he was forced to retire. I was feeling like putting off the attempt for another time. "Aye, well, I don't think we should do that," said Tom. "Come along now, we'll just make a wee traverse across that slope under this wall, then we'll be well on our way."

We traversed and Tom went into top gear, hacking steps in the ice pitch after pitch without stopping. While Tom was busy making steps I had time to brood about the weather. A curious cloud formation had got me worked up and I called out: "Don't you think that we're pressing our luck a bit far?" He took no notice. About five minutes later the clouds disappeared and overhead was a clear sky and bright sunshine. Tom looked down: "What was that you were saying about the weather. Are you sure that you are feeling all right?"

We carried on till we were about 3,000 feet up the face. In front of us a band of ice sloping at 50 degrees went across a pillar. The ice was very hard and it took many blows with an axe to cut a step in it. Tom persevered till he came to a rock blade where he belayed. At the stance he beckoned me forward into a line of overhanging chimneys filled with ice. This was supposed to be my kind of ground. I had to use some pegs even to get up the first few feet. I soon felt pretty harassed, digging away at the ice and occasionally getting a hand-jam between the rock and the ice. The chimneys went up for 300 feet; the climbing was very hard all the way.

Two alternatives were clear from the head of a couloir. I chose the wrong one and found myself on extremely difficult rock again, whereas the second alternative was much easier. Tom led the final section on snow and ice up to the summit ridge.

Looking in the direction of Mont Blanc we saw the mountain covered with a vast black cloud in which lightning was flashing. We went down as fast as we could. The storm hit us just before we reached the glacier. A violent wind dashed hail and snow in our faces. We sat down there and then and pulled a bivouac sheet over our heads. We had stopped in a very bad place at the foot of a couloir. What with the booming of thunder and crackling of lightning I was expecting all the snow in the couloir to slide on top of us.

We remained in this position until 2 a.m. The storm was still raging but Tom was fed up and wanted to get moving. I argued that if we waited a couple of hours we would have daylight to help us. Besides we still had to rope down one pitch on to the glacier and I did not fancy doing this in the dark. So we waited.

We reached the Charpoua hut quite quickly, where I had to lie down for three hours because I felt so ill after sitting up all night in a very cramped position under the bivouac sheet. Lightning was striking the Aiguille de l'M as we approached the Montenvers. Climbing up the ladders off the Mer Glace to the hotel we received electric shocks from the metal rails. Looking back at the Dru when the clouds parted for a moment, the peak was cloaked in a mantle of white. Two Italians who had bivouacked with us before our climb had gone on to the West Face and were caught in the blizzard. One died and the other was five days getting back to Chamonix.

Don Whillans had arrived in Chamonix and when I spoke to him he wasn't interested in climbing. I persuaded him to come with me and try the South Face of the Fou, which I had set out to inspect with Robin Smith and others in 1960. I had been aware of its possibilities for a long time and Don and I carried enough artificial equipment to the hut to cope with anything— or so I thought. At the hut we learnt that a strong American party was on the face. The Americans had been going up and down the peak for a month between periods of bad weather. Just after we rose the following morning the Americans walked in with victorious smiles on their faces.

We decided that as we had carried all the gear up, we might as well try the climb anyway.

Don and I soloed up the couloir till we came to some very bad rock. I suggested that we should put the rope on. Our sacks weighed 45 or 50 lb each and I had already just missed falling off. After the loose section the rock was much better and we started up the face.

The first 600 feet were very interesting and continuously difficult. We got into the diagonal crack line leading right up the face. This fault formed a slab varying from about two feet wide to fifteen feet, with a crack in the back where the slab met the impending wall above. The angle of the slab averaged perhaps 55 degrees. It seemed best to climb the fault by the layback method, and in this manner we went up for 600 feet. We found wooden wedges and a number of other pieces of artificial equipment all the way up the crack. Hardly any of it was necessary. Because of the diagonal line of the fault we could only haul one of the sacks. We put all the heavy gear into one sack, until it weighed about 80 lb, and filled the other with spare clothing and light articles. The leader climbed without a sack and hauled up the heavy one behind him, while the second climbed wearing the light sack.

Whereas it took only about five minutes to climb each pitch, hauling up the big sack took thirty minutes. Clearly this was ridiculous and it wore down our stamina and patience. We reached the point where the American route entered the diagonal fault. An overhang had to be turned to continue up the very steep final wall. Don had taken the lead and was half-way up the crux pitch. He had a great deal of trouble pulling up the sack. I could almost read what he was thinking by the grim expression on his face. I thought, if I have to haul that sack up a pitch like this once more I'm going to suggest we go down. Moving across to join Don, I was just making a hard step when he called out: "I've had enough of this. I am not hauling that sack any farther." I thought, Great, and reversed back to the stance which I had just left.

It was nearly as much trouble getting down with the sack. You couldn't lower it straight down because gravity took it well away below the line of the route. One of us had to climb down, anchor the rope and then the man above lowered the sack which was clipped to the climbing rope held along the fault line. At one stage the sack came off the lowering rope, shot down the guide rope at a terrific rate and hit me. I couldn't jump out of its path because I was tied on to the belay for the guide rope.

By midday we were back in the couloir. Don had a septic foot and suddenly felt unwell. This made us think it was a curious piece of luck that we had been foiled in the attempt by having a sack too big for pulling up the face; if Don had fallen ill high on the face it might have been a bit too exciting.

My second season with Tom Patey began less successfully. We attempted a route on the North Face of the Migot but there was still too much winter ice on the face and we had to retreat after only one rope length.

After that Tom produced his plan for the Aiguille de Leschaux. He had photographs of the West Face, which promised a good climb. A large group of us went to the Leschaux hut and four started early the following morning. The approach was as for the normal route on the West Face of the mountain, below the Petites Jorasses, in a wild and remote corner of the range. We made an intricate ascent of a steep glacier riddled with crevasses. On the way up we noticed a set of tracks going straight across one of the worst parts of the glacier and then up a sheer slope. Having traversed on to the West Face a herd of chamois appeared above us; if only we could climb like them! As soon as they caught our scent they bounded across a snow slope, disappeared behind a ridge and reappeared in a couloir to our left. They went up this at express speed and vanished over the col at the top.

We traversed on to the West Face; the rocks were little more than scrambling for most of the way. I was climbing with Tom although we were not roped together, and Chris Bonington and Robin Ford were close behind. Later on the rocks became quite steep, probably Grade V, so we put on the rope for two pitches, then took it off again. Altogether we took three hours to go up the face to the summit.

We made a bad mistake in descending the normal West Face route, instead of climbing down the way we had come. The rock was so loose that shock waves from an echo were almost enough to start the stones flying. It was a very dangerous place. I was not looking forward to finding a way through the slushy obstacle course on the glacier back to the hut, but Tom went charging down it, making a trail for the rest of us to follow.

It was now ten days since we had been rebuffed on the Migot. We went back and found the entry couloir, originally full of snow, now fairly clear, but the great ice cliffs at the top of the couloir were no less menacing. It was a place where you didn't care to linger. The object was to force a route up the North Face of the peak. Well away from the couloir, we started the climb over a little overhang. After that the rocks were fairly straightforward for the next 400 feet, up to a patch of ice at the lower end of a long ramp slanting across the blank wall of the face.

Tom was leading the ice pitch and I was belayed to a block sticking out of the ice. Suddenly he shot off and I managed to stop him before he went over the edge of the slope and down the precipice below it. I called him a few names, which he thought were not warranted, and he got quite shirty about it. He must have been quite angry with himself. "Hadn't you better put some crampons on," I suggested. "You might not be so lucky next time." Tom put them on. Blocks of ice skidded down the slope as he chopped some steps and he disappeared over the ramp.

Following Tom, I was struck by the resemblance of the ramp to Longland's on Cloggy—a narrow slab about 55 degrees steep and some 500 feet long. At the top of the ramp Chris Bonington and Robin Ford were close on our heels. A number of alternatives presented themselves on the upper part of the face and one of them enabled the Bonington rope to get ahead of us. Tom put on a spurt and regained the lead on the final 300 feet to the summit. The descent was uneventful.

Frank Davies, an equipment dealer, arrived in Chamonix. I had always wanted to climb the North Ridge of the Peigne, and this seemed a good choice for Frank who was completely out of training. We galloped up the first slabs until the ridge steepened. The climbing was not as easy as I had expected. In fact although the Peigne is a low peak I thought the climbing was as hard as anything on the West Face and South-West Pillar of the Dru. Merely because the mountain was so accessible, half an hour from the cable railway, you assumed that none of the climbing could be serious—which was why Frank went on it.

Some of the pitches were superb. I was fairly certain that Frank had done very little artificial climbing, so when we came to a pitch with four pegs in it—a little overhanging wall—he had a painful struggle to get up. I felt very sorry for him.

Frank had a very false picture of my ability to climb. Coming down the couloir of the normal route, which is quite difficult in places, I told him to speak up if the climbing became too hard, when I would stop and give him a tight rope. Frank went down in front of me and after a steep pitch I called out: "What's it like?" He gave me a brief description. The first time he said a pitch was "hard" I shuffled down it without difficulty. When he saw this, the next time I asked him to give me directions he said: "Oh, it's dead easy. You'll have no trouble at all." I found myself in the neck of a bottle-shaped chimney that suddenly widened. I nearly fell out of it before I could bridge across the walls and secure myself. This went on all the way down to the glacier, Frank saying that I would find the climbing easy and me having a little epic on every pitch.

The Midi television programme was something of a fraud, but then so are many forms of entertainment on film. I was asked to take part in a Eurovision TV broadcast of climbing the South Face of the Midi. The team was an international one under the direction of the veteran mountaineer, Guido Magnone. I was put up in one of the best hotels in Chamonix, which made a pleasant change from camping and staying at the Biolay. Instead of toiling up the mountain to make our preparations, we travelled by cable railway to and from the Midi summit and were treated like royalty. My companions were already known to me and I was paired to climb with Réné Desmaison.

We arrived "on stage" for a rehearsal in a terrible blizzard. It was bitterly cold and the snow froze on your face. As usual, Robert Paragot, a Parisian, was walking about only in a sweater. We went down to look at the face. Magnone was keen to have us limber up and discover if the route was climbable in these terrible conditions. I thought it was folly to try; a strong wind was blowing and the snow was being driven horizontally. We walked to the foot of the climb, had one look and walked back.

Next day we did the climb. Desmaison led my rope and I was

tremendously impressed at the way he tackled the verglassed rock. Instead of making some effort to cut steps in the ice he simply smashed it off with a hammer and got down to the rock beneath. I would have been tapping away at the ice, making nicks to stand on. The climb was quite pleasant and everything went smoothly till we were about two-thirds of the way up. Here the climbing was less open, in corners and deep grooves. At one point I noticed that Desmaison was having a great deal of trouble. He tried a move three or four times and finally put in a peg before getting up. I thought I could see a good hand-jam, and when I reached this point it was by no means the hardest part of the pitch. Indeed there were hand-jams galore and they made the climbing quite easy. We continued until the top was only 200 feet away. The last part was not going to be televised and we finished by traversing off with fixed ropes.

For the programme it was fairly important for the climbers to be in the right places on the climb at the right time; camera positions had been planned precisely, and it would not be possible to change them after the broadcast had started. To accomplish this timing the technique was to traverse right round a ridge on to the face to reach our appointed places. On the day we went on the air the weather was as bad as ever. The lower part of the route was televised in a snowstorm, which made it quite interesting for the climbers. Having climbed the first part, we roped down to the bottom during a break in the programme and walked round to the cablelift station to eat and drink. Meanwhile the viewers thought we were still battling our way up the face in a blizzard. When the time came round for the next broadcast we roped down to our new positions higher up the face.

The rock was wet at first but later ice coated. The ice began building up on the rock to a thickness of two inches. Then I was told that a particularly difficult pitch was to be my lead. I started up it on verglassed rock and noticed that the ice, instead of lying smoothly on the rock, was rough and its surface corresponded to the slight disfigurations in the rock beneath. I had never seen this happen before. The pitch was considered so tricky that a sling had been left hanging at the crux, which I was told to use as a handhold. The viewers will never see you using it, they said. The camera could not pick up an object so vague as a sling in the prevailing visibility. However, I reckoned that if I used it, the curious position of my hand would betray what I was doing to some of the viewers. As I was making the last movement on to a ridge the rope went tight behind me. I had no idea what Desmaison was doing below but he had certainly stopped paying out the rope. I almost came off, which would have given the viewers a thrill that they were not entitled to see. I just managed to recover my balance and stretch over for the large finishing holds.

I pressed on and joined Paragot, and together we brought up Desmaison. The elements were howling round our ears and it sounded as if all hell had been let loose. Paragot screamed to us that it was too icy to get on the top, so it was decided to traverse off and come down to a terrace where we were interviewed in our appropriate native tongues.

At home I was now doing quite a lot of television and broadcasting, and Val had been on Woman's Hour to say her piece about what it was like living with a fellow like me. Two BBC producers were anxious to have a "return match" with some of the Midi team in Britain. They approached me for advice. "Where's the best place to go, Joe?" said Andy Wiseman. "Cloggy, obviously," I replied. I gave them the alternatives of Castell Cidwm and Kilnsey Crag, which was done later in any case. They decided that Cloggy had more atmosphere than the other locations and there remained the technical problems to solve. I went up with a group of them to make a test to see if the tele-radio signals, which would have to be transmitted across Europe, could be picked up. The radio men decided that everything was all right.

The route up Cloggy for the programme was to be a combination of Llithrig, Pigott's and the Pinnacle Flake. I said the only thing that could spoil the transmission would be bad visibility. We all knew what the weather might do on the day of the programme. Privately I was also concerned about whether the route combination was climbable in the worst conditions. Dave Alcock and I decided to go up and try it in really foul weather. It was pouring with rain and I said to Dave: "Let's go up there today. The weather can't possibly be worse than this for the transmission."

Llithrig in a deluge was surprisingly unaffected, but by the time we had reached the top of Pigott's, bedraggled and soaking wet, our enthusiasm for the exercise waned. So we didn't bother with the Pinnacle Flake.

Tractors carried piles of equipment up to Cloggy and the whole area was a hive of industry before the programme went out. Several flimsy huts were erected to house the power equipment. The weather turned bad and I remember going into one of the huts and everything inside was dripping with water. When the technicians started putting juice through the equipment the whole lot went up in sparks, flashes and smoke. I thought, if they don't make everything watertight, there would be no chance of getting any signals through.

The team assembled at the cliff: Don Whillans, Ian McNaught Davis, Robert Paragot and myself. Christopher Brasher and Guido Magnone acted as commentators.

I was climbing with Mac and Don with Paragot. During one of the rehearsals Big Dave Thomas, who was always around to lend a hand, caught his hair in a device called a descendeur, which is used at waist level for roping down. He ripped out a large part of his hair, which caused quite a bit of excitement.

The final rehearsal on the day before the actual broadcast went perfectly. All the cameras were working well and everyone had been thoroughly briefed and felt very satisfied. As luck would have it, next day the cameras in the best positions were out of action and consequently the most dramatic climbing scenes were missed.

I had quite a long spell away from climbing on Cloggy, mainly because of the difficulties of getting down to Wales frequently, but also because I was preoccupied with exploring the crags in the area to the south of Snowdonia. Then I returned to my old haunt during a long spell of good weather in 1965 and made three more new routes on the Far East Buttress, to the left of Woubits. Although these were very pleasant climbs, they were not really of the quality of my earlier routes on Cloggy. In fact the best cliffs in Snowdonia really did seem to be worked out.

During this period there was much talk about the young generation of climbers exploring a "secret crag" on Anglesey. Martin Boysen, Bas Ingle and Pete Crew were spending most weekends beside the sea. Rumours and speculation were flying about, as they usually do when a "secret crag" is found, and finally I was tempted to go and have a look at the cliff. I had no idea where to find it, and the place I eventually found was the horribly loose and vertical cliffs around South Stack on Holyhead Island. The wall was certainly impressive, but also very off-putting. I thought, if this is where the young lads are climbing, then I really have been left behind this time.

I was having periods of losing interest in climbing altogether. There seemed to be little left to stimulate my passion for exploration. Occasionally I drove myself to action and this usually resulted in one or two minor discoveries. It was during one of these dull moods that I first visited Anglesey.

I next went there shortly after we had opened the shop in Llanberis when the BBC was making a film of climbing on these cliffs. The programme was actually on the cliffs of South Stack, which I had seen on my first visit. But the location was chosen more because of its convenience for staging a television programme than because of the quality of the climbing. The route we did was completely artificial and my first impressions of the quality of the rock were certainly confirmed.

Soon after this I found out exactly where the "secret crag" was situated. It was about a mile away, in the back of the bay between the North and South Stacks. The cliff is called Craig Gogarth. I had been to Cornwall in the past, but had not really enjoyed climbing in the holiday atmosphere that sea cliffs tend to produce. So I was pleasantly surprised to find that I really enjoyed the climbing at Gogarth. The routes were long enough and serious enough to make up for anything they might lose through not being in a mountain setting. Although something like a dozen routes had already been climbed there were obvious possibilities for many more, and I quickly became excited at the chance to explore this mile and a half of cliff.

I had now achieved the almost perfect life for a climber. These new cliffs stimulated my enthusiasm, and my new home and business made it possible to climb almost whenever I wanted. A new world of interest had suddenly been opened to me.

POSTSCRIPT

THE DINING-ROOM TABLE was covered with photographs, slides and diagrams. Val's head came round the door to the kitchen.

"Are you two staying for tea?" she said to Robin Collomb and Peter Crew.

They answered that they thought not.

"I'll make a brew, anyway," said Val.

"Val," I said, "can you find that photograph of me taken when I was in the army?"

Val returned with the photograph. It was a yellowed and cracked print of two soldiers standing outside a hut in an army camp.

Collomb and Crew studied it.

"Not good enough. It won't reproduce well at all," stated Crew.

Then Collomb said: "Which one is you?"

He hadn't intended to make us laugh but he did.

"So that's it," said Crew. "We'll collect the rest for you in London and bundle them off to the publisher."

"What are you going to say at the end of the book about your plans for the future, Joe?" asked Collomb.

"On that point," I replied, "I'm telling no one. You'll just have to wait and see. I'll draft it out in the next few days and Pete can bring it down to London."

"Now that the shop is doing well," continued Collomb, "will you be doing more guiding?"

"That's an interesting point," I said. "I get lots of people wanting me to take them out and I haven't had much time lately. One of the problems is that many of them think that if they go climbing with me their standard will rise rapidly, as if I was some miracle worker. So it's much better to have someone who is already capable of doing Severe or Very Severe climbs, and who wants more experience of doing routes at this standard, than novices who think that I can show them short-cuts. I can't, nor can anyone else."

"I don't suppose you would consider guiding with clients in the Alps," remarked Crew.

"No, because there is too much I haven't done myself yet, and in those circumstances it is always best to climb with people you know well and on whom you can rely in an emergency."

Val brought in the tea and we sat discussing the latest routes on Craig Gogarth.

I think my interest in mountaineering will go through the same stages that it has done in the past. I have been climbing seriously now for about twenty years and in that time I have had periods of intense enthusiasm and periods of lethargy. All the same I have always remained interested in going out to the mountains, even if it is just to walk around.

At the moment I have a number of new climbs in mind that I would like to try in the Alps, and, of course, there are expedition-size targets that I would like to aim for overseas. One of these is the Tramgo Towers in the Karakorum. Achieving these objectives now depends on whether I can travel abroad for several months without disrupting the comparatively settled life I have made for myself and family in Llanberis. When you have a business to look after you think twice before dashing off to the other side of the world. I have passed the stage of acting on impulse and I have a duty to look after my home and the people who depend on me.

I don't think I will ever settle down completely in the accepted sense of the term. Mountaineering, by the nature of things, is a very unsettling activity. I do not like to think of myself as growing old comfortably, and in view of this I hope to find ways of living the sort of life that I have enjoyed so much to the present moment, while keeping those around me quite happy at the same time.

THE LEGEND OF JOE BROWN

by Tom Patey

(To be sung vaguely to the tune of *North to Alaska*)

Many tales are told of climbers bold, who perished in the snow,
But this is a rhyme of the rise to fame of a working lad named Joe.
He lived in good old Manchester, that quaint old fashioned town,
And his name became a legend—aye—the legend of Joe Brown.

> *Chorus:* We've sung it once, we'll sing it twice,
> He's the hardest man in the Rock and Ice.
> He's marvellous! He's fabulous!
> He's a wonderful man is Joe!

He first laid hand upon a crag in the year of Forty-Nine,
He'd nowt but pluck, beginner's luck and his mother's washing line.
He scaled the gritstone classics with unprecedented skill,
His fame soon reached the Gwryd, likewise the Dungeon Ghyll.

In the shades of Dinas Cromlech, where luckless leaders fall,
The Corner was towering high, and Joe uncommon small.
But his heart was as big as the mountain and his nerves were made of
steel,
It had to go, or so would Joe—in a monumental peel.

He crossed the sea to Chamonix, and to show what he could do
He knocked three days off the record time for the West Face of the
Dru.
On the unclimbed face of the Blaitière, a pitch had tumbled down,
So he cracked the crux by the crucial crack now known as the
Fissure Brown.

When Evans raised his volunteers for far away Nepal
'Twas young Joe Brown who hurried round to rally to the call.
On mighty Kangchenjunga his country's banners blow
And the lad who raised the standard was known by the name of Joe.

In the cold, cold Karakorum where crags are five miles high,
The best in France had seen the chance to pass us on the sly.
You may talk of Keller, Contamine, Magnone, Paragot,
The man of the hour on the Mustagh Tower was known by the
name of Joe.

With Colonel Hunt on the Russian Front he paved the paths of
    peace
And helped to bridge the gulf that lay between the West and East,
That climbers all might brothers be in the kingdom of the snow.
And the man who led the summit talks was known as Comrade Joe.

He's happy as an eagle soaring up the face,
Swinging in his étriers on a thousand feet of space.
Watch him grin when the holds are thin on an overhanging wall,
He's known by every nig-nog as the man who'll never fall.

Like a human spider clinging to the wall,
Suction, faith and friction—and nothing else at all.
But the secret of his success is his most amazing knack
Of hanging from a handjam in an overhanging crack.

They said that Joe Brown was sinking down in mediocrity,
He'd even climbed with useless types like Dennis Gray and me;
He'd lost the pace to stay the race and keep up with the van,
And Baron Brown, that sorry clown, was now an also-ran.

   Chorus: They sung it once, let that suffice
            For the faded flower of the Rock and Ice.
            What's he doing? He's canoeing!
            Old long-gone, hand-jam Joe.

So said Martin Boysen and young Bas Ingle too,
Ranting Allan Austin and Peter "motley" Crew.
When from the outer darkness a voice like thunder spake
As Baron Brown with troubled frown, from slumber did awake.

INDEX